Aksel Sandemose and Canada

Aksel Sandemose and Canada

A Scandinavian Writer's Perception of the
Canadian Prairies in the 1920s

edited by Christopher S. Hale

2005

Copyright © 2005 Canadian Plains Research Center, University of Regina
Copyright Notice
All rights reserved. No part of this work covered by the copyrights hereon may be reproduced or used in any form or by any means — graphic, electronic, or mechanical — without the prior written permission of the publisher. Any request for photocopying, recording, taping or placement in information storage and retrieval systems of any sort shall be directed in writing to the Canadian Reprography Collective.

Canadian Plains Research Center
University of Regina
Regina, Saskatchewan S4S 0A2
Canada
Tel: (306) 585-4758
Fax: (306) 585-4699
e-mail: canadian.plains@uregina.ca
http://www.cprc.uregina.ca

Library and Archives Canada Cataloguing in Publication

Sandemose, Aksel, 1899–1965
    Askel Sandemose and Canada : a Scandinavian writer's perception of the Canadian Prairies in the 1920s / Christopher S. Hale [editor and translator].

(Canadian plains studies, ISSN 0317-6290 ; 46)

Translation of the articles and stories originally written in Danish.

Includes bibliographical references and index.

ISBN 0-88977-184-7

1. Sandemose, Aksel, 1899–1965—Travel—Prairie Provinces. 2. Sandemose, Aksel, 1899-1965--Translations into English. 3. Danes—Prairie Provinces—Anecdotes. 4. Prairie Provinces—Anecdotes. 5. Prairie Provinces—Description and travel. 6. Authors, Danish—20th century—Biography. 7. Authors, Norwegian—20th century—Biography.

I. Hale, Christopher S., 1942- II. University of Regina. Canadian Plains Research Center III. Title. IV. Series.

FC3250.D3S35 2005   971.2'004'3981
C2005-905845-5

We acknowledge the financial support of the Government of Canada through the Book Publishing Industry Development Program (BPDIP) for our publishing activities.
Cover design: Donna Achtzehner, Canadian Plains Research Center
Cover photo: Aksel Sandemose, courtesy Christopher Hale
Printed and bound in Canada by HoughtonBoston, Saskatoon
Index prepared by Adrian Mather (amindexing@shaw.ca)

Contents

Introduction 1
Factual Articles 53
    Prairie Women 54
    The Emigrant's Start 58
    Life on Canada's Prairie 63
    Culture on the Prairie 71
    Canada's Horse 74
    On the Rails 78
Anecdotal Articles 81
    From Belle-Isle to Montreal 82
    Harvest Time in Canada 85
    Winnipeg 90
    The Prairie Night 96
    A Canadian Pastor 100
    Medicine Men 105
    See for Yourself 110
    Winter and Spring 113
    Saskatchewan 116
    Redvers 123
    Moving Day 128
    East Coulee 131
    Simon Hjortnæs, King of the Danes in Canada 135
    The Last Duck Hunt 140
    The Whisper of the Blood 143
    Go Back 147
    The Prairie—Long Ago 149
Fictional Stories 153
    Cover-Up 154
    Norwegian Amazons 158
    Happiness 163
    The Wolf Trap 166
    Horse Thieves 170
Bibliography 175
Index 181

INTRODUCTION

Aksel Sandemose (1899–1965) is considered by many Nordic scholars to be one of the most significant Scandinavian writers of the 20th century. He is widely read in Denmark, Norway and Sweden, and it is virtually impossible to get through secondary school in those countries without having read some of his work. In addition he has been translated into other languages such as English, French, German and Polish, though he is still not particularly well known outside of Scandinavia.

In 1927 Sandemose made a trip to western Canada sponsored in part by the Canadian Pacific Railway. The idea was that he would write about conditions in the Danish settlements there and consider the advantages in immigrating to the country. The result was a series of articles and stories about Canada and three novels, *Ross Dane* (1928), *En sjømann går i land* (*A Sailor Goes Ashore*) (1931), and *September* (1939) which take place there. *Ross Dane*[1] is the story of the ideal immigrant, Danish pioneer Rasmus Dansker or Ross Dane, who establishes a colony in the fictitious Beaver Coulee in southern Alberta. The settlement goes through internal conflicts, but eventually prospers with Ross becoming its virtual king. In *A Sailor Goes Ashore* Sandemose's alter-ego, Espen Arnakke, is introduced. Espen kills a man in Newfoundland and flees to Beaver Coulee where he settles and tries to come to terms with the fact that he is a murderer. *September*, also set in Beaver Coulee, has a love triangle as its central theme, but it is also concerned with the extent to which first-generation immigrants have become real Canadians or still remain a part of the old country.

Sandemose moved to Norway in 1930 and wrote most of his remaining works, novels primarily, in Norwegian. These include, besides *A Sailor Goes Ashore* and *September*, probably his most famous book *En flyktning krysser sitt spor* (*A Fugitive Crosses His Tracks*) (1933), a semi-autobiographical book about a young man and how he is cowed growing up in a small town called Jante. During World War II and the German occupation of Norway, Sandemose was forced to flee to Sweden where he remained in exile from 1942 to 1945. During this time the central novel to come from his pen was *Det svundne er en drøm* (*The Past is a Dream*) (1944), which portrays the identity crisis of a Norwegian immigrant to the United States on a visit to his homeland during the war. After the war Sandemose returned to Norway where he lived until his death in 1965. Probably the most important work to appear in his later years is *Varulven* (*The Werewolf*) (1959), which deals with an aging man and his search for "self."

This volume is an English translation of most of Sandemose's articles and stories that deal with or are set in Canada, and a critical introduction starting with a survey of Danish immigration to Canada, then covering Sandemose's early years up to his immigration to Norway and stressing the role Canada played in his life. In order to facilitate the reading of the articles and stories, notes on the texts have been relegated to a separate section after the translations.

Danish Immigration to Canada: the Background

The oldest Danish settlement in Canada is that of New Denmark, located near the town of Grand Falls in the province of New Brunswick. A group of about 30 people arrived there in June 1872,[2] the same year that Canada passed its Dominion Lands Act providing immigrants to the country with the opportunity to acquire homesteads under similar conditions to those which prevailed in the United States. During the next 55 or so years an additional dozen or more rural Danish communities were established across the country, including those at Pass Lake, Ontario, Ostenfeld, Manitoba, Alida/Redvers, Saskatchewan and Dalum, Standard, Holden and Dickson in Alberta. As well, relatively large numbers of Danes settled in Canadian cities such as Montreal, Toronto, Winnipeg, Calgary and Vancouver.

In this section, I would like to look at some of these settlements or colonies, in particular those on the western prairies that Aksel Sandemose visited, and some of the people he met. Then I will briefly discuss Danish immigration to Canada generally, in particular during the 1920s, in order to furnish some background for Sandemose's Canada trip in 1927. Here I will also discuss the reports, with which Sandemose was familiar before he left, made by three separate writers after their journeys to Canada.[3]

All the rural Danish colonies in western Canada were founded by Danes who emigrated from the United States in the early years of the 20th century, and all except one, the Alida/Redvers settlement, were started by one of the Danish churches.

By the end of the 19th century there were two distinct Danish churches in the United States. The Danish Church had been founded in 1872 and was heavily influenced by the teachings of N.F.S. Grundtvig (1783–1872), the Danish minister and hymnist who in reaction to pietism on the one hand and the high church on the other preached "den glade kristendom" (the happy Christianity) based on the living word. His followers became known as the "happy Danes." He had also been instrumental in starting the folk high school movement in Denmark. These were usually rural boarding schools with terms lasting from one week to a full academic year, which had neither entrance requirements nor degree-granting status. The subjects offered were mostly in the humanities with emphasis on class participation and discussion. The Danish Church also laid stress on helping immigrants and encouraging the retention and cultivation of the Danish language and culture in Danish colonies. The other church was the United Church, founded in 1896, which was heavily influenced by the Inner Mission, a fundamentalist and revivalist group in Denmark. These people took the Bible literally, stressed conversion and missionary work, and were not concerned with the retention of Danish language and customs in the immigrant communities.[4] Most of the western Canadian Danish settlements were founded by the United Church.

The oldest of these United Church colonies is that of Dickson, located near Innisfail, Alberta and established in 1903 by a group from Omaha, Nebraska.[5] In 1910 the settlement of Standard east of Calgary was organized on Canadian Pacific Railway land by colonists from Elk Horn, Iowa.[6] Dickson and Standard were the largest United Church communities in western Canada, though Danes belonging to this church had congregations in the major cities on the prairies like Winnipeg, Calgary and Edmonton.

The only United Church colony outside of the cities which Sandemose appears to have visited is Ostenfeld, about 30 miles east of Winnipeg. This settlement was founded in 1926 by Niels Damskov, the Danish immigration pastor in Winnipeg, who had come up from Sidney, Manitoba in 1919. In the 1920s he became well known among Danish immigrants for meeting the trains in Winnipeg bringing Danes who wished to settle on the prairies. He would see to it that they were housed and fed for a few days until arrangements could be made for them to move on further west. Until 1926 he had sent most on to Simon Hjortnæs in the Redvers/Alida colony, but in that year he arranged with the government of Manitoba to have a tract of land set aside for purchase by a number of young Danish immigrants. He called the settlement Ostenfeld after the Danish bishop Henrik Ostenfeld (1864–1934), who had visited the Danish congregation in Winnipeg in 1923 and had managed to obtain a large grant to build a Danish church in the city. This colony was never very large. The land there is heavily forested and quite rocky, which makes clearing it quite a lot of work, and this likely prevented extensive settlement.[7]

The first Danish colony Sandemose visited was that of Alida/Redvers in the southeastern corner of Saskatchewan. Unlike most of the other Danish rural settlements it had been founded by a private individual unconnected with any church, a farmer by the name of Simon Hjortnæs who had come over from Vrensted, Vendsyssel to South Dakota at the age of 11, sometime in the early 1890s. The story of the colony's founding has become a virtual legend amongst Danes in Canada. As Frank Paulsen says,

> I collected variants of it in every Danish settlement I visited, from Dickson, Alberta, to Ostenfeld, Manitoba… Hjørtness [sic] variously lost his horses in Minnesota, South Dakota, North Dakota, and Montana. In some cases he was led to their whereabouts by a Norwegian wizard, in others by a woman fortune teller. In one instance, the horses got away from him when he slipped and broke his shoulder bone; in another, when the wind made a commotion by blowing against the side of his tin-covered wagon; in yet another, he allowed the horses to forage for the winter, and they strayed off.[8]

But Paulsen continues, saying that those who knew Simon Hjortnæs best maintained that the whole story is false and something that Simon himself had made up. In reality it seems that Simon's father sent him to the Redvers district to look over the land in 1902. He returned home with a good report and his father decided to sponsor his move to Canada.

After establishing himself, Hjortnæs encouraged as many Danes as possible to come over from the old country, and it was rumoured that he was paid $25 by the Canadian Pacific for every immigrant he persuaded to do so. He became quite wealthy over the years, owned several farms in the region and was given the epithet "King of the Danes." Sandemose was to use him as a model for his title character of the novel *Ross Dane*. Though many of the new arrivals continued on to other areas of western Canada, by the mid-1920s this settlement had about 300 Danes.[9] A Lutheran congregation was formed called "Dannevirke" after the ancient rampart along the old border separating Denmark from Germany, the name by which the colony was known, and a church was built in 1925 halfway between Redvers and Alida.

A small number of Danes came up from the United States just after the turn of the century and homesteaded near the town of Holden, Alberta, about 70 miles southeast of Edmonton. One of the first of these to arrive was Peter Sorensen, who homesteaded in the area in 1905 and later became known for helping new immigrants. It was with him that Sandemose stayed while visiting the settlement. The population of the Holden district was mixed, having a fairly large number of Norwegians and Ukrainians, and the Danes never formed a real colony here as happened at other places in the province. By the mid-1920s they comprised about 50 people.[10] Nevertheless, they formed a Danish Lutheran congregation that met in private homes and was served by Pastor Peter Rasmussen from the colony of Dalum who came up several times a year to hold services.[11]

Dalum, located above the coulees formed by the Red Deer River system near the mining town of Wayne, Alberta, east of Calgary, was the principal colony in Canada founded by members of the Danish Church. In 1887 a son of N.F.S. Grundtvig had formed *Dansk Folkesamfund* (The Danish People's Society) in Iowa which had as its objective the strengthening of Danish culture among the immigrants in North America, with weekly meetings consisting of such things as lectures, the exchanging of Danish books, and the singing of Danish songs. This organization soon had chapters in many parts of the United States and took upon itself the task of establishing new Danish colonies. In 1917 it sent a representation to Canada to negotiate the setting aside of an area of land in Alberta for Danish settlers. The reserve was named Dalum after an agricultural school in Denmark, and soon Danish immigrants began arriving; there were about 200 by the mid-1920s.[12] A Danish Lutheran congregation was organized in 1918 which chose as its minister Peter Rasmussen. Rasmussen had been running a folk high school in Ashland, Michigan, and he arrived in Dalum in May 1920. Shortly after his arrival, the community built him a house next to Home Coulee, later to be immortalized as Beaver Coulee in Sandemose's Canada novels. Here he set up a folk high school which he conducted in his home, the students living upstairs, and later also in a couple of bunk houses he had constructed on his farm.[13]

Rasmussen's Danish folk high school was not the only one established in Canada. There was Danebyrd folk high school in New Denmark, Danebod in Edmonton, and Dannevang and Dana in Calgary. The only other one outside of Dalum that Sandemose visited was the last mentioned. Dana was founded in 1924 by Pastor Mathias Gammelgaard Christensen of the United Church, who had come to Calgary the previous year. At that time Calgary had the largest population of Danes of any Canadian city with the exception of Vancouver, so it was felt this was a logical place for such a school. Christensen resigned, however, in 1926 and was replaced by Pastor Jens Knudsen from Brooklyn, who had also served in Danish churches in the Dakotas where he had been director of another folk high school. These schools all had as one of their main functions the assisting of newly arrived Danes in acclimatizing to Canadian conditions and teaching them at least the rudiments of the English language.[14]

Though a number of Danish settlements had been founded, there had been little emigration directly from Denmark to Canada before World War I. After the war, Canada, like Denmark, suffered an economic depression, and it was felt in many circles that an influx of immigrants would help the situation. The Canadian Government encouraged immigration from Europe. Immigration was definitely in the interests of the railway companies, as well as other businesses, which wanted new settlers, particularly in the prairie provinces, to increase their business in grain and passenger transport, and to farmers who needed workers, especially during the harvest season. Preference was given to those immigrants who could easily be assimilated with the predominantly Anglo-Saxon population, and so northern and western Europeans became those chiefly in demand. Stimulation for this movement of people to Canada came also from the United States in the form of the quota system on immigrants, which was set up there starting in 1921. This meant that anyone wishing to immigrate to North America now had a far better chance of getting into Canada than into the United States.

In 1921, the Information Bureau for the Trades was established in Denmark and connected with the Foreign Ministry. It became the function of this bureau to provide information about conditions in those countries which were of interest to Danish emigrants. However, there was no real policy on the part of the Danish government in regard to emigration, and no stand was taken on whether or not to encourage it. Already, though, the Canadian Pacific Railway had set up an office in Copenhagen with M.B. Sorensen, associated with the railway's Department of Colonization and Development, as its head, and this office was actively engaged in propaganda extolling the virtues of Canada as a place for immigrants.[15] Advertisements picturing prosperous and idyllic Canadian farms and pointing out the desirability of immigrating to the country began appearing in Danish newspapers and other periodicals.

In order to help the Danish Government form an opinion about Canada's suitability for Danish emigrants, the Canadian government and the Canadian Pacific Railway issued an invitation to the Danish Government to send representatives to Canada to see for themselves. A delegation was chosen for this purpose, headed by the editor Christian Reventlow and the agricultural expert Marius Gormsen, which travelled to Canada in 1923 and spent from August 15 to October 15 visiting the various provinces of the country. On its return the delegation issued a report on its findings. Based on information given to the Danish Foreign Ministry by the Consul General in Montreal, the delegation assumed that farmers were the only type of emigrants to whom Canada offered good opportunities. Therefore, they looked into the possibilities Canadian farming and related occupations, as well as winter employment, might extend to Danes and where the opportunities would be. The question of the advisability of Danes setting up colonies was also examined. To find answers to their inquiries, the delegation talked to numerous people, from government and railway officials to Danish farmers living on the prairies.

The report turned out to be quite objective. It was careful not to paint too rosy a picture of conditions for immigrants in Canada. While stressing that those starting out would need to have lots of endurance and work very hard, if they did so, they could make a go of it. Though most immigrants had gone to the prairie provinces in the past and grew grain, those who settled in areas where mixed farming was conducted were more likely to succeed, and it would be easier for Danes, who were usually used to that sort of farming, to adapt there. In fact the region most suited for Danes, in the opinion of the delegation, was southern Ontario. Grain farming had the disadvantage that while it was usually very easy to get work and make good money during the harvest season, in the winter it could be difficult to earn anything. If one considered the prairie provinces, Alberta probably offered the best possibilities because of the natural conditions there, but grain farming in particular was always a gamble, dependent on weather and world market prices. Before leaving Denmark, the prospective emigrant should acquire as much information as possible about the place he intended to go to, and before buying land should stay in Canada at least a year in order to be certain of his choice. It was recommended that Danes not settle in colonies, as this would not be favourably looked upon by the population already there, and their formation could hurt the prospects for assimilation of future generations. In addition the report gives some information about such things as living conditions, farm prices, weather conditions and attitudes toward immigrants. Its concluding statement sums up the opinions of the delegates: "What is being referred to is a kind of business in which the emigrant is to be considered a form of merchandise and is made the object of exploitation which he through *his own* strength and ability must try to turn to his own advantage."[16]

During the 1920s, others made journeys to Canada to report on conditions there. For example, in 1925, the writer and "emigration expert" Olaf Linck sailed over and spent from May to December in Canada. He travelled from Quebec all the way to Vancouver, then back east to Montreal, and on his return he wrote a book about his experiences and with advice for potential emigrants from Denmark.[17] While in Canada he visited Winnipeg, where Pastor Damskov showed him the provisions that had been made for Danish immigrants during their wait to find a place further west. Then he took the train on to the Danish colony which had been founded by Simon Hjortnæs near Alida, Saskatchewan. He stayed with Hjortnæs for a while and was an invited speaker at the laying of the cornerstone for the "Dannevirke" church between Alida and Redvers where he met, among others, the farmer Rasmus Madsen. The continuation of his trip took him to Standard, Alberta in time to witness the harvest and then to Calgary where he had a long visit with the Danish consul Peter Pallesen. In British Columbia, Linck interviewed two of his countrymen in a copper-mining town and afterward spent some time in Vancouver before returning east.

Linck's basic advice to those wishing to emigrate to Canada was to be prepared to work hard physically and, before coming over, to know what they wanted and where they were going. Older people, city folk and those looking for "cushy" jobs such as office workers should stay at home. It was advisable to have some money, but not to buy any land before seeing it. Also it was a good idea to know English before arriving. Those following this advice were likely to do well, since Danes were considered favourable and desirable immigrants from the Canadian point of view. The book gives quite a number of examples of Danes who were successful in Canada, including Simon Hjortnæs, who had become almost an ideal farmer in Linck's eyes as well as a leader in his community, and Peter Pallesen, the Danish consul in Calgary who had become a major producer of dairy products and the manager of a mine in British Columbia. Other success stories, though more modest, were a wheat farmer in Saskatchewan and a carpenter's apprentice who had put his training to good use on the prairies constructing farm houses and churches.

The negative aspects Linck brings out about Canada are few, and his examples of failure are most often due to a person's laziness or failure to follow the author's advice. Mention might be made of the plainness of the farmhouses, the lack of good beds for farm workers, and the fact that winter work is sometimes hard to get, but on the other hand the food was excellent. At one point a Dane from Wayne, Alberta complained about the railroads making large profits selling their land, but it was pointed out to him by another farmer from Standard how much benefit the railways had brought to the province.[18] On the whole Canada could be considered a very good place to immigrate to, and a suitable emigrant from Denmark could benefit those at home by giving them more space and opportunity since he was then no longer in competition with them.

The year after Linck's visit, the editor of the Hjørring newspaper *Vendsyssel Tidende*, C. Mikkelsen, also made a fact-finding trip to Canada. Since so many of the Danish immigrants to Canada came originally from the province of Vendsyssel, Mikkelsen was a fitting person to embark on such a journey. On his return, he published a number of articles on the country which he later collected and supplemented in a book, *Canada som Fremtidsland (Canada as Land of the Future)*.[19] Though the dates of his trip are not mentioned in the book, it would seem from his descriptions that Mikkelsen left Denmark at the very end of July 1926, sailing across the Atlantic on the CPR ship *Metagama* and returning sometime in the fall of the same year. After a couple of days each in Montreal and Toronto, he travelled by train and Great Lakes steamer to Winnipeg where he met with Pastor Damskov. Then he moved on to Redvers and Alida where he talked with a number of Danes including Simon Hjortnæs and Rasmus and Godtfred Madsen.[20] After having visited Dannevirke he took the train on to Calgary to see Consul Pallesen and then to Standard to watch the harvest work. On the west coast Mikkelsen stayed both in Vancouver and Victoria and afterward took the train east to New Brunswick to see the Danish colony of New Denmark, before returning home.

Just a little over a quarter of his book is devoted to Danes in the prairie provinces, with an additional nine pages dealing with New Denmark and the final ten summing up some of Mikkelsen's ideas on emigration. The rest of the book talks about such things as the trip across the Atlantic, the cities of Montreal, Toronto, Vancouver and Victoria, and what it is like to ride the train across Canada.

Regarding Danish immigration to Canada, Mikkelsen is upbeat and paints a rosy picture of emigrant life there. He says that he is only an observer and is merely describing what he sees on his journey, but all the people he meets have been basically successful. Even those who have had setbacks in the beginning have come through and are now reasonably prosperous if not downright wealthy. Mikkelsen says that obviously one should be young, healthy and willing to work before considering emigration, but that anyone with the right frame of mind and wanting to get ahead can do so in Canada. Damskov, for example, tells him that he can always find work for those wanting a job, even during the winter, that it is a relatively straightforward thing to buy a farm, and that it is better for those involved in agriculture to emigrate to Canada than to the United States. Farmers such as Simon Hjortnæs say the possibilities are limitless, and advise Danes who want to succeed through hard work to come. One of the Danish immigrants mentions how the work is actually easier in Canada than in Denmark, and the food is excellent. The trouble is that some Danes when they arrive want luxuries like a car and waste their time and money on these. Such people are bound to fail. Indeed a farmer's wife has a lot of work, there are hailstorms and crop failures, but these things can be overcome. However, those who have an occupation back home already or who are old or married should hesitate. The unemployed would be well advised to leave Denmark as any social help they get in their homeland is a drain on society. As far as a loss to Denmark through emigration is concerned, why should an overpopulated country not send its surplus to a place where the opportunities are great?

Of the three works discussed above, Mikkelsen's is the most biased in favour of Danish emigration to Canada. The reasons for this may lie in the circumstances under which he made his trip. Throughout the journey he travelled first class, something that is clear in his depictions of life on board the ship, the railway journey and his descriptions of the hotel rooms he stayed in. At several junctures he mentions his travelling companion, though never by name. Who this person is becomes apparent in an entry in Sandemose's diary from his Canada trip the following year.[21] Here Sandemose mentions that he was told in Redvers that Mikkelsen's companion was M.B. Sorensen, head of the CPR office in Copenhagen, which likely financed the journey. Thus it would only be natural for Sorensen to show him the most successful Danish settlements and steer him away from those that were not.

Soon after Mikkelsen's book appeared, Aksel Sandemose wrote a review of it for the local newspaper of which he was editor at the time.[22] In it he recommends the book to anyone thinking about emigrating and wanting guidance. But Mikkelsen, he feels, should rather have written more about what would interest an emigrant and left out the introductory part dealing with the trip to Canada itself. Reference to passport requirements, ticket prices, and so on would have been more relevant. Sandemose goes along with the assumption that ignorance about Canada is great and that Mikkelsen takes this into account. His descriptions of the political and geographical conditions of the country are clear and concise, and in general he gives a good overview. Among other things Sandemose notes, the author considers the possibilities for the future Canada offers and, though dealing perhaps somewhat superficially with the Canadian people, it is with the Danes in Canada the emphasis lies. His descriptions of them are especially readable, and "there is no doubt for a moment that C. Mikkelsen speaks the truth in addition to being a man with sound sense." One must agree with his admiration for these people who know no other nobility than that of work: "The book is appealing precisely in its quite non-literary style. Through and through it is the voice of a man with a clear view and standpoints free of prejudice." On the whole Sandemose hopes the book will reach both those wishing to leave and older people wanting to know more about the country which the young people have made their own. All in all the review is quite positive, but as we will see, Sandemose formed other opinions after his own trip to North America.

Danish immigration to Canada between the wars reached its height in the years 1927–28.[23] But two years after Sandemose's trip, things began to change. After the New York Stock Exchange crash in October 1929, the number of immigrants began to fall sharply. By the summer of 1930 Canada had essentially closed its borders to new arrivals, unless they had enough means with them to support themselves. A fairly large number of Danes returned to Denmark from Canada in the 1930s, but a majority remained.[24]

Sandemose's Early Years[25]

Aksel Sandemose was born March 19, 1899 in the town of Nykøbing on the island of Mors in Jutland, growing up as the youngest boy and second youngest child of eight[26]— a total of six boys and two girls. His father, Jørgen Nielsen, was a smith at Schourup's machine factory in Nykøbing where he worked most of his life. Jørgen had had a difficult childhood, as his father had been injured during the Dano-Prussian War in 1864 and had become a vagrant, inventor and local eccentric, often turning his children out on the street to beg. In spite of this, Jørgen became a diligent and punctual worker as well as a very strict teetotaller. Aksel's mother, Amalie Jakobsdatter, had been born in Norway on a farm called Struterud in Skedsmo (now Lørenskog), Akershus. In 1883 she went to Denmark, like a number of other Norwegian girls at the time, and worked as a milkmaid at Lyngbygård, a large farm near Silkeborg. It was here that she met and married Jørgen Nielsen who was then a stable boy and coachman at the same farm. Shortly afterward they moved to Nykøbing.

At birth Sandemose received the name Axel Nielsen, but in 1921, while living in Copenhagen, he decided to adopt a more distinctive name. While examining an official list of names which supplicants could choose from, he came across "Sandmose." This seems to have called to mind the Norwegian farm "Sandermosen," about 15 kilometres from where his mother was born, and from which his mother's family had supposedly originally come. It was probably under the influence of these two names that he finally chose the surname "Sandemose." About the same time, Sandemose adopted the spelling "Aksel" of his first name. According to an article he wrote in 1934,[27] the letter "X" reminded him of a cross, in particular the one on the grave of his little brother who had died at the age of 2. Since he had determined to live in three centuries, and thus had to reach a minimum age of 102, he did not want a cross in his name. However, Johannes Væth feels this is a later rationalizing. He points out that in 1920 Sandemose had fallen deeply in love with a girl in Copenhagen who was already engaged. In the attempt to win her hand, he lost out to a man named Alex, and this must have given rise to, or strengthened, his aversion to the original spelling of his name.[28]

The family lived in small house with a garden on Færkenstræde 12 in the workers' area near the outskirts of town.[29] Sandemose's younger sister, Anna, later Anna Paris, has given the following description of the inside of the house at the time:

> There were two rooms and a kitchen, and, of course, a nice-looking outhouse. In one of the rooms there was a double bed for Mom and Dad. In the other room there was what we called a "kanopé." It was like a wooden bench, and it opened up, so two people could sleep there, or if you wanted, just one. There was a table that stood in front of that "kanopé." Then as the family got bigger, of course, there wasn't room. There was a loft, and Dad made that into sleeping rooms for the boys. So that's where they slept, and I stayed downstairs in the "kanopé." So the boys slept upstairs, and then as they grew older, they left home. There was a skylight in the roof upstairs. We called it a "tagvindu." The Danes were great for putting up the flag. They flagged for everything. And Dad had a long flagpole, and when something went on, this window in the loft was open, and his flag was out that window.[30]

The Nielsens were poor, certainly by today's standards, but the fact that they owned their own home made them better off than many proletarian families in small-town Denmark at the turn of the last century. Nevertheless, Sandemose paints a rather dismal picture of family conditions while he was growing up in his supposedly autobiographical novel, *En flyktning krysser sitt spor* (1933). Here he mentions how cramped the house was with all the children and how his mother would work from morning until late at night to keep house, cook, clean, wash and mend old clothes. His father would plod off to his job at the machine factory early each morning when the whistle blew, along with all the other workers in the district, and would not reappear until late the same day. His wages were probably not much above subsistence level, yet due to the resourcefulness of both parents, there was never real want in the house, as Anna Paris notes:

> They were good parents. Mother made all our clothes for all those boys, as long as they were in school. And both Mother and Dad, they were proud people. Poor, but proud. When we were kids, you could borrow schoolbooks, and we tried, but we couldn't, because we had decent clothes on, and looked halfway decent, I guess. You had to be ragged and dirty in order to get help. If you came to school looking good, no help.

> We were never hungry. In the morning, we had to have our oatmeal cooked the old-fashioned way. There was no such thing as instant. And we always had a big meal at noon. But all Danes did. And then we would have rice porridge or some other kind of porridge. There was usually just one course. On Sunday, we would always have meat and potatoes and gravy. A big meal was at noon, and then at suppertime, it was sandwiches or something. We had a lot of potatoes, one day, and the next day they were fried.[31]

Aksel was clever in school and got good grades, but he felt it very restrictive. It seemed to him that the curriculum was narrow and left little room for individual thought. In addition, as a member of the proletarian class, he was relegated to the so-called B-class, designed to give workers' children only the basic subjects, as opposed to the A-class for the children of members of the upper echelons.[32] At the age of 9, in order to supplement the family's income, Aksel had to take on after-school jobs running errands, delivering newspapers, and selling programs at the local movie house where his father also had an after-work job as a doorman. Also as a child, he had an interest in nature, collecting butterflies, and he liked taking long walks along the coast or inland. This perhaps honed his abilities as an acute observer.

According to *En flyktning krysser sitt spor*, Sandemose was very close to his younger sister, Anna. They kept together in the daily struggle against their older brothers who teased and persecuted them constantly. It has been speculated that their relationship developed into one bordering on incest.[33] However, Anna Paris gives quite a different picture of her brother than he gives of her:

> We didn't get along like a brother and sister really should. He was always the good one. I mean he was more like a pet. It seemed to me like my mother always looked up to him and took care of him before me. He was better than me, for the simple reason he was smarter than me.
>
> In school, I remember, my dad told him he should help me. I went through school all right, but I had to work hard with my homework. So my dad suggested that Aksel should help me. Oh, he would help me all right. There was a problem of some kind, and he fixed it for me. I took it to school, and it was all wrong. He really fixed me up good.
>
> Of course every time he did something, I came home bawling or crying. And I remember as the boys grew older, they had to get a job. When Aksel came of age, he had to do something too. So he got a paper route, and he decided I should help him. He divided the paper route up, so we each had the same amount. And it was in the wintertime, bitter cold, snow and ice, and we wore homemade stockings - knit, woollen stockings. My dad could never understand why he came home so much earlier than I did, and what I was doing that I didn't get home the same time he did. Finally one day they found out that he had split the paper route so that I had all the customers on the outskirts. I walked maybe two or three miles, whereas he had every one right in the center of town, and could do it in no time. I used to come home crying and wet and everything. So that was the end of the paper route, as far as I was concerned.
>
> That was just one of the things he did to me, and I couldn't have been more than maybe nine years old. There were little things. He was always after me, trying to make it look like I was the one in the wrong, not him.
>
> We lived in Færkenstræde, and I can remember sometimes Mom and Dad would go away for the evening. Then he would get the idea that we should clean the house while they were gone. It wasn't that big of a house. He would pick up the rugs and shake them, and I was supposed to sweep the floor. So I got mad. I said, 'I don't want to sweep the floor. I'll shake the rugs.' And we got in a big fight over that. In the meantime, my parents came home, and there we were fighting. So that was the end of the cleaning.

> I used to be scared to death of the dark. I would never go out after dark. And right on the corner of the house there was a streetlight. I guess it was gas. When it would start to get dark, the one who took care of it pulled a thing up there to turn on the light. And if we kids were outside, that was a sign to come in, that the lights went on. But not Aksel. When it was time to come in, he had disappeared. So, of course, I was questioned. Where was Aksel? Well, how should I know? I didn't know. I didn't see him. So it was my fault that he didn't come in the same time I did. And things like that.
>
> I guess it grew on me. As we got a little older, I was against him, because I thought he had mistreated me. When I visited him in Norway in 1952, I got the feeling at that time that he was trying to apologize for when we were kids. He didn't come right out and say anything, because it wasn't in Aksel to apologize to anybody.[34]

Alcohol and girls were Aksel's biggest problems during puberty. After his confirmation in 1914, he was a gardener's apprentice for a year and a half, but he began drinking heavily and hanging about with some of the seedier elements of town. He had no success at all with girls, and it bothered him, as this was one of the prerequisites to becoming a man. If one were unhappy in love, then one was expected to drown one's sorrows in drink. Perhaps, too, the fact that his parents were such avid teetotallers may have contributed to his sprees, though he tried his utmost to keep them hidden. It is not inconceivable, though, that his parents found out about his drinking anyway, since Nykøbing was after all a small town.

In 1913, after the death of Schourup, Jørgen Nielsen was asked to take over the machine shop at his place of work. This improved his financial situation, and he and his family were able to move to a larger house near the harbour. As well, his parents could now afford to give Aksel some further education that might also get him away from his life of carousing. This took the form of a term at a teacher's school in Staby near Ringkøbing. The school, Staby Vinterlærerseminarium, specialized in educating *vinterlærere* (winter teachers). Because of long distances between schools in western Jutland at the beginning of the last century, many children could not get to school during the winter. Thus on the larger farms, schools were set up where the children of one district could get instruction. This usually consisted of one class which children of all ages attended. The "winter teacher" was housed on the farm and could earn between 75 and 100 kroner for the winter semester. Sandemose passed his exams in October 1915 with good grades, and shortly after his return to Nykøbing, he became a teacher's apprentice at Nykøbing Mors' Private School. He also got a part-time job at Schourup's machine factory where his father was now in charge, but he fell back into the life of drink and carousing he had led before going to Staby, and did not do the work expected of him.

By March 1916, Sandemose had given up his position of teacher's apprentice. Late that month he left Nykøbing with the intention of going to sea. He realized he was accomplishing nothing at home, had acquired an inferiority complex, and probably had guilt feelings toward his parents. World War I was at its height. He arrived in Ålborg and there signed on with the Swedish schooner brig, *Ragnar af Gäfle*, a leaky, dirty boat with a drunken skipper that sailed the Baltic. Life on board was, needless to say, extremely unpleasant. In April, *Ragnar* arrived in Stettin with a load of coal, and Aksel witnessed first hand a German city on a war footing. Then the ship sailed to Rønne in Bornholm with a cargo of gunpowder. But conditions were so bad that Aksel could not tolerate them any longer, and so he signed off.

In Copenhagen, on May 21, 1916 Sandemose took work on board the Marstal schooner, *Katrine*. The *Katrine* was one of the small ships from Marstal on the Danish island of Ærø which were engaged mostly in the transport of fish from Newfoundland across the Atlantic. Conditions on board were a significant improvement over those on *Ragnar*, but nevertheless, Aksel was not content. From Copenhagen *Katrine* sailed to the Faroe Islands and then back to Copenhagen, but in spite of his dissatisfaction, Aksel did not leave the ship. In August she left for Newfoundland via Iceland, reaching Saint John's in October. Proceeding to Fogo Island, the *Katrine* stopped there to take on a cargo of fish, and it was here Sandemose made a decision that was to colour his life for years to come.

On the night of October 29–30 he sneaked off the ship while it was at the dock and attempted to find a hiding place on the island. The reasons for his jumping ship have been debated. He mentions in his diary from the trip[35] that life at sea for a common seaman was like that of a slave, and in addition he tells of an altercation with the first mate. Espen Haavardsholm is of the opinion, based on a letter Sandemose wrote many years afterward to the Norwegian author Sigurd Hoel, that Sandemose was actually sexually abused on board.[36] However, there is no direct evidence that this was in fact the case. After a couple of days, Sandemose was discovered by two local men, William Walter Ludlow and Charles Chaffey, who hid him while the skipper of the *Katrine* and his men scoured the island for him. Ludlow became his lifelong friend, and later Sandemose dedicated his first book to him and named his son after him.

Just after the *Katrine* sailed on her way, Sandemose left Fogo for the mainland, having been told of good-paying work in the forests near Millertown. The logging concern he hired on with was part of the newspaper empire of Lord Northcliffe, who had bought up most of the wooded tracts in the area a number of years earlier. It was a dismal existence, far from civilization, with constant rain and slush, and work from dawn to dusk. There was nothing to do but sleep or play cards in the off hours. Only 17, Aksel had to make out as though he were three years older, and he also had to learn from scratch the exhausting job of chopping down trees with a double-bladed axe. When he was not working, he roamed around the area looking at nature or writing in his diary. Because of his strange behaviour and the fact that he could not speak English, the other loggers, most of whom were illiterate, soon became suspicious of him, and even suspected him of being a German spy.

After less than two months, he quit the job and went to Saint John's where he signed on with another Danish ship, the Marstal schooner *Chr. H. Rasmussen* bound for Portugal and Spain with a load of fish. This trip across the Atlantic was an exceedingly rough one because of bad weather, and the ship barely made it to Leixoes near Lisbon on February 12, 1917. When the ship had been repaired, she continued on to Cartagena, arriving in March during the Easter season. While in Cartagena, Aksel and his shipmates frequented the bars and bordellos of the city. Sandemose's diary contains vivid pictures of life in this port with its beggars and prostitutes, as well as its Easter ceremonies. Particularly noteworthy are his descriptions of the brothels along a street to which the Scandinavians had given a name so bad that he did not want even to mention it in his diary. He thus called it X-Street.[37] The *Chr. H. Rasmussen* continued on to Ibiza in April to load salt, returning via Gibraltar and the Faroe Islands to Denmark. The ship arrived home at the beginning of September after a very slow journey due to unfavourable winds.

On his return to Nykøbing, Sandemose fell deeply in love with a local girl. Though she broke off the affair after only six weeks, it affected him greatly, and he never forgot her. This first love is depicted in many of his later works, for example, *En flyktning krysser sitt spor, Det svundne er en drøm, Varulven* and others. As Sandemose says in *Vi pynter oss med horn (Horns for Our Adornment)*:

> [The first love] functions with prodigious power. Having found its channel, it surges forward like a mighty spring freshet, wild and insatiable, with frantic exigency. But its coarser aspects are matched with day-dreaming and tenderest elegy.
>
> Afterward comes the parting. It goes without saying that collapse comes fairly soon. The searing pain is that of a knife-thrust; the victim waves his arms, falls to his knees, and shrieks. Queer that anyone should ever live through it.[38]

Having had enough of life at sea, he now considered the possibility of pursuing a career as a teacher. Between November 1917 and May 1918 he was a substitute instructor at Glyngøre School, across the fjord from Nykøbing, but he found his home region stifling and in August 1918 left for Copenhagen to attend a course of further study. In the city he rented a small room, and for the first time he could now be free and his own master. The winter and spring of 1919 found him back in Nykøbing, living in a rented room instead of with his parents. That summer he went for the first time to Norway, with his mother and one of his brothers, and saw where his mother had spent her childhood. He returned to Copenhagen in August to continue his studies, this time at Døckers Kursus, an institute which prepared adults for taking their student examinations. Here he made friends with people with whom he had things in common.

Sandemose, as mentioned above, had already been keeping a diary during his time at sea, and while at Glyngøre the idea of becoming an author had occurred to him. In the spring of 1919 he completed a manuscript entitled *Blandt Søens Vagabonder (Among the Vagabonds of the Sea)* and submitted it to Hasselbalch, a publisher in Copenhagen. It was refused, but this did not keep him from continuing to write; in fact he seems to have spent more time writing than following his studies. One of his friends at Døckers Kursus was Leo Estvad, later a painter and art critic. Through him Sandemose became acquainted with and then fell under the spell of decadence literature, especially the poetry of the brooding *fin de siècle* Norwegian writer Sigbjørn Obstfelder. Later Estvad and Sandemose had a prolific exchange of letters for a year or so.[39]

During this period he made a number of attempts at writing novels. Some of these foundered after his inspiration ran out, but others he completed and submitted to Gyldendal, Denmark's most prestigious publisher. They were all turned down. None of the drafts have survived, but many or most seem to have been endeavours at self-analysis, frequently set against a background of life at sea. He also wrote some drama and poetry. His first published work was a prose sketch, "Hjemløse Fugle" (Homeless Birds), about a sailor's homecoming which appeared in *Morsø Folkeblad* (July 2, 1921). In December 1921 he managed to get several essays and stories published in *Folkerevyen Skandia*, a new journal founded in Helsinki, Finland as a cultural pan-Nordic organ. These appeared in Swedish translation. Though the journal was short-lived, Sandemose's confidence was increased considerably by having his work appear in it.

On December 8, 1921, he married Dagmar Ditlevsen whom he had first met shortly before he had gone to sea. She was from a town on Mors, and she and Sandemose had been seeing each other on and off for the previous several years. While he was in Copenhagen, she had been helping an elderly couple there. At the time of their marriage he was virtually out of money, and so this new state of affairs did not help his economic situation; nor did the birth of their twin daughters on April 8, 1922. As a result Sandemose had to return to Nykøbing, feeling that here was the only place he could really support his family. Back in Nykøbing he got a job as a construction worker on a railway line, but the work was so strenuous that he gave it up after a short time. Then he became a travelling salesman for Gyldendal books. Though this position gave him only a small income, he was able to spend part of his days sitting in a ditch partially covered with pine branches where he could write undisturbed. Because he felt a great deal of pressure from his family and others to get a permanent job, he then moved with his wife and children to Vamdrup, further south in Jutland, and worked there as a peat cutter. It was while living here that he received his first breakthrough.

In November 1922, Johannes V. Jensen, at the time one of the most famous and influential authors in Denmark, had started up his own periodical called *Forum*, and in it he called on new literary talents in the country to contribute. Sandemose sent in a prose sketch, and Jensen had returned it, but he encouraged Sandemose to submit something else. He then sent in a short story called "Den blinde Gade" (The Blind Street) for which he was paid 100 kroner, and it appeared in the March 1923 issue of *Forum*. Other stories followed. Encouraged by Jensen, Sandemose went back to Copenhagen in the late summer of 1923, moving into a small house in Hareskov on the outskirts of the city. Jensen became a sort of mentor for Sandemose and a father figure as well, and his influence on Sandemose and his writing became quite marked.[40]

One of the most important things Jensen did for Sandemose was to persuade him to put his short stories, including those that had already appeared in *Forum*, into a collection and send them to Gyldendal. Jensen wrote a recommendation to accompany the manuscript.[41] Gyldendal accepted the collection, and it appeared under the title *Fortællinger fra Labrador (Stories from Labrador)* on November 7, 1923. Jensen had recommended using "Labrador" in the title, even though Sandemose had never been there, feeling that the word had a new ring to it and would be attractive, even for English readers.[42] The stories are influenced by Sandemose's experiences during his time at sea and are set against the harsh background of the eastern Maritime provinces in logging camps, fishing stations and on the ocean.

Fortællinger fra Labrador received good reviews on the whole, and this, as well as his precarious economic situation, caused Sandemose to attempt to publish three additional books at three different publishing houses the following year. This he succeeded in doing, but as a result he got a bad reputation in the publishing world, and literary critics came to regard him as a pompous upstart.[43] These works, *Storme ved Jævndøgn (Storms at Equinox)*, *Ungdomssynd (Sin of Youth)* and *Mænd fra Atlanten (Men from the Atlantic)*, are primarily reworkings of earlier refused material and most have life at sea and its effect on sailors as their main theme.

The poor reviews the three books received made it very difficult for Sandemose to get anything major published for the next few years. He was getting desperate for money, and at the beginning of 1925 he was forced to get a job. He was offered a position as a guard by the director of the Ny Carlsberg Glyptotek museum, and Sandemose accepted.

Prelude to Canada

By the beginning of 1926, it had been a little over a year since Sandemose's last book had appeared. To be sure, he had been having articles and short stories published in periodicals and newspapers, primarily *Berlingske Tidende*, and in the summer of 1925 had become editor of the local paper *Hareskov Grundejerblad*, for which he also wrote a good deal. But according to correspondence between Sandemose and various publishing houses, in particular Gyldendal, every novel he had submitted was refused.

His job at the Ny Carlsberg Glyptotek naturally helped to a certain degree; but as a couple of letters to his friend and mentor Jørgen Bukdahl[44] during the first months of 1926 show, this job interfered with his writing and by no means solved his economic problems: "It's just that [I] have almost no time, since for now I have to work at the Glyptotek into the night. Am having unbelievable money difficulties."[45] "I have to appropriate one of the Glyptotek's stamps in order to send you this letter…"[46] "I think it's necessary to remember that before the sun is up I start a tiring job and am working into the evening each day. The elasticity of my brain is gone those 1 to 2 hours I am able to write."[47] He had also acquired a substantial debt when *Mænd fra Atlanten*, which had been published by the firm Forlaget af 1924, formed by Sandemose and an acquaintance, Johannes Carstensen, failed to earn enough money to cover its printing costs, and his creditors were knocking at the door.[48]

On account of his precarious situation, Sandemose began considering the possibility of leaving his homeland, at least for a while. The earliest concrete evidence for the idea of escaping from Denmark comes in a letter he wrote to Jørgen Bukdahl in August 1926, where he asks his friend whether he thinks it possible for him to live in Norway:

> I can't stand it here. I'm suffocating. No progress, no time, I can't take any greater leaps—the furthest one is Norway. Can I live there? Can I get hold of 3000 kroner there every year? How does the land lie? Can one even get permission to live there? This isn't a whim of mine, it's serious—anyway you, of course, know the conditions in the country.[49]

Two months earlier Sandemose had written to Bukdahl that he had been considering taking an eleven-day vacation with his family in Norway to visit relatives,[50] but now the matter was serious.

Bukdahl responded to his friend's letter by saying, first, that he could not say whether Sandemose could make a go of it in Norway, because their situations were totally different. He pointed out that he himself had no children and made his living giving lectures and writing articles primarily for Norwegian newspapers, as well as having books and articles published abroad. Prices in Norway, especially rents, were higher than in Copenhagen:

> Your intention seems rash to me—remember I have a strong point in that I know Norway better than the Norwegians, and because of that I have a point of action and a source of income.
>
> But what do you want to do up here? Correspondent for a Danish newspaper? *Berlingske Tidende* or *Københavneren* [?]. *Politiken* has two up here besides me.[51]

For the time being, at least, Sandemose seems to have given up his plans to move to Norway.

A real chance for getting out of Denmark presented itself to Sandemose in the fall of the same year. He was offered a job as a guest lecturer in a high school in the Danish settlement of Cascallares, Argentina, near the town of Tres Arroyos. Sandemose, it seems, was not going to let this opportunity keep him from writing, as *Berlingske Tidende* informed him that it would like to receive correspondence from him during his stay there.[52] Evidently he had made an agreement with the school's principal and was ready to go[53] when something unexpected occurred.[54] According to Johannes Væth,[55] Sandemose once told him that the school was closed by a homosexual scandal of some sort, and thus he was unable to take the position.

The beginning of 1927 saw Sandemose, as always, up to his neck in debt. He was overdue on the payment of his rent, as evidenced by a lawyer's demand note for 218.40 kroner, on behalf of the co-operative housing association which owned Sandemose's apartment.[56] About the only light on the horizon was an offer from the Icelandic writer Gunnar Gunnarsson, on behalf of Gyldendal, to translate some Icelandic sagas into Danish.[57] This offer seems to have encouraged Sandemose to ask Herbert Jerichow[58] at Gyldendal for an advance of 1,000 kroner on future publications with that company.[59] Sandemose had already received advances on *Fortællinger fra Labrador* and *Storme ved Jævndøgn* from Gyldendal and was by now running up a considerable debt with them. The translations were never completed.

But a measure of success was indeed achieved by the publication in March of a new novel, *Klabavtermanden (The Klabauterman)*. This is the story, partly realistic, partly fantastic, of Adam Klinte, the aging skipper of the ship *Ariel*. While abroad, Klinte learns of his wife's death in Denmark. During the long and arduous sail home, he becomes fixated with desire for his young ward, Anna, who has been living in his home. On his return he asks for her hand in marriage. She refuses, repulsed by the idea. Thereupon Klinte abducts her and hides her in his cabin aboard the *Ariel*. Later at sea she is discovered by the crew, and her almost sacred aura of femininity binds the crew to her and to the ship in a worshipful adoration. As revenge against the skipper, Anna refuses to have anything to do with him after the first night when he rapes her, and life in the close quarters of the captain's cabin becomes a hell for Klinte. For years the ship sails the seas with the same men. One of the crew eventually falls in love with Anna, and one day in port he stabs the skipper and marries Anna. The rest of the ship's men are consumed with jealousy and hatred because their Madonna has been desecrated. As the couple celebrates their wedding night below deck, the crew steer the *Ariel* onto the rocks off the coast, and the ship sinks with all aboard. But Adam Klinte must continue to pay for his crime by being transformed after his death into the klabauterman of sailors' folklore, the ghost that appears on board a ship just before it sinks.

It was while he was writing *Klabavtermanden* that Sandemose hit upon the concept of the *lykkemand* and *nidding*. This idea goes back to the Icelandic sagas, most particularly Grettis saga where the Old Norse term *lukkumaðr* refers to the man who is born with luck or good fortune, the one for whom everything goes right, whereas the word *níðingr* denotes the opposite, the born loser, who from the beginning is destined never to have anything work out. Sandemose finds the *lykkemand* in the *Flying Dutchman* and the *nidding* in the *klabauterman*. He expressed this in a letter to Jørgen Bukdahl,[60] where he talks about plans for upcoming books, including one called *Den flyvende Hollænder (The Flying Dutchman)*:

> The fact that the Dutchman is a blasphemer is his entitlement to the eternal life he has. He is the ideal seaman who overstrains himself in the struggle against God himself, but he is victorious also through this straining and becomes eternal…

> The *klabauterman* is his counterpart… This is the reason that the Dutchman is an object of admiration, the *klabauterman* of the blackest fear: the master of good fortune and the man without luck—not to be understood inanely as lucky and unlucky.

> In the latter sense I guess we all are lucky and have rescued ourselves in a boat of illusions, even he who is the unluckiest and luckiest of all in his lucklessness.

The concept is formally dealt with first in the article "Den flyvende Hollænder"[61] and in the Norwegian version of *Klabautermannen*, which came out in 1932. It actually plays a role in all of Sandemose's books from *Storme ved Jævndøgn* and on, not the least in his first two Canada novels, *Ross Dane* (1928) and *En sjømann går i land* (1931), though it was not until the late 1920s that Sandemose gave it actual form.[62]

Klabavtermanden was a welcome success after the poor reviews and slow sales of his past three books. The critics were almost unanimously favourable in their assessments of the novel. Many felt that Sandemose was Denmark's long-awaited poet of the sea and the common sailor and compared him to England's Joseph Conrad. Others remarked on his mastery of the Danish language and his improvement as a novelist, while pointing out some weaknesses. Most agreed he had talent and would be an author to reckon with in the future.[63] His friend Jørgen Bukdahl was quite effluent in his praise. "It was an inner victory for you. You have made progress in self-knowledge… Deep sensual-sexual, sea-calloused metaphysics marked by reality is indeed your domain."[64] In fact the only really unfavourable criticism came from the professor and literary critic Hans Brix, who commented:

> It's difficult for him [Sandemose] to construct a work of any size, difficult to get those characters he sees before him to interact naturally, difficult to gather everything around one concept so that it becomes a BOOK.[65]

There was yet another triumph of sorts the same spring. On April 25, 1927, Sandemose was awarded Carl Møllers Legat, an annually presented stipend of 1,000 kroner to a humorous author. This grant had been set up, among others, out of the estate of the writer Carl Møller (1844–98), and was intended to go primarily to a writer of humour under the age of 30, though for the previous few years mostly more serious authors had received it. The year before, much to Sandemose's chagrin, it had been given to Johannes Weltzer (1900–51), a youthful poet who only briefly in the 1920s made any real name for himself.[66] In 1927, according to the author Tom Kristensen,[67] Sandemose was an obvious choice to receive the award, and as far as the grant's committee was concerned, it was only a matter of selecting which year this ought to happen in, before Sandemose turned 30. Because Sandemose needed money at the time, he listed his birth date with the committee as 1897, so that the committee, if they were going to choose him, had to do it in 1927. Thus he made the committee's choice, so to speak, easier.[68] According to an interview in *Nationaltidende*[69] when asked what he would use the 1,000 kroner for, Sandemose replied he would pay his rent and any other debts he had at that moment. Since this meant that he would probably have no money left, the interviewer remarked that Sandemose would likely get little pleasure out of receiving the grant, to which Sandemose responded, "Well, then I'll be rid of my creditors… It's been a long time since that's been the case."

The fact that Carl Møllers Legat had not been awarded to a truly humorous author in recent years was not lost on the reading public. For example, an article signed "Ej" in *Social-Demokraten* for April 26, 1927, noted:

> The complement of authors in recent years is pitifully lacking in humorists. Even a grant such as Carl Møller's for humorous writers, which ought to have an enhancing influence on humour, has lately had the misfortune necessarily to be awarded to those of a more tragi-comical nature, such as last year to the elegiac poet Johannes

> Weltzer. Yesterday Ritzau's Bureau announced that this year it had been awarded to the author Axel [sic] Sandemose, and with all due respect to his better qualities: a humorist he is not…

Nevertheless, Sandemose was invited to give a reading of appropriately humorous sketches. In reply, Sandemose stated he was impossible as a reader, but would come anyway. He also included a sampling of titles of things he could recite, including "Description of How the Reverend Hansen on March 5, 1916 Got a Bullet from a Revolver in his Rear End," "The Incredible Account of Jonas Who Swallowed the Whale," and "Proof that Negroes Belong to the Human Race."[70] Whether or not any of these sketches existed or were ever recited at the unnamed association will probably never be known.

Carl Møllers Legat did not get Sandemose out of his financial difficulties. At about this time, Sandemose noted in a diary entry for April 13, 1929:

> Once before I went to Canada, I was in desperate financial difficulties on account of a long overdue rent payment of approximately 600 kroner. At that time I spoke several times with Jonas who suggested I write a series of short stories for Göteborg Handels- och Sjöfartst. I never did so but offered them as a serial the novel "Sin of Youth" which they didn't want. In the meantime at the direct request of Jonas, who was indeed going to save the situation, I gave to the lawyer, who was responsible for the collection of the rent, a letter of conveyance for approximately 600 kroner from G.H. och T. Later on it led to an incredible mess of complications, when the lawyer found out that there was no security.[71]

Göteborg Handels- och Sjöfartstidende wrote back to Sandemose on May 17, 1927 that, though the book was very good, it would have to be turned down:

> The paper is so heavily laden with serious and factual material that the poor female readers find almost nothing in it for their sentimental souls. There must also be *something* for them, and therefore the paper has always kept to quite unliterary English and American idiot-novels for serials… They have to contain rich people who love each other in international luxury if the serial readers are to be kept from protesting.[72]

The letter of conveyance in the amount of 346.50 kroner was forwarded to the co-operative housing society "Paa Bjerget" (On the Hill) on June 7, 1927.[73]

The first we hear of the possibility of a trip to Canada is in a letter Sandemose wrote to Jerichow in May,[74] where he mentions having negotiations with Canadian Pacific's General Agent M.B. Sorensen in Copenhagen concerning such a journey:

> Until I am in the country, the company will not ascribe to me its support for fear of talk of bribery, etc. But I can straightaway and without committing myself have a pass for the Canadian railway lines issued to me which is also valid in a few of the northern states. The pass will for the time being be valid for six months and include the roundtrip Copenhagen-Montreal. The implied understanding is of course that I as a writer will do my best to keep the name of Canada alive in the Danish consciousness.

It seemed now as though Sandemose would finally get his chance to leave Denmark.

As was noted earlier, the mid-1920s was a good time for a writer to travel to Canada. Canada was in the news, there was much discussion about it, and it was obviously the place to head for. Indeed, while Sandemose was making preparations for his Canadian journey, he was reading some of the literature that was being published on the subject. That he was acquainted with Olaf Linck's book is known from the fact that he mentions it in his Canadian diary. More importantly, though, he read Mikkelsen's book. As we have seen, he wrote a very favourable review of it for *Hareskov Grundejerblad*. Mikkelsen, of course, had been accompanied by the CPR agent M.B. Sorensen on his trip, and it turned out that Sandemose ended up visiting a number of the same places and people as Mikkelsen. Though there is no direct evidence to support the theory, it would seem as though Sorensen gave Sandemose these peoples' names and addresses, in particular that of Simon Hjortnæs, before he left and had perhaps even prepared the way for Sandemose by writing ahead to them. From various diary entries, it is clear that he was expected by most of the people he stayed with in Canada.

However, to embark on such a long journey, even if one's transportation and some of the hotel costs were covered, would take money, something of which Sandemose was in short supply. Also, he recognized that his family would have to have support in some form or other while he was away. According to his letter to Jerichow of May 22, 1927, he felt he needed around 2,000 kroner. In this letter, he holds out hope for the future, as he mentions that the newspaper *Berlingske Tidende* would sign a contract to accept articles sent to them from Canada, though they would not offer any further economic help except possibly by writing off some money Sandemose owed them. Furthermore, he expressed confidence that the CPR would foot the cost of pictures for a book he planned to write about Canada, probably something along the lines of Mikkelsen's and Linck's books, and that they might indeed put up a guarantee to cover the costs of producing such a book.

In spite of his outstanding debt with them, it seems that Gyldendal at the end of May was willing to offer Sandemose some financial assistance, at least for his family, while he was in Canada. At the bottom of a letter Sandemose wrote to Jerichow on May 23,[75] concerning a new book he planned to have out that summer, is a pencilled note by someone at Gyldendal, dated May 27:

> Informed Mr. S. verbally that we are willing to give him 150 kroner a month (to Mrs. S.) for 6 mos. (at the most 7 mos.) on condition that he is away that long; as an advance on royalties(!) (no book in particular): We will pay nothing immediately. We were not directly interested in his journey to Canada but did want to support him.

Now Sandemose could plan his trip in earnest.

The final agreement made between Sandemose and Gyldendal concerning the financial support for his wife can be pieced together from various bits of correspondence among Sandemose, Gyldendal and the housing co-operative *Paa Bjerget*.[76] Gyldendal would pay Dagmar Sandemose 150 kroner per month. Out of this Gyldendal would pay her rent of 89.55 kroner per month, leaving her with 60.45 kroner per month. Of whatever Sandemose earned on articles while he was away, half would go to Gyldendal to pay off his debts until these debts were brought down to the sum of 1,200 kroner. After this, Gyldendal would take one-third.

On July 24, 1927, M.B. Sorensen wrote to Sandemose,[77] telling him that he had to leave Copenhagen no later than Aug. 10, if he wished to sail with the *Montcalm* on August 12 for Canada. In addition, Sorensen mentioned that he would try to reserve a single cabin for him on the ship.

The Canada Trip
Copenhagen to Winnipeg
Sandemose left Copenhagen August 10 for the port of Esbjerg, and on the afternoon of the

same day took the boat to Harwich. Arriving in Britain the next day, he boarded the train to London. The following morning he headed for Liverpool, and set sail aboard the Canadian Pacific ship S.S. *Montcalm* bound for Montreal that afternoon. Before heading for the open sea, the ship called at Dublin, Belfast and Glasgow. He recorded his experiences and impressions of Canada quite meticulously in a diary he kept while abroad. Much of this material he used in his later articles, stories and novels about the country.

About the only thing Sandemose noted in his diary about his voyage over the ocean was his impression of the Americans on board:

> On the steamer I got the impression of Americans being big, robust children. Their women are also children, most often having an aura of sexlessness over them, I saw only one I really desired. ... They acted various parts. A certain *vampire* was particularly conspicuous. A little too coarse, with a stupid face and red hair, fitted out in comical clothing, which did not suit her at all. All of them were there from Mary Pickford to Pola Negri.[78]

The *Montcalm* made its North American landfall off Belle Isle about noon on August 17 and stopped near Father Point in the evening of August 19. Here Sandemose took the opportunity to send off a few letters with the little boat that came out to get mail. In one letter to Schmidt,[79] he mentions that manuscripts and correspondence to various newspapers will be sent through S. Hurwitz, a lawyer's assistant and acquaintance of his, whom he trusts implicitly. In addition, he sent a note to his friend Poul Munk-Madsen:

> We're going in to the above-mentioned little harbour, and I wanted to send you off quickly a greeting. I have had a good trip with no real surprises, have eaten and drunk well—first-rate service. Have just exchanged money, boy, how it shrunk. You'll look in on my family?[80]

The *Montcalm* docked at Quebec City in the early morning of August 20.

Arriving in Montreal on August 21, Sandemose stayed in the Place Viger Hotel. It was in Montreal that he actually started writing his diary. On his first day there, he landed in a birthday party for the son of a young minister, John M. Jensen, who had been born in the United States though he had spent his youth in Denmark. Sandemose mentions in his Canada diary how fanatically Lutheran Pastor Jensen was, but that the minister's views on immigration corresponded very much to his own. For example, the first period would seem like a regression to the well-accustomed Dane, and he would suffer many defeats. He would need a strong will, because no one would help him, and many who tried would break during the process.

Sandemose left Montreal on August 24 by train, arriving in Toronto the same day in the late afternoon. His diary mentions that he had difficulties finding a hotel room, but he finally found one on the outskirts of town.

The next day, August 25, he left Toronto, taking the train down into the United States, headed for Erie, Pennsylvania, where both his brother Anton and sister Anna lived. Virtually the only information extant about this trip is what is found in the article "I Pennsylvanien" (In Pennsylvania)[81] as his diary is basically silent. It seems as though he had not planned to visit his relatives until Christmas time, but after examining the map in Toronto, had seen how short the distance was, and had decided to make the trip immediately.[82] After a hassle with the American customs officials (noted in the diary) because of a campaign against cocaine and morphine smuggling, he evidently went to his brother's summer cottage outside the city. Quite likely he stayed with his brother for the next several days, rather than with his sister; she recalled nothing of this particular visit.[83]

The article and the diary mention his meeting a man from Mors, Mads Christensen, who had immigrated to Erie 16 years previously and had done quite well for himself in the United States. The article goes on to discuss how successful most Danes had been in America and how none of them would consider moving back to Denmark. Most of them would not have been nearly as well off in the old country, and, of course, their children had become totally Americanized. In addition, Sandemose here talks about prohibition in the United States and how he and Anton felt the prohibition laws were doing more harm than good to the country. The diary mentions his sending the article "From Belle-Isle to Montreal" off to S. Hurwitz to be forwarded to *Berlingske Tidende*. Thus, this appears to have been the first of his articles written on this trip.

On September 7, Sandemose left Erie and returned to Toronto.[84] There he caught a westbound train for Winnipeg.

Winnipeg I

On his arrival at the CPR station in Winnipeg at 8:40 A.M., September 9, Sandemose took a long walk down Main Street and on the way back stopped in at the as yet unfinished St. John's Cathedral. Sitting on a beam of wood up against the back wall of the church, Sandemose started jotting down his impressions of Winnipeg in his diary, many of which he used in the article "Winnipeg":

> This is the first time I've felt at peace in the month that's now past since I left Copenhagen—It's hard to imagine that 6 weeks ago I was living at home. A whole world has been thrust in between. Here it is peaceful and secluded... There's shade here, but a short distance away the sun is blazing. The sky is so far away over here. There are no towers or spires on the church, but there will be. Catholicism has time, another generation after this one will come to build the towers. All in good time, all in good time, we are eternal. You have to go out into the world to see how mighty Catholicism is.[85]

In the margin beside this passage, however, is a note: "Was an Episcopal church." The rest of this day's experiences are described in "Winnipeg."

The next day Sandemose was again strolling around town. He wrote in his diary:

> The cityscape is dominated by blocks of buildings erected by public institutions—by banks, Hudson [sic] Bay, Canadian National and Canadian Pacific Railway and churches. The contending religious sects vie with each other in the building of churches—from an architectural point of view not always with fortunate results.
>
> Strangest characters and ways of dressing.
>
> Parliament Building with Q. Victoria (a spirit in the lady, sceptre, crown, good looking the old girl—symbol).[86]

As with the day before, most of the other events and impressions found in his diary entry for this day are in "Winnipeg."

Maryfield

Sandemose's diary informs us that he left Winnipeg on September 12 on the train to Maryfield, just across the provincial border in Saskatchewan, arriving at his destination in the evening. However, it is not immediately clear why he went to Maryfield as there was no concentration of Danish settlers there. One clue may be the name "John Østergaard" which appears in a diary entry for September 17. After having spoken with a number of older people in the Maryfield/Redvers district, I found no one who remembered a John Østergaard. Fortunately, however, a few years before his death Martin Jensen, a Danish settler in the Maryfield area, wrote a short article about John (Johannes) Østergaard for a book of local history. Here Jensen mentions that Østergaard had been born in Haderslev, Southern Jutland and had served in the German army during World War I. He came to Canada in 1924 and to Maryfield in April 1925, where he worked a section of land near the town. In 1926, he returned to Denmark, married his girlfriend Sorine and came back to Canada in the spring of 1927, renting a half section six miles southwest of Maryfield. Though John liked Canada, his wife was very homesick, and so in the fall of 1929 they went back to Southern Jutland.[87] The diary says that as soon as Sandemose arrived, he rode in a wagon for six miles out on the prairie, and this confirms the fact that the John Østergaard mentioned by Martin Jensen, who had land four miles south and two miles west of Maryfield, is the same person Sandemose names. On the other hand, how John Østergaard and Sandemose became acquainted is not known.

Most of Sandemose's diary entries for the week he spent in Maryfield contain very little narrative and consist primarily of single words and short phrases, and so it is difficult to ascertain exactly what happened to him. About the only information we have concerning the intervening days is contained in the article "Saskatchewan" where Sandemose describes exploring the province on horseback. The account of some of his Maryfield experiences in this article may be compared with the notes he made in his diary, and thus to a certain extent its accuracy can be verified. Most of these entries were made on September 17 as he was waiting for the train to take him back to Winnipeg.

For example, the validity of the description in "Saskatchewan" of the Chinese restaurant in Maryfield appears to be confirmed here:

> Chinese cafe in Maryfield, half raw, hot potatoes, ham, coffee with liquorice and a slimy, yellow sediment—dissolved loam which the Chinaman had taken with him in his pocket from the Yangtze-Kiang. Dirty. Black hair like silk on a group of children who crept around like rats on the table and snatched whatever you didn't put into the middle of your plate. Fell greedily over the remnants the moment I got up from the table.

Both accounts about the restaurant seem to have racial overtones, and this is surprising in light of what Sandemose discovered later on in Alberta.[88]

There might be some truth in the story about shooting the turkeys in the article. In the same diary entry for September 17, he says:

> Cold, windy day, started at 8 in the morning from the farm (probably John Østergaard's), at the Irishman's and paid for the turkeys, sat like a criminal on a box in the bottom of the wagon. The face of the Irishman.

Though the diary says nothing about the purchase of a horse, it is mentioned there that Sandemose rode on an old nag through Saskatchewan.[89] However, the few words said there about the farm workers he observes while waiting at the station could well fit the horse owner in "Saskatchewan":

> Workers walked in and out, cutting looks, the cold steely glance which does not steal up on one in a roundabout way, but strikes one in the face like a snowstorm, the ice-cold sterile American eyes, evaluated and found to be too lightweight in *his* circle.[90]

Earlier diary entries mention remarks he makes on the landscape of Saskatchewan in the article, for example, "the distant smoke from the steam threshing machines," "bush rabbit," "the coyotes' howling," "soil like a black diamond, bluish tinge, rich."[91] But on the train back to Winnipeg he makes some entries, which are almost identical to some of the descriptive passages in "Saskatchewan":

> The cold wind sends disconnected shreds of coyote howling from the north.
>
> The typical fall shape in the wheat producing districts, the straw stack, falling abruptly on the side facing the thresher, gently sloping on the opposite side. Here and there grey stacks which have stood for years like sinister habitations of subterranean creatures, narrower toward the bottom than higher up, like a reef at sea which has been licked by the waves for millennia.
>
> In the dark night the straw stacks were burning in the land, a sacrificial fire to the gods of autumn on the horizon. Men take the grain and give the trolls the stalks. The dark September nights in Alberta, Saskatchewan and Manitoba when the straw fires… From these districts comes our white American flour, the fires shine in blessing on the whole world's daily bread.[92]

Certain passages in the diary confirm other things mentioned in "Saskatchewan." For example, "Experience that deserted farms are haunted (foghorn). 2) that you shouldn't wake up a sleeping farmer."[93] One other passage uses almost the same words as in the article: "Flaming straw stack, burnt out fire, which had once gnawed its way into the earth and made a sight as though a muddy subterranean river shows its face here for a moment."[94]

The account of the train ride back to the city in the diary[95] is nearly the same as that at the end of "Harvest in Canada."

Redvers

The next trip Sandemose made out from Winnipeg into the Canadian prairie would prove far more profitable for him than the previous one. This time he would visit a real Danish community and have a chance to meet and talk with its more prominent members. The impressions he would get there would influence to a considerable extent both his Canada novels and his articles. Fortunately a considerably more complete personal record of this trip than of the previous one exists in the diary.

Sandemose spent over a week in Winnipeg before going to Redvers. There are very few diary entries from this stay, but we can assume that at least part of the time he spent writing articles. One entry dated September 24 mentions that he has written four articles, "Høst i Canada," "Saskatchewan I," "I Pennsylvanien" and "Saskatchewan II," listed in that order. Also it is noted here that he had written "Winnipeg" during his first stay in the city.

The diary recounts that on September 26, the day before he left, the flag was flying over the Manitoba Free Press Building in commemoration of Christian X's birthday.[96] In the train near Elm Creek, Manitoba, the next morning, Sandemose made notes about the view from the train window, for the most part the straw stacks:

> Year-old straw stacks like large, spongy mushrooms.
>
> Whenever stacks are formed short distances apart by variable winds, they lie there like giant snails on the way over to each other.
>
> The old stacks, furrowed by cold and heat, snow storms and rain, fantastic pachyderms, lying with head and legs twisted under their bodies in grief over how the land has changed.

> Tumbleweed, which scatters sheaves, rolls in the wind on top of the grain or over the stubble fields, a half dozen or more pursuing one another.[97]

It had been chilly and windy the last few days in Winnipeg, and Sandemose had caught a rather bad cold and fever. When the train stopped in Souris, Manitoba, Sandemose got out and lay down a while on a grassy field, which seems to have helped a bit.

On arriving in Redvers late in the afternoon, Sandemose checked into the town's only hotel on Railroad Street, across from the station. However, judging from the description in his diary, the hotel was not of the better sort, confirming his account of it in "Redvers":

> Just arrived here (Redvers) and am sitting in a dirty room. The oil lamp, the girl, no lock on the door, no table... It is unusually cheerless in this grubby place, the staff stupid, holes in everything... It is so strangely quiet in the deserted room where I have for the time being been stranded. What an idiotic place: Redvers, Saskatchewan. The roads lead from a dozen wooden houses straight into the prairie, the ancient wilderness. God knows how long I'll be staying here. Preferably not too long at the hotel, at any rate, with a privy for a neighbour so you keep yourself occupied by counting how many pieces of paper the visitors pull off the roll.[98]

It turned out he would have to stay here several days, and as we shall see, things did not improve.[99]

The next morning he walked around trying to find a farmer, Godtfred Madsen, who was supposed to be bringing grain to one of the elevators in town. He was not able to find him, however, and went back to the hotel

That evening Sandemose took a walk outside of town and was almost run down by a box wagon hauling wheat, as is described in "Redvers." He then returned to the hotel, but things there had not improved:

> Chattering, talking and hullabaloo everywhere in the hotel still at almost 11 o'clock. The privy seems to be a favourite place of sojourn. If a couple of girls are not amusing themselves loudly inside, besides producing the various sounds which are peculiar to a privy, there are a couple of men who go in together and discuss the threshing results in Saskatchewan. I have got out of bed where I have been lying since 8 o'clock and have been rolling cigarettes on the off chance that the day will still be long.[100]

The next morning, Sandemose came downstairs only to find a note on the door, saying the hotel dining room would be closed for four days after breakfast. Evidently he met some Danes in town this day and they discussed Mikkelsen's visit of the preceding year. According to the diary, many Danes were very critical of Mikkelsen's book, which had, as we have seen, painted a rosy picture of life on the Canadian prairies. Sandemose himself was now beginning to wonder whether a lot of what Mikkelsen had said was in fact true, especially now that he had been in Canada for a couple of weeks. For example, Mikkelsen seemed to find it easy to have contact with English Canadians. Now Sandemose was told that Mikkelsen had been accompanied by M.B. Sorensen during his trip, and thus he would have visited only the "safe" places, since Sorensen would not have taken him to visit his enemies.[101]

That evening Sandemose again spent in the hotel. He complained that his formerly unusable bedclothes had now been exchanged for absolute rags, and that the hotel seemed to be just an ordinary whorehouse. Fortunately his headache had improved.[102]

The next day, September 30, around noon, Godtfred Madsen fetched Sandemose in his car, a Chevrolet which he was very proud of, and it appears that Sandemose spent the rest of his time in Redvers at Madsen's farm. They visited Godtfred's younger brother Rass and went out to observe the threshing. There they ran into Rass's son Harald. Godtfred and Rasmus Madsen had immigrated to Redvers from South Dakota in 1919, and set up a farm a few miles southwest of the town itself. It is not certain why Sandemose had got in touch with Madsen and how arrangements had been made for him to stay at Madsen's farm, but Mikkelsen had met Madsen when he was in Canada,[103] and it is quite likely that M.B. Sorensen had known him and given Sandemose Madsen's name.

According to Sandemose's diary, Godtfred Madsen praised Canada and felt that those who were starting out had better possibilities than those who had come 20 or 30 years before. Perhaps this was because they were more used to things. Even though money was worth less than before, land was not as expensive. As far as Sandemose was concerned, Godtfred was the first person he had met who looked at things objectively. Yet Sandemose also noted that Madsen had a desire to return home.[104] Later on Madsen did return to Denmark several times. He also spent some time in the Dakotas in the United States.[105]

Saturday night, October 1, the town of Redvers was alive with people. Godtfred and Sandemose drove into town and Sandemose gave a picture in his diary of what a Saturday night was like in a small prairie town:

> Slim, tender prairie girls, patent leather shoes, silk, bashful smiles. A bearded Irishman in dirty working clothes, fat cigar with a band. Redvers Saturday evening. Dancing so the post office shakes. The various types: Danes, Russians, Canadians, Frenchmen, their clothes, the faces, their character. What's the name of this town? Extra show at the movie house. At the Chinaman's café sits a newly washed lad with his girlfriend licking ice cream. Harvest workers stand under the lamps, chomping bananas and rolling cigarettes... After midnight, the cars spread out into the prairie, where straw fires lick toward the starry sky.[106]

On Sunday, October 2, Sandemose went to the newly erected Danish church between Alida and Redvers, where he met the minister Pastor Larsen and Simon Hjortnæs. Hjortnæs accompanied him back to Godtfred Madsen's and invited Sandemose to come and visit him in Alida. At Godtfred's they drank wine in the garage. This might have occasioned the description of visitors on a farm in "Culture on the Prairie."

In the evening of October 4, it started to rain and snow, and the next day the weather was so bad that everyone had to stay inside. A couple of young people, however, were out driving their car on the almost impassable roads. "The muck shot out behind it like a mud volcano" when the car left Madsen's farm.

Alida

Alida, Saskatchewan, is located about 25 miles southwest of Redvers. A few miles to the east of town was the farm of Simon Hjortnæs, the founder of the "Dannevirke" Danish settlement. Since Hjortnæs was very influential in getting Danes to immigrate to western Canada, at any one time, especially during the busy seasons, there would be a large number of Danes on his farm.

On October 6, Sandemose was driven to Alida by Godtfred Madsen. It took 3.5 hours, according to the diary, but this was because the car evidently broke down on the way. Mrs. Hjortnæs prepared food, while Simon went out to plow. Sandemose also gave the plow a try, while Simon and Godtfred talked together:

> A bit of an experience to sit on the huge double plow and drive with five horses. Wherever large stones were in the soil the plow flew several feet in the air as if flung out of the ground. Behind me the thousand-year-old prairie turned its black face toward the sun.[107]

Sandemose found it difficult to part from Godtfred Madsen, whom he had grown to like quite a bit: "A sadness smoulders in this silent farmer who doesn't know if he wants to be here in the States [sic] or in Denmark."[108]

After two days of staying on Hjortnæs' farm, Sandemose had begun to admire his host. He liked the fact that Simon had both experience and knowledge about farming and also had a nice personality. He would be an ideal farmer in Denmark. Sandemose remarked on how Hjortnæs told him that his favourite work was plowing:

> He will certainly stand in my consciousness as one of the finest men of his type I have met. It feels good in our muddled world to meet a man who has both heart and strength.[109]

On the night of October 7–8 it snowed, so that by morning the prairie was covered:

> Out here on the farms one is put back to an earlier point in time in Denmark's history when a distinctive social life was led on each one of the solitary farms in a thinly populated country. While it is still night, one hears voices from the stables, the horses are being given feed, the cows milked and the dung cleared out of the stalls. Toward daybreak the cream separator raises its whirring voice, and the housewife calls to breakfast. After the meal, the master of the house at the end of the table gives the orders for the day. The difference from that life one has lived in the city is felt very strongly. Out here the mystery is continually *the night*. The lights are turned out and the people sleep. A night one is awake, one sees in the living room the white light from the snow, hears the flight of birds over the farm, a sound from an animal, which in the stillness has come near the houses. And one again closes his eyes, hears other sounds of breathing like a whispering in the great night.[110]

On October 9, there is a diary entry concerning an immigrant by the name of Strate whom Pastor Damskov in Winnipeg had taken for his colony—presumably Ostenfeld in Manitoba—and about whom Simon Hjortnæs felt guilty. Strate was evidently an immigrant with some money, and Damskov had managed to get him to his colony, even though he might have preferred to go to Dannevirke. But Hjortnæs did not try hard enough to get him, and at the time Simon's farm was overcrowded with immigrants. He also had not thought that Damskov would have been able to entice Strate, whom he thought to be intelligent. A page or so later in the diary Sandemose remarked: "The poor ones are relatively lucky as Damskov doesn't want them in his colony."[111]

Most of the next few days Sandemose spent hunting and observing the farm work. The morning of October 12 he left Simon Hjortnæs and headed back to Winnipeg. Travelling from Alida to Winnipeg meant switching trains several times. Between Schwitzer and Redvers he noted that the train was full of harvest workers going east toward Winnipeg, but when he changed trains in Schwitzer and went in the opposite direction, it was almost empty. Plowing had already begun, though the harvest was not yet complete. Some flax was still left in the fields, and wheat, barley and oats were still standing in sheaves.

Sandemose also mentioned how the farms themselves were so different from those in Denmark. There were, for example, no red bricks sticking out of a grove of beech trees nor any manor buildings with towers:

> *A farm is a factory* for the exploitation of the soil. It seems forlorn and gloomy. The farms appear just to lie there, feeling it themselves. I always get the impression that the houses are grieving over their not being able to hide in the newly plowed earth, a wound in the prairie.[112]

Again Sandemose had to change trains, this time in Reston, Manitoba. Near the station was a small park with a statue in memory of those who had served in World War I, which he described in "The Prairie Night." A similar figure was also to be seen in Redvers.

Arriving back in Redvers that evening, Sandemose booked into the same hotel as before to stay the night until taking the train to Winnipeg the next morning. To his surprise the hotel had changed considerably since the last time. It had a new manager, everyone was polite, and things were clean. He also had to admit that this time he had no fever either.

Around noon on October 13, Sandemose boarded the train in Redvers bound for Winnipeg.

Winnipeg II

Sandemose's second Winnipeg stay was to prove to be the lowest, most unproductive point of his travels in Canada, as this time he wasted over a month in the city waiting for money to come from Denmark. He appears to have spent most of his time wandering the streets or going out hunting in the country with his host. Very few of his impressions from this stay in Winnipeg found their way into his novels or other works.

Four days before he left Redvers, Sandemose had noted in his diary: "Around noon the train goes to Winnipeg, I'm taking it and have to see about getting hold of some money while I'm there. Right now I'm totally broke." While in Winnipeg he lived with a relative of his wife, Christine Mikkelsen, and her husband John, on Queen's Street in the St. James district. The quarters were quite cramped, as the house was very small, and John's brother, Carl, was also living there at the time. Nevertheless, because of his financial situation, the Mikkelsens probably had little choice but to put Sandemose up for the next month.

The day after his return to Winnipeg, Sandemose mentioned in his diary about going out hunting with John Mikkelsen and his brother Carl to "the minister's land," which he described as desolate steppe. It was

> not forest, not grassland, it was wilderness, a quiet, dead land where neither people nor animals lived... The river, the railroad, the cemetery, here they had toiled and laid their bones as the wilderness grew over their dust: Peace Perfect Peace...[113]

After reading the diary passage, a number of older Danish settlers in Saskatchewan told me that it must refer to the area around Pastor Damskov's colony of Ostenfeld. Christine Mikkelsen later confirmed that her husband often went hunting in the region.[114] In the Ostenfeld district, near the hamlet of Nourse, is an old graveyard with just two gravestones, situated close to a river and railway tracks. One of the stones from 1914 is, in fact, inscribed, "Peace Perfect Peace," and the landscape is much like the diary description.

Sandemose had already acquired a pass to ride on the CPR from M.B. Sorensen before he left Denmark. CPR had also paid for his roundtrip passage to and from Canada, and seems to have put him up in their hotels in a couple of cities.[115] However, he did not have a pass to ride on the Canadian National, something he would need if he were going to take the train to several of the Danish settlements further west. A note in his diary for October 20 mentioned that he had visited "Press" the previous day, who was going to try to get him a pass with CNR in the next three or four days. This must have been H.S. Press, who was the district passenger manager for Scandinavian-American Lines. That Sandemose was successful in getting this pass is indicated by his later travels on the CNR, trips he would not have been able to afford on his own money.

As mentioned above, Sandemose often went out hunting with John Mikkelsen and his brother Carl. On October 20, the diary notes that he and John had been near Headingly, a short distance to the west of the city, where they shot three rabbits between them. On October 26, according to the diary, Sandemose and Carl drove 70 miles out to Lake Manitoba, via Portage la Prairie, to do some duck hunting. Carl was disappointed because, as around Headingly, the people from Winnipeg had secured for themselves all the hunting rights in those areas that were easiest to get to. Sandemose was surprised that though the land was prairie, there were no sloughs like in Saskatchewan. After wading in water up to their knees through swampland full of rushes and low red plants, they came to a tree-grown row of dunes. Climbing onto the top of them, Sandemose was surprised to see the lake, which looked like the sea: "The surf rushes toward the coast and booms like the open sea, was as if a longing had suddenly been satisfied, you look out into the lake, no land in sight."[116] This trip was the inspiration for the article "The Last Duck Hunt."

On the evening of October 29, Sandemose visited Danish Vice-Consul Fremming on Inkster Avenue. He noted in his diary[117] that Fremming's remarks on immigration were much the same as those of Pastor Jensen in Montreal. He felt that under current conditions there was more use for Germans, Ukrainians and Hungarians in Canada than for Danes, and agreed with Sandemose that the loose relationships among Danes were due to a lack of intelligence, and that muscular strength determined the tone among them. There were some small people who judged the new country from their own narrow horizon and did not really discover it at all. Any feelings of homelessness and disregard in such a person took the form of grumbling and sulkiness.

In a diary entry for October 30 is a description of the St. James area of Winnipeg where Sandemose was staying. It was a muddy district with small, strictly wooden houses. There was no sewage system, and the sidewalks were made of boards on top of earth. Along the back lanes were privies and chicken coops.

Sandemose was now beginning to realize that he was running out of time. He said in the diary that he was supposed to have visited the west and been in Chicago by the middle of December. Now October was already gone. He had wasted a lot of time in Canada because of lack of money.[118] The money he was waiting for, though, does not seem to have come. On November 3, he felt he had had enough of Winnipeg and caught the train for Edmonton in spite of his poor financial position. The question arises, how did he get enough money to travel on to Alberta? As noted above, he probably got the free railway pass he had requested, though later in his diary, he noted that the cost of the CN ticket roundtrip was $12.[119] But in a letter Valdemar Henriksen, Christine Mikkelsen's father, explains what perhaps really happened.[120] In this letter, Henriksen described how Sandemose told the Mikkelsens he was expecting money from Denmark but that it had got lost on the way, and he did not know what to do. The Mikkelsens took pity on him and loaned him the equivalent of 1,000 kroner (over $200 at the time) against an IOU Sandemose wrote out on a postcard. Later, when Sandemose moved to Norway, Henriksen tried to get the money paid back, since he had sent his daughter funds to help her and her husband build a house in Winnipeg and was thus somewhat short of money himself. Sandemose never answered Henriksen's letters, and the loan was never repaid. It is possibly this money Sandemose was referring to when he wrote in his diary on the train through Saskatchewan to Alberta: "Have now a debt of 107 dollars which is supposed to be paid very soon and strictly speaking should have been paid long ago."[121]

Holden

To get to his next destination, Holden, Alberta, 70 miles southeast of Edmonton, Sandemose took the CPR northwest from Winnipeg through Yorkton, Foam Lake and Saskatoon:

> Here toward Saskatoon I finally see the prairie, which I visualized in my childhood, and which I have expected to meet here in Canada. Only now do I see it—the endless flat lowland without trees. It's miles between human habitations. The world, life and time must come to a standstill here when the snow arrives... Burned-off stubble fields or straw stacks break the monotony, it is as though a god of fire had stirred under the heavens one night and now and then stretched a finger down and written on the earth. The telephone poles look like Christmas trees with their variously coloured porcelain isolators.[122]

Saskatoon he described as a large pioneer colony with skyscrapers and low wooden houses mixed together, its station the same model but an enlargement of those found in the country towns. Having now a chance to reflect on things, Sandemose pondered his own feelings about Canada:

> Now that all the steam has gone off and you're travelling in the midst of Canada's dry reality, can you recommend to the Danes that they come over here? The emigrant is not your type, he generally has no interest in the beauty of nature, etc., he is in a worse position than you in every respect.[123]

Continuing his musings in his diary, he put down some observations about Canada as a land for immigrants. Canada was building itself up inwardly, and it had a lot to learn from older countries like Denmark. Because Canada was backward in everything, it needed immigrants. Emigrants should either go to an unfinished country like Canada or to one in the same situation as Denmark. Since the latter was impossible, the only choice was to stay home or go to a place like Canada. It was best to think it over very carefully before emigrating. It was always easier to come over than to go back. Many Danes had regretted emigrating, but they stayed where they were, because they knew they would not be satisfied in Denmark: "It is an unfortunate condition which is often incurable. It is often said: If only I never had laid eyes on this country, I would be happier today."[124]

Sandemose arrived in Holden at noon on November 5. He had to take the CPR all the way to Edmonton and then change there over to the CNR, which serviced Holden. While in Holden, he stayed with Peter Sorensen who had a farm not far from town. Sandemose had gotten his name from Simon Hjortnæs in Alida, and the two had exchanged letters.

In the Holden-Camrose area the prairie was rather different than in the southeast corner of Saskatchewan:

> More wooded here, more rolling and varied landscape. There are stretches here which are reminiscent of Denmark—a combination of all Denmark's districts except western Jutland and the coasts.[125]

The day of his arrival Sandemose and Sorensen went out hunting, and both of them shot two rabbits each. They also got a horned owl. Sandemose mentioned how the owl sat on the road looking at him and Sorensen's dog and the strange way it turned its head. "You can wring the neck of an owl by walking around the tree it's sitting in."[126] The snow sparrows in their large flocks also caught his attention:

> They rush into the air, but up there each individual turns around on its wings, each one rushes in its own direction, like a pile of paper scattered by a whirlwind. Then it can turn into three flocks, throwing themselves down and once more becoming one.[127]

Sorensen was well informed in local matters and knew most of the people in the area. He was always telling anecdotes about events that had happened there. A number of these people served as models for characters in *Ross Dane*. Already on the second day of Sandemose's visit, Sorensen evidently was relating all kinds of information to Sandemose, judging from the diary.

On November 8, Sorensen took Sandemose to visit another Danish family, the Christensens. The patriarch of the family, Hans Christensen, according to Sandemose's diary, had come to Canada 24 years earlier, with his whole family, when he was 50 years old.[128] He had been farming on the same land for 20 years. Hans was then a widower, his wife having died 6 years earlier. Sandemose described him as being a large man with a long beard, "laughing, sometimes bragging, but none of it came from deep within him, he was armour-plated under his skin like his youngest son." The oldest son, Chris, then 40, had had to stay in a cold shed as young man to recover from tuberculosis. Sandemose described him as wise, kind-hearted, capable and sceptical, a good father to his sister's children. He had been on the school board and was a bachelor. His complexion was dark with a pair of lively eyes and warm features. The younger son, who was 30, was constantly chewing tobacco. He wanted to get married, but needed to get a bit of capital together before he could do so. These three members of the Christensen family were to become models for Pedersen and his two sons, Theodor and Frederik, in *Ross Dane*.

It was in Holden that Sandemose had his first real contact with racial prejudice. People of western European origin looked down on those of eastern European stock. The latter were usually called Galicians and were normally Ukrainians, but others of Slavic or southern European background could be included in the term. In an entry for November 7, Sandemose noted, "The Galicians are considered surly and quarrelsome. The town's lawyer lives off them. They fight murderously, beat their wives." He got the idea for his article "Whisper of the Blood" in Holden.

November 11 was one of the coldest days Sandemose had up to that point experienced:

> Nowhere is there mercy, there is no place to seek peace except by the stove. If you take shelter under trees, the cold sneaks quietly into the marrow of your bones. If you walk around outside, it rides up around the empty universe like a nightmare, slashing, merciless. As the cold settles in your joints you are overcome with inertia, let your hand hang down at your side though you know it would warm up if you put it in your pocket. You remain standing and let yourself be overwhelmed by the cold instead of walking, give up in advance an unequal struggle. If you take off your mitten it becomes immediately like ice inside, frost grows on your nose, your hands are dead. You don't notice it when you move your jaw.

The next day, Sandemose drove with Peter Sorensen into Camrose to meet Peter Rasmussen, the pastor of the Danish congregation in Wayne, near Drumheller, who arrived on the train. Sandemose observed that Camrose was about the size of a Danish provincial town on a gently sloping river valley and with a Norwegian school and a seminary:

> The town is mostly residential—people who live here for the sake of the children's schooling. Nicely situated. A single column here has replaced the otherwise awful soldiers' monument.[129]

Pastor Rasmussen came up once or twice a month to conduct services in the Holden area, usually held in one of the farmers' private houses. That evening he performed a baptism.

The following morning the church service, which Sandemose describes in "A Canadian Pastor," was conducted in the house of a Danish farmer. That afternoon, packed in bedclothes, Sandemose accompanied Rasmussen back to Camrose in a Transport-Ford. It would appear that Rasmussen invited Sandmose to come to Wayne during his visit in Holden.

On November 16, Sandemose mentioned in his diary that he was that day in Edmonton. According to an entry the following day, he seemed to have gotten someone to drive him there to telegraph Gyldendal, probably to ask for money. This, he said, would mean using the last of the money he had with him which he could have spent getting a ticket to Wayne. Whatever the circumstances, Sorensen drove him the 26 miles to Camrose in an open truck where he was able to get on a train to Wayne November 17. As mentioned above, it seems quite likely that he had gotten a railway pass from the CNR before leaving Winnipeg, and that his concern about having to choose between a trip to Edmonton and one to Wayne was totally without basis.

Wayne

Passing through Stettler on the train between Camrose and Wayne, Sandemose mentioned seeing a burned-down grain elevator, its ruins still smouldering. A smell of burned bread filled the car:

> I saw before me the prairie being turned by the blade of the plow, harrows and small machines followed drawn by eight or twelve horses. And summer came, autumn came, the yellow plains were mown down. The autumn worker toiled, the threshing machine thundered, a parade of slow wagons to the grain elevator. There a match put an end to it all, leaving only a pile of burned pig feed.[130]

In the evening of November 17, he arrived in Wayne, situated at the bottom of a coulee about six miles from Dalum. He was met at the station by Oscar Sørensen, a seminarist from the Løgstør area of Denmark, in a sled, since all car traffic was impossible because of a snowstorm:

> The land here rises to the west with hills of sandstone, earth, minerals, coal, metals. Wayne is situated on a plain, completely encircled by hills, an impressive place. The sleigh trip up from Wayne to the plateau, the frosty mist, bitterly cold, blurred stars. Sky and land the same greyish white colour, you could wander around here some nights without knowing why or where you are going. The coyote howls through the canyons and is answered with a baying from the other end.[131]

For the first few days Sandemose stayed with Pastor Peter Rasmussen (1877–1963), the minister portrayed in "A Canadian Pastor," on his farm just north of the Dalum crossing on the edge of Home Coulee. The house, in which a couple of rooms upstairs served as dormitory accommodations for newly arrived Danes attending Rasmussen's folk high school, was very crowded. In addition the pastor's wife was in the hospital in Drumheller. As a result, most of the housework and cooking fell on the shoulders of Rasmussen's oldest daughter, Thora, later Jorgensen, and her siblings.[132]

In addition to the folk high school students and Sandemose, a Pastor Juhl and his wife were staying at the Rasmussen farm. Juhl was living in Saskatchewan, but had a hard time making a go of it there, and thus he frequently came to Dalum on visits.[133] Sandemose was evidently not particularly at ease in Mrs. Juhl's presence. "The little round pastor's wife with the dead eyes. Her self-satisfied song, her sweet smile which makes a cold shiver run down your back."[134]

Since Dalum had no church in the 1920s,[135] Rasmussen held services each Sunday during these years at an assembly hall, built by the colony's members,[136] and located on the Rasmussen farm. Here also some of the folk high school students were housed. Most of the Danes in the area attended, even if they were not particularly religious, as this was about the only chance people had for social intercourse.

On November 28 Sandemose attended a meeting of "Dansk Folkesamfund" (Danish Peoples' Society)[137] at the house of Peter Rasmussen (not the Pastor), the chairman of the church congregation. Sandemose had evidently given a talk at the school the previous Sunday, but as can be seen from the following report, his ideas on religion and evolution did not exactly correspond with those current in Dalum:

> A song, afterward the agenda was run through in two minutes, but there was nothing on it. Then again a song, and the chairman of Folkesamfundet, Ostergaard, stated that he had been told that Pastor Juhl would like to give a talk. He did so based on one I had given at the school last Sunday on evolution. For an hour and a half he spoke blackly about creation and prophesy, about whales with air chambers, etc.,[138] after which we sang again. Pastor Rasmussen asked afterward if I would like to speak and if the audience on the whole wanted to listen to me. No one answered... It can be added only that the song after Juhl's sermon was a ridiculous tune without poetry about Darwin. It was an outrageous show, which I was distressed at having come to experience. But naturally I knew ahead of time that "tolerance," "freedom" etc. only apply to those who blather perversely about drivel, but yet stick to the drivel.[139]

Thora Jorgensen remembered Sandemose as always being a gentleman and well dressed. Because she was so busy with the housework at the time, she didn't remember having any time to converse with him. However, Sandemose did mention Thora several times in his diary and also that he did on occasion speak with her.[140] November 29 was Thora's birthday, and Sandemose mentioned this as well.[141] Thora said that a party was given for her and that Sandemose wrote a song for her. This song, which Thora showed me a copy of, was written down by someone at the party. However, Sandemose is nowhere else known to have written a song, and the lyrics do not resemble any other work of his. Judging from the text, it would seem to have been composed by someone who knew her reasonably well and who had been staying at the school for a fairly long time, rather than just the twelve days Sandemose had so far been there.

Probably on account of the crowded conditions at Pastor Rasmussen's, Sandemose moved over to Peter Østergaard's farm on November 30. He had already made the acquaintance of one of the few people in Dalum who had strong intellectual interests—Østergaard's brother-in-law, John Andersen,

> ... generally popular also among the extreme religious elements, referred to by the pastor with reservation. Faithful Communist, believes in the possibility of the betterment of mankind... Tries above all to be objective, yet becomes subjective when it comes to his own ideas. The typical gentle, accommodating man who defends the

wildest excesses. Characteristic that he does not believe in a Communist victory in the U.S.A. and Canada and does not even consider such a victory desirable, but believes in a closely impending victory in Europe. He knows American conditions intimately, not European.[142]

On December 3, John Andersen got a team of eight horses to move an old granary six miles down into a coulee not far from the town of East Coulee. Another farmer named Thorkil who, according to the diary, shot at a coyote, which approached the men, accompanied Sandemose and Andersen. In the article "Moving Day" Sandemose gives a fictitious account of how he helped a farmer in Saskatchewan move his house down into a coulee, which is obviously based, to a large extent on this experience.

For the next five days Sandemose stayed with John Andersen down in the coulee. There the two men spent some of the time discussing literature, according to the diary. John Andersen's favourite writer was Thoreau, in particular his book *Walden Pond*. Since there was little to read in the shack, Andersen leafed through a half-finished manuscript of Sandemose's, and Sandemose picked his way through one of Andersen's on national economy. Sandemose thought that Andersen's writings, though, were very boring.[143] Sandemose mentions an old, broken safe in the coulee. In order to get a bit of exercise, the two men would compete by throwing stones at it. The one who lost the competition would have to get up in the ice-cold morning and light the fire in the stove.[144]

On the morning of December 5 they ran out of tobacco. They also went through a hailstorm and later in the day a snowstorm. Thorkil had gone out hunting wolves and had not come back. That night Sandemose began to be afraid,[145] and if we are to believe the diary, this feeling continued into the next couple of days. Thorkil returned to the shack the next morning when the storm had abated, having gotten shelter with a farmer. Sandemose's stay with John Andersen is described more fully in "East Coulee."

On December 8 Sandemose left John Andersen's shack and came back up onto the plains. The next day he was at Carl Dresen's. Dresen was another sort of intellectual with whom Sandemose might well have had something in common. He was a dreamer, loved music and played the violin. He eventually gave up on farming, though, and went to work in one of the mines.

By December 9, according to the diary, Sandemose was back at Pastor Rasmussen's school. During the next few days he made many diary entries. Most of these were drafts for articles and stories, many of which he later used. Also he started making plans for a novel which he called "Folket paa Præ rien" (The People on the Prairie) and which would later evolve into *Ross Dane*.

Sandemose left Wayne at 6:45 P.M., December 14 after waiting an additional hour and forty-five minutes, as the train was late:

> Bitterly cold, nose so sore that it couldn't stand to be touched... it was quiet and clear, but searingly cold, it shrieked as though a giant knife were cutting through a giant cork, a raw sound grating inside your head! When you walked the sound shrieked and cut like knives, certainly the coldest day of the year up until now.[146]

Because he was not dressed for the weather, he became sick and spent the afternoon in the waiting room where it was warm.

Calgary

While in Calgary Sandemose stayed at the CPR Hotel Palliser, the most luxurious hotel in Calgary at the time. From here he had a commanding view of the city and its surroundings:

> Outside lies Calgary, I have a room high up and am looking far out over the city where the smoke in the twilight is drawn in compact masses in the crisp air. The snow-covered square roofs form a broken, tangled, but nevertheless calming mosaic. Calgary is located in the Red Deer (?) [sic] River valley, the river lies with ice packs, here and there the current breaks through, black and alive. To the west you look into the mountains, pinnacles and spires, they are not stage sets like mountains in the distance often seem to be, you look into them and sense their timelessness… Calgary's streets are like all other Canadian ones: a couple of main streets well lit, the others pitch black crevasses, so that you instinctively move your revolver into your coat pocket before you go through them.[147]

On his first day in Calgary, Sandemose went to visit the Danish consul, Peter Pallesen. Pallesen was the son of a smallholder from a village near Silkeborg, born in 1873. After serving in the military, he had come to Canada and begun work as a milk deliverer. Over the years he had worked himself up to become a successful farmer and dairyman, with a dairy in Calgary, next to which he had built his home that also served as his office. He also owned a number of smaller dairies in other districts.[148] He and Sandemose discussed, among other things, the winter conditions on the farms for the hired hand where usually $10 to $15 a month could be earned. However, these positions often went unfilled, because it was difficult for a man who had been used to the relatively high pay during the busy season to adjust to this lower remuneration.

That afternoon Sandemose met with Pastor Jens Knudsen. Knudsen had been ordained in 1910 and had served several congregations in the United States. He had been director of a folk high school in Kenmare, North Dakota for a couple of years and had then spent six years in Brooklyn. In 1926 he came to Calgary as pastor of Sharon Lutheran Church, the United Danish Evangelical Lutheran Church there, and the one most Danes frequented. He also became principal of Dana Folk High School which was situated in a stately mansion on the north side of the Bow River on a bluff overlooking the city.[149] As he had done with Pallesen, Sandemose talked with Knudsen about the immigrant's situation in winter—that those who had the will and physical ability to do work had many possibilities for success. They also examined the question of health insurance for Danes in Canada, something Sandemose had already considered with Fremming in Winnipeg.

Another prominent Calgary Dane Sandemose visited the next day was Charles Waldemar Petersen (Charles Walter Peterson, 1868–1944). Petersen was from a military family in Denmark and had attended a private school in England. In 1887 he came to Canada, first to Manitoba where he farmed for a few years and then became Assistant Dominion General Immigration Agent and Colonization Agent for Manitoba Northwestern Railway. He moved to Alberta in 1892 as a rancher and became Deputy Minister of Agriculture and then entered the service of the CPR in various capacities. He was also an author and editor of *The Farm and Ranch Review*.[150] The two discussed immigrants, Petersen claiming that in general northern Europeans didn't make good pioneers, because they had been brought up in countries where everything was unchanging. Danes had to get rid of their Danish point of view, he felt, before they could make a go of it in Canada. They had to accept that a person in Canada wasn't evaluated by how many hours he put in at work, but by how much he produced.[151]

In the afternoon Sandemose went to Dana High School where he gave a lecture entitled "Concerning What an Immigrant is Going to Give up or Keep." This he characterizes in his diary as being "neutral enough to make a hit with the Mission people."[152]

It appears from a diary entry[153] that Sandemose was asked to pay in advance for one night at the Hotel Palliser and that he did so, even though he must have had very little money at this point. Thereafter, according to the same entry, he was constantly being paged on the telephone or by bellboys, but he kept himself low for fear that he would have to pay for the additional nights:

> I am staying now outside of the borders of Denmark for the fifth month until I am left holding the bag in the good city of Calgary in the most expensive room in the best hotel in town without a penny to pay for all this magnificence. When you cannot pay anyway, you might just as well have a run for your money.[154]

However, he was expecting a telegram, and when he was paged on the morning of December 18, he revealed himself:

> [Ouch!] It wasn't the telegram… from my free pass it seemed to appear I worked for the CPR, the hotel's owner—we just want your name—I was more frightened than hurt, but my fingers began to tremble anyway—for the fact is, that Alberta is a very, very cool country and I didn't want to make a bed up right on the street when the thermometer stands thirty below zero.[155]

Ever since arriving at Redvers, he had been sick, sometimes not so badly, at other times quite badly. On December 17 he mentions that now was one of his worst periods. He also talks about having nightmares when he has a fever. The next day he was better.

As late as his stay with John Andersen in East Coulee, he had planned to continue on to the west coast.[156] These plans would now have to be abandoned. However, he was still hoping he might be able to visit the Maritimes and Newfoundland before returning to Denmark. In a letter to Schmidt, written December 17,[157] he asked whether or not the former had received his telegram from Edmonton, dated November 16, in which he had requested money. If he did not receive any, then he would have to give up plans to travel in eastern Canada and return straight home. On the evening of December 18 he seems finally to have made his decision to leave Calgary. Just above some drawings showing a skeleton head, men with wide open mouths and a pistol pointing to a head with the caption "Stemninger fra Calgary" (Moods from Calgary) he wrote:

> I am tired of this country now and long for home. Yet I don't actually suffer from homesickness, just get tired and sluggish, don't remember well, forget everything. I wish I were back in Copenhagen. You have to deal with the most pressing problem here and now which is to escape safe and sound from Calgary.[158]

Perhaps also his fear of having to pay for his hotel room helped him to make his decision.

On December 19, Sandemose was on the train to Toronto.

To Erie and Beyond

"I telegraphed Erie for fifty dollars, but they weren't able to get more than thirty-five and then I was back again where I started, meanwhile, I was able to get away from Calgary to Toronto where the story can then begin from the beginning."[159] If this is true, then the money must have come either from his sister Anna or his brother Anton, but the tone in the diary almost makes it seem as though in reality nothing was forthcoming. He also telegraphed a request for money to Chr. Mikkelsen, the editor of the newspaper *Vendsyssel Tidende*, and was expecting it to be there when he reached Toronto.

The following day he passed Brandon, Manitoba on the way to Winnipeg. He remarked in his diary that the absolutely flat prairie in this region was almost the same as that east of Saskatoon. At 5:05 the train came to Winnipeg and then continued on. Most of the third day the train spent going around the northern part of Lake Superior. Sandemose wrote how desolate the countryside was and described the seemingly endless forests:

> The spruce trees stand with white veils, devout as nuns at vespers. The branches of the poplars become as fine as threads at their tops, bridal veils, a vision of the wheat, which will grow here sometime.[160]

On arriving in Toronto December 22, hungry and broke, Sandemose discovered that no money had been telegraphed to him. He wondered whether Mikkelsen might actually have sent him some but that it was sitting somewhere else, since he observed that the address he had given Mikkelsen was not the best one. Then he sent a telegram to Col. J.S. Dennis, Chief Commissioner, Department of Colonization, Montreal in a last ditch hope. While waiting in the telegraph office in Toronto a telegram with $25 from another person in Col. Dennis' office, since Col. Dennis was out of town, did in fact arrive. Sandemose was elated, exclaiming to his diary that this was the greatest amount of money he had ever received in his life. Perhaps, he speculated, the man had thought the $25 was something that Sandemose and Col. Dennis had made an agreement on earlier.

Thinking he was to clear customs in Hamilton, he had sent his trunk there and was expecting to have to wait in the city for some time while doing so. He remembered, undoubtedly, the problems he had going across the border that fall. When he arrived the customs official was not there. The possibility was offered to him to leave his bags with the keys there and have them forwarded to him, but Sandemose felt he should stay with them and go through the ordeal. While waiting in Hamilton a customs official did arrive and explained that the inspection would be done on the train. "Slipped remarkably safe and sound into the U.S.A. The immigration officer must have missed me, didn't see him, am thus probably here illegally."[161]

That evening, December 22, he arrived in Erie, Pennsylvania, where he spent the next six weeks with his sister Anna and her husband Paul Paris. Anna Paris lived not far from Lake Erie with her husband and two young daughters, Velma and Flora. Their apartment was not far from an ironworks, and in the next few diary entries[162] Sandemose mentions the nearby gas flame that created a stench in the air that was frequently impossible to get away from.

His diary entries for the next few days were usually short and contained a few sketchy comments about his surroundings and the weather. He also wrote a draft for a short story or a chapter of a larger work, copied some information on the conditions around Holden, given him by Peter Sorensen and speculated on various aspects of life, often in a pessimistic vein. On January 12 there was a long entry on capital punishment in the United States, the methods used, its frequency and how it is treated in the press. It is almost as though he had reached the bottom of a depression that had been building since his arrival in Erie. The remaining entries from his Erie stay were few and far between and said virtually nothing about his visit with his sister.

Anna Paris recalled the visit of her brother.[163] According to her, Sandemose and Paul Paris were always arguing politics:

> Now Aksel was pretty good at English, if he put his mind to it. He could follow a conversation in English. My husband was quite a... Well, I must say he was quite intelligent. And they got in the biggest conversations, those two. I'll never forget one incident where we had had... See, that was during the depression [prohibition], you know, there wasn't much of liquor of any kind. But we had some wine, and Aksel just loved this wine. And he had had quite a bit of wine this one night, and, I guess, got a little sick, and complained, "Oh, my God!" So Paul looked at him, and he said, "Why do you call for him, you don't even believe in him?" Well, Aksel didn't have much to say. He didn't believe in God.
>
> I think it was my oldest daughter. I don't know, if she had whooping cough or what she had. I don't remember. She had a terrific cough, I know that. And she coughed her poor little lungs out, and he complained, and he couldn't sleep for that coughing. So I just looked at him. I says, "Well, how do you think she feels. If you can't stand it, well, you know what you can do." That was it. Nothing more said.

Sandemose had a small room, and Anna remembered his spending a lot of time in it writing. The question arises, if he wasn't writing much in his diary, what was he writing? At the beginning of part VI of the Canada diary, the first entry of which is dated January 24, 1928, Sandemose listed the articles he had already written and had published while away, those he had finished, but presumably not yet published, and those he was at least planning to write. Of these, four had been already published, ten had been written and 32 had been either started or considered. Likely he was working on some of these while in Erie.

Toward the end of his stay in Erie, Sandemose had finally decided that he would have to go directly home instead of visiting the Maritimes. Anna Paris recalled his talking about going to Newfoundland, but remembered nothing about his cancelling the trip.[164] On February 4 he wrote to his friend William Walter Ludlow in Joe Batt's Arm saying he would not be able to come, but the letter took some time to arrive. Ludlow had expected him and had even gone to Fogo on February 15 to meet the boat he thought he would be on.[165]

No money appears to have come to him during this period. Accordingly his brother and sister decided to help him as he was leaving on February 8:

> [He] didn't have much while he stayed with us. And when he came, he had a kind of a raincoat on, not a very warm one. And like I said, it was bitter cold. And I can remember we kind of took turns with a visit from my brother, Anton, who also lived in Erie here. We talked it over between the two of us that we should try to get him something warmer to wear. So between the two of us... I shouldn't even say, "me." My husband, Paul, and Anton went together, and they got him a new suit of clothes and a good, warm overcoat. So that he had. And when the time came that he had to leave, of course, he didn't have any money, so he got $60 out of us. In 1928 $60 was a "formue" [fortune]. It was something. ... And he took off then. And from then on we didn't hear whether he had gotten off on that boat that he should, or... As a matter of fact, we didn't hear at all from him. Never got a word of thanks from him afterwards. And I didn't appreciate that. So then I thought, "Well, that's Aksel."

About a year after having visited Erie, Sandemose wrote a short story, the characters in which were based on Paul and Anna Paris, called "Grækernes Flytning (The Greeks' Move)."[166] It is about a married couple related to the author, living in Erie, Pennsylvania and named Paris, though the husband, like Paul a Greek, is called "Stratos," not "Paul." They are portrayed as constantly quarrelling with the man always taking credit for everything, even his wife's ideas:

> He had [the article] in a newspaper, and he had made, or somebody made like a caricature, picture of Paul. He made a funny face and all. See, Paul had black, curly hair. He had bushy, curly hair and a knife in his box. A picture like that. And then he had a... I can't think of the name now. "Den ville Græker" [The Wild Greek]. And I didn't like that. No, I didn't. I really didn't like that. Because whether it was to be funny, or what, I don't know. But the way he was treated here, he had absolutely no business to write anything like that about Paul that had been so good to him. Because, after all, it wasn't me, it was Paul's home, you know, and Paul's money. And Tony. Even so I didn't like it. I really didn't. If you'd have been in my place, you wouldn't have either. That was bad news. I felt, very, very bad. I saw [the article]. Somebody showed me that picture, and I thought to myself, well, that's what you get when you're good to people.[167]

Again Sandemose had no problems crossing the border to Canada. He reached Toronto at 9:45, but did not stay in the city this time. Instead he rode in a sleeper that night to Montreal where he arrived the next day, February 9 at 7:00 A.M.[168]

February 9 was a busy day, according to the diary, as he had a number of appointments. One of the places he went was to the Department of Colonization and Development, Canadian Pacific Railway, where he was interviewed by a reporter from the *Montreal Herald*. He had gone there, according the article in the *Herald*, which followed the interview,[169] to get letters, photographs and maps. In the interview he talked a bit about his experiences in western Canada and how the Danes were doing there. Portions of the interview later appeared in at least two western Canadian newspapers.[170]

That evening Sandemose was on his way to St. John, New Brunswick to catch the S.S. *Metagama* back to Great Britain. He arrived in the city the following day around noon. The next day at 1:00 P.M. the ship put out from St. John in fog and a snowstorm.[171]

There were only 35 cabin passengers on board, and Sandemose was the only Dane. He travelled first class. The diary entries made during the sailing were few.[172] He mentioned the rough seas on much of the trip, which cut down on the liveliness of the passengers and kept him to his bed a great deal. Mention was also made of his remembering his first trip to Newfoundland in 1916–17.

On February 17 Sandemose had a very strange experience:

> As the days passed I became more and more convinced that I would never reach Liverpool alive. The feeling began to develop just before I went aboard Metagama and became stronger day by day. The night between February 15 and 16 I got out of my berth almost convinced that now the moment had come. But since I had been in an especially calm and determined condition, I saw myself giving up the struggle against the wild ocean, which was going on. The joy of being on the way home was rather dampened, for it was only a matter of three to four days at the utmost before I would be eaten by sharks—I wouldn't reach home at all.[173]

The feeling culminated after dinner on February 17 as he was walking on the deck near the entrance to third class:

> Then I called on the evil spirits, the klabauterman. And he came right away. I was in terror. He yielded but came back after a few seconds. Dazed I went into the light, where canvass had been set up to make a shelter—but which also closed off the view to the sea. I stayed there a long time, listening to the raw sounds. That night was unbearable. Some one was walking outside the side of the ship and looking through the porthole into my cabin. Later in the night I got out of my berth, walked over to

the porthole with my head turned away and drew the curtain tightly in front of it. The eeriness lasted until daybreak and had not quite passed when the steward rang.[174]

The morning saw better weather, and Sandemose wondered whether the whole thing wasn't a result of seasickness. Later a group of young people asked him for a contribution for a dead boy's parents:

> I looked unsympathetically at them—and then got the story, which, because of my seclusion, I had not heard anything about before: a little boy had struggled with death on board since we had sailed from St. John. He expired February 18 early in the morning. Then the spirits of death left the ship. I had heard and seen them and believed they were coming after me.[175]

The *Metagama* arrived in Liverpool shortly after midnight on February 19, and in the morning Sandemose boarded the train bound for London. Judging from his diary entries, he seems to have been almost ecstatic to return to Europe:

> No, I must ask for the old world where farm girls wave to the train and serrated tiles are outlined over forests. England, wonderful misty Nordic land.
>
> A little bridge with a brick parapet over a river—that's worth all of Canada.[176]

In London Sandemose stayed at the National Hotel, Russell Square. The morning of February 20 he went to visit the British Museum in the thick morning fog and then strolled around the city. At 6:00 P.M. he took the train to Harwich where he boarded the boat for Denmark: "There came over me a strange absurd happiness as soon as I was on the deck of the Danish boat. I had to control myself not to tickle the cabin maid under the chin and say 'Hurrah' to the steward."[177] The next evening at 9:05 he was back in Denmark.

Post-Canada

Shortly after returning to Copenhagen, Sandemose attempted to get Gyldendal interested in taking over two of his earlier books, *Ungdomssynd* and *Mænd fra Atlanten*. In a letter to Jerichow[178] he asked Gyldendal to consider his proposal, saying that while he had not spoken with Mr. Jespersen since the former book's publication, the publishing house that published the latter had since collapsed. He had heard it said that these books were the best ones he had written, and pointed out that neither of them had been critiqued by Gyldendal. Schmidt replied[179] that his company could not look into Sandemose's request until it was found out how many copies of the book runs were around. While *Mænd fra Atlanten* was probably not a problem to take over, Sandemose himself would have to have contact with Jespersen to find out what the situation was with *Ungdomssynd*.

Meanwhile Sandemose was working on his next novel:

> I am now well into my new book... It's going to be on a greater scale than my previous ones. I am doing my utmost to have it ready in the course of the summer, but it's of course sometimes hard to be able to work in peace.[180]

In May the manuscript was sent to Gyldendal. The consultant, Ludvig Holstein, was quite enthusiastic in his assessment:

> The material has been waiting a long time for its author. And now he is here... The book can be absolutely recommended for publication. It is the most significant book Sandemose has written and the first in which he fortunately has overcome the difficulties that until now have blocked the way for his great talent. For the first time he knows fully what he wants and where he wants to go... I can imagine that with this

novel Sandemose will win the victory that is more than a mere tribute due to a new talent... [The book] in its style and its character portrayal is like a saga.[181]

Holstein also recommended that the book should carry the name of its main character, Ross Dane.

On July 6, 1928 an agreement was reached between Aksel Sandemose and Gyldendal that his new book, provisionally entitled *Folket paa Prærien (The People on the Prairie)*, would be printed in an edition of 2,000 copies.[182] An arrangement had also been made with a German publisher that was to include all foreign editions of it. The book, under Holstein's proposed title *Ross Dane*, appeared on September 29, 1928. The first edition was printed in 1,500 copies, but later in the year an additional 500 were issued.

The reviews in various newspapers and periodicals were overwhelmingly favourable. An almost insignificant exception to this was Hans Henriksen's assessment in *Morsø Folkeblad*.[183] While Henriksen described Sandemose as having, "a good deal of imagination himself," nevertheless "One would only wish that the lines in Rasmus Dansker's (Ross Dane's) work were penned in a bit more strongly. It lacks breadth and rarely reaches higher than the everyday." Most reviewers felt the book was Sandemose's best to have appeared so far, and many remarked on its superiority to *Klabavtermanden*. The one dissenter in this regard was the author Tom Kristensen:

> *Ross Dane* is not up to the standard of *Klabavtermanden*, as its themes are not fully elucidated. The fact is Aksel Sandemose proceeds too quickly, lines up his figures quickly and quickly leaves them; but there is this great and exceptional imagination in him, and there is the grandness and freshness of the first draft over his book.[184]

That which was perhaps most praised was his character portrayals, in particular that of Ross Dane, and his nature descriptions. "Sandemose has energetically completed the portrait of this strapping fellow."[185] "Where the book is best, its form becomes a characteristic of Rasmus's nature... Ross Dane [is] glorious reality, and the book about him is fast-paced and exciting, signs in the sun and the moon that Aksel Sandemose's talent is growing and developing fruitfully."[186] "Around his Rasmus Aksel Sandemose gathers a gallery of characters, drawn with clear and confident lines, and with the most penetrating understanding of human beings."[187] "Aksel Sandemose also has an exceptional ability to portray his people so one will recognize them, and to describe nature in such precise connection with events and character description that it is never felt he has the specific objective of telling about the landscape, animal life and changes in the weather."[188] "Sandemose's natural descriptions of the prairie in all seasons, of its plants and numerous animals, virgin nature's ever changing moods are those of a great artist."[189] "A rich fullness of nature descriptions in Sandemose's strong, personal language, simple human figures who stand out alive for the reader, a complete compact catechism for Canadian colonists."[190] "Neither in the portrayal of [Ross Dane] himself nor the other Danes ... does Sandemose exhibit a psychological ability that goes into depth. But it isn't really missed—his descriptions are so lucid, so organic and so atmospheric that one's own imagination supplements what is given."[191]

Harald Bergstedt in *Social-Demokraten* remarked, "Fresh, brilliant, without digressions and at the same time with its own ironic or sarcastic psychology which has both a lively and salty quality... Seriousness and humour alternate in this book from modern Canada ... a book with the pulse of modern life and a book for everyone."[192] Like Consulent Ludvig Holstein, Axel Broe compared the book to a saga. "It is ... great in its outline, of an exceptional simplicity, written in a harsh, perhaps slightly massive but precise language. It is on the whole a narrative close to the sagas, also its humour only distances itself from them in the description of remarkable mystical states of mind, reproduced with a visionary's erotically coloured imagination."[193] Perhaps Oscar Geismar should have the last word. "Some people will ... happily maintain that now in Mr. Sandemose Denmark has an outstanding writer of prose from whom there is reason to expect first-rate things. The many efforts from his earlier books have become here the decisive leap. Now he is capable of inspiring the facts, and art is nothing more."[194]

That Sandemose might have an opportunity to make use of his Canadian experiences in a capacity other than that of writer is first indicated by a letter from M.B. Sorensen to J.S. Dennis.[195] According to this letter, Dennis had evidently been considering Sorensen for a post with the Canadian Pacific Railway in Canada and had asked Sorensen to suggest a replacement for him in Copenhagen. Sorensen recommended two people. The first one was Svend Broby who at the time was working for the Department of Agriculture in Montreal. While pointing out that he was held in high esteem in Denmark and had been interested in Danish emigration, Sorensen was not certain that Broby would want to move to Denmark. His second suggestion was Aksel Sandemose. He presupposed a Canadian Pacific objection to Sandemose by saying his Canadian experience might be considered too short, but mentioned his visiting all the Danish settlements in the west and also his having been in Quebec, Labrador and Newfoundland during the war, which of course was only partly true. He said as well that Sandemose had been very productive writing articles about Canada, "and I feel certain that he with his pen could do far more effective propaganda work here than can I and given opportunities to visit Canada as I have had, he can augment his Canadian experience." Sandemose had, in addition, held lectures, and Sorensen felt that he must be good at that or he would not have gotten engagements.

Sandemose had received a copy of Sorensen's letter, and he included it in a letter to Schmidt.[196] Here he said, "If things go the way he wants, my position in the course of about nine months will be totally changed." He also requested that the letter be treated with discretion. No further communication is known regarding this matter, but it must be assumed that Sorensen's recommendation of Sandemose was not acted upon by the CPR.

The next that is heard about Sandemose and his possible future involving Canada was in a letter he wrote to Jerichow at the end of October.[197] Right at the beginning of the letter he said that he and his family intended to go to Nova Scotia to settle there, for various reasons, some of which were private. One of the reasons he mentioned is that he wanted to be able to concentrate on his books and not spend time getting involved in other things which would likely distract him in Denmark:

> In Nova Scotia it's my intention to start up a small farm. Simple farming makes it possible for a person to have large parts of the year at his disposition. And I have always found myself best up against tangible realities. I am in no doubt that my authorship gains in value as a result—the last book proves that, I think.

Sandemose proposed that all his income from his writings go into Gyldendal's account and that he be paid a certain amount each month out of this. He hoped that the publisher could assure him an amount of $125 Canadian from the day he left Denmark. The next day Sandemose talked to Schmidt on the telephone, and was informed that Gyldendal was not willing to go along with Sandemose's request.[198] This was confirmed two days later in a letter from Schmidt.[199]

Less than a month later Sandemose was telling journalists about his plans to emigrate. In an interview with *Berlingske Tidende*[200] Sandemose mentioned he was leaving Denmark in order to secure a new future for himself. When asked why, he answered that he was superfluous in Denmark. "The country is so small that there is a remarkable discord among all things, for example, that I, a mediocre author, am proclaimed a genius." When asked if he found this unpleasant, Sandemose answered that when one sees the great degree there is between what one is considered to be and what one is in reality, and that this is a peculiarly Danish phenomenon, then one is in the middle of the lie oneself and one gets a distorted view of oneself. As to why he had chosen Canada, he replied that it was one of the few countries open to immigrants, but that he could not really explain why he could fall in love with a certain place.

On January 1, 1929, Sandemose was interviewed by John Frimand of *Aalborg Venstreblad*.[201] In this interview he gave his reasons for wanting to emigrate and said, "We can easily assume that there are a maximum of three proper poets per one million inhabitants. That makes a total of nine in Denmark." He said he was not one of them, and "If I can't be number one with a fair distance down to the next one, then I'd rather run a farm." In response to the question as to why not do so in Denmark, he replied that for a provincial who has gone to Copenhagen there is no way back. If he did start farming in Denmark he would be a cotter and just end up leaving his children with debt, since he had no capital. As to whether or not he could run a farm, he said that he would have to or die of hunger. Sandemose would not recommend anyone to go to Canada. "Proper people don't try to unload the responsibility onto others with that kind of question." Did Danes like Canada? "The first year they usually curse it. Few end up blessing it. But most people make comparisons—and do *not* go back."

Sandemose mentioned he felt as a soul mate with the sailor and pioneer and was going off to take land in Canada.[202]

Since returning from Canada, Sandemose had had contact with Godtfred Madsen from Redvers by letter. In one, partly in Danish and partly in English, dated February 26, 1929,[203] Sandemose let Madsen know that he could not hold out any longer in Denmark:

> Min Kone følger mig gerne, og Børnene, ja, de er jo for smaa til at blive spurgt. (My wife would like to follow me, and my children, well, they are of course too little to be asked.) The twins (two girls) are seven years, they will not miss Denmark but turn out to [be] real Canadians with no immigration-fever in their hearts as we who waited to [sic] long—a fact I will not try to deny.

However, he told Madsen that he had to postpone his trip indefinitely because he had to redeem his six books that were sitting with various publishers, though everything else was in order.

Later in the year Sandemose started having dealings with the Canadian railway companies again. In a diary entry for November 2, 1929,[204] he mentioned that he had stopped by the office of La Cour of the CNR office in Copenhagen, who was very preoccupied with the fact that the travelling inspector of the CPR in Denmark was preparing to move to Canada. La Cour, Sandemose stated, was nervous as to what kind of person the inspector's successor would be, in part because "the successor might be me." La Cour cautioned Sandemose that if he wished to enter the business, then he should approach Scandinavian-American Lines, since that was where the future lay. Sandemose also noted in the same diary entry that he had written a greeting to M.B. Sorensen in order to bring himself to Sorensen's attention. Sorensen had replied, asking Sandemose whether he could supply passengers for CPR cruises. Sandemose said he had then written back to Sorensen giving the impression that he took matter of getting such a job with the CPR as a joke:

> When it comes down to it, I hardly think I would accept an offer from any of them. But I like this little game. If S.A.L. gets its new boat and the new office in Edmonton opens, it certainly wouldn't be the worst thing for me to sit there a couple of years. And the part of a travel manager here at home with a trip to Canada once in a while—I dare say that's also something to be considered.

For the next few days Sandemose continued his "little game" with the railway companies. On November 5 he had had a telephone conversation with La Cour about the possibility of his getting work with the CNR.[205] However, La Cour had not been successful in arranging this. Later Sandemose met with M.B. Sorensen at a restaurant in town. He told Sorensen that he thought he had certain qualifications for the job of travelling inspector for the CPR in prairie Canada, the job La Cour had been so worried about, but he asked what defects he had that made it such that Sorensen did not seem to want him in that position? Sorensen said that no one but Sandemose was better fitted for the post, and that his concern was primarily that he might quickly tire and neglect details.

According to a diary entry for November 8, 1929, Sandemose received a letter from M.B. Sorensen dated the day before and which he quoted in full in the diary. According to this letter Sandemose had told Sorensen that he was unable to follow a schedule and that he was only able to work according to his inspiration and when it suited him. This, Sorensen said, would not be appropriate behaviour at the CPR. Sorensen continued:

> Of course I have to judge you by the knowledge I have of you. You are not reliable in money matters and have a weakness for alcohol. Under its influence you would not shrink from incurring debts and swindling.

> In our business where so much depends on our sincerity and ability to inspire confidence in ourselves, it would not do to be careless in money matters or with alcohol.

> Finally it's indeed also a question whether you can get a driver's license, and if you got it, whether it then would be defensible to allow you to drive.

> What speaks in your favour I don't have to go into.

Sandemose replied to Sorensen's letter in a clear and quiet manner, according to the diary, but he was actually quite upset:

> But accordingly that's the way you're looked upon when you go outside the land of the poets. That's the way I'm looked upon, and that's the way poets in general are looked upon. Though I knew it well enough, it was still like feeling the earth slip away under my feet. And stronger than ever it came down on me that now very soon it will be a question of life, an inexorable either-or. Living on only as a poet means death by strangulation. Through this [job] positive rehabilitation could be had. And if it fails, a long time can pass before anything similar comes up.[206]

Sandemose waited for further communication with M.B. Sorensen, but the diary ends before anything is learned about the outcome of these efforts. It can be assumed, however, that Sandemose was not offered the job.

One further attempt was made by Sandemose to get a job in Canada. According to a letter written by M.B. Sorensen to an assistant in the service of the CPR in Kentville, Nova

Scotia[207] there was a rumour going around that the Nova Scotia Government was thinking of hiring a Dane to look after and help Danes arriving in the province. Sorensen explained that he was writing in order to recommend Aksel Sandemose for such a position, should it materialize. He mentioned that while Sandemose was not familiar with Nova Scotia, having visited only Halifax and Sydney, he felt it would benefit the province to employ someone who was acquainted with the "mental attitude of the Danish immigrants." Furthermore, since Sandemose was an author, "The story of the success of Danish Immigrants in Nova Scotia many times told and a view of the possibilities rightly told with the colour of an author's pen and with the weight of a government office's authority would soon add new interest to Nova Scotia and see new settlements spring up." Most Danes were suspicious of what private companies and railways promoted, but Sandemose could conduct a publicity campaign that would be astonishing. In conclusion, Sorensen pointed out that Sandemose had published a considerable amount about Canada.

Sorensen must have told Sandemose about the Nova Scotia rumour before he wrote his letter, because on January 27 Sandemose had already written to the Department of Industries and Immigration in Halifax.[208] He said he had decided to "register" himself as an applicant for any CPR position. Afterward he gave some biographical details, such as that he was born in 1897, went to Newfoundland in 1916, later worked for a while in Sydney and Halifax and then went to sea again. The things he had written about Canada are noted, and he mentioned how he had decided to emigrate long ago but did not do so because of his wife's health. In fact it was to Nova Scotia he had intended to immigrate, even though his knowledge of that province was very meagre. He felt he could be valuable because of his "connection with Scandinavian publicity" and that he "in a very short time could influence many tillers of the soil to stay in Nova Scotia." Superintendent, Land Settlement, H.H. Congdon, of the Department of Natural Resources, Nova Scotia replied to Sandemose's letter on February 15, 1930.[209] In it he said, "I regret, however, to advise you that our plans are all made for the coming season and consequently there will be no openings of which you speak." However, Congdon says he will keep Sandemose's letter on file and let him know should anything arise. This appears to be the last attempt on the part of Sandemose to get a job in Canada.

But Sandemose did leave Denmark in 1930—not to Canada, however, but rather to Norway, the homeland of his mother, a move he appears already to have considered back in 1926, judging from his correspondence with Jørgen Bukdahl. From then on he wrote almost exclusively in Norwegian.

Notes

1. Besides Danish and Norwegian editions *Ross Dane* has been translated into English. Aksel Sandemose, *Ross Dane*, translated with an introduction by Christopher Hale (Winnipeg: Gunnars and Campbell, 1989).
2. For a history of the early years of the colony, see, for example, Palle Bo Bojesen, *New Denmark, New Brunswick, Canada: Udviklingen i en dansk udvandrerkoloni 1872–1914* (New Denmark, New Brunswick, Canada: The Development in a Danish Emigrant Colony 1872–1914) (Århus: Aarhus Universitetsforlag, 1993) and the same author's survey in English, "New Denmark—The Oldest Danish Colony in Canada," in Henning Bender and Birgit Flemming Larsen (eds.), *Danish Immigration to Canada, Udvandrerarkivets Skriftserie: Udvandrerhistoriske Studier Nr. 3* (Ålborg, 1991), 49–70.
3. A survey of Danish settlement in Canada is found in Christopher Hale, "Danes" in Paul Robert Magocsi (ed.), *Encyclopedia of Canada's Peoples* (Toronto: University of Toronto Press, 1999), 406–13.
4. For a discussion of the role of the churches in the Canadian Danish colonies, see Christopher Hale, "Happy, Holy or Anglican: Danish Churches in Canada," *Religious Studies and Theology* (1998): 47–58, and Henrik Bredmose Simonsen,

"The Early Life of the Danish Churches in Canada," in Bender and Flemming Larsen (eds.), *Danish Immigration*, 91–105. A history of the Danish churches in America is Henrik Bredmose Simonsen, *Kampen om danskheden. Tro og nationalitet i de danske kirkesamfund i Amerika (The Struggle for Danishness. Faith and Nationality in the Danish Church Congregations in America)* (Århus: Aarhus Universitetsforlag, 1990). Except for several paragraphs devoted to each of the more important Canadian Danish settlements, this volume contains only scattered references to Canada.

5. On the Dickson colony see Frank M. Paulsen, *Danish Settlements on the Canadian Prairies: Folk Traditions, Immigrant Experiences, and Local History*, National Museum of Man Mercury Series. Canadian Centre for Folk Culture Studies, Paper No. 11 (Ottawa, 1974), 1–27, which contains transcriptions of reminiscences of several of the original settlers; *Dickson Koloniens Historie. Et Mindeskrift om vore Pioneerer (History of the Dickson Colony. A Memorial Volume about Our Pioneers)* (Blair, NE: 1948) (typewritten English translation, *History of the Dickson Colony*, in the Provincial Archives of Alberta, Edmonton); Margrethe Nissen, Esther Thesberg and Andy Kjaersgaard, "A History of Dickson, Alberta, Canada," in Bender and Flemming Larsen (eds.), *Danish Emigration*, 71–90; and *Dickson: Grub-Axe to Grain* (Spruce View, AB: Spruce View School Area Historical Society, 1973), 29–68, which includes short family histories of both Danish and non-Danish residents.

6. For further information about Standard see Paulsen, *Danish Settlements on the Canadian Prairies*, 44–47, and *From Danaview to Standard* (Standard, AB: Standard Historical Book Society, 1979), which contains short family histories of both Danish and non-Danish residents.

7. When interviewing Danish-Canadians who were living on the prairies in the 1920s, I heard a number of them tell stories of how Pastor Damskov would look over the immigrants as they got off the train. If he found one who appeared to have some money he would strongly encourage him to consider buying land in Ostenfeld, rather than continue on to Saskatchewan. There were also rumours that the pastor was paid $25 by the Canadian Pacific Railway for each immigrant he managed to bring to Canada.

8. Paulsen, *Danish Settlements on the Canadian Prairies*, 73.

9. H.O. Frimodt Møller, *Dansk Bosættelse i Canada (Danish Settlement in Canada)* (Copenhagen: Dansk Traktatselskabs Forlag, 1927), 37.

10. Ibid., 43.

11. *Hemstitches and Hackamores: A History of Holden and District* (Holden, AB: Holden Historical Society, 1984), contains an account of the settlement and growth of the town of Holden and its institutions, but little is mentioned about the Danish community. The book has personal family histories, though, which include most of the Danish families.

12. Møller, *Dansk Bosættelse i Canada*, 42.

13. For an account of the history of Dalum and the folk high school written by members of the community, see *The History of Dalum* (Drumheller, AB: The Big Country News, 1968) and *Reflections—Dalum and Area* (Dalum, AB: Dalum History Book Committee, 1990), both of which also include family histories of a number of the Danish settlers. See also Paulsen, *Danish Settlements on the Canadian Prairies*, 48–71 which has interviews with some of them.

14. On the Danish folk high schools in Canada, see Rolf Buschardt Christensen, "Danish Folk Schools in Canada," in Bender and Flemming Larsen (eds.), *Danish Emigration*, 106–24.

15. See Poul Erik Olsen, "Emigration from Denmark to Canada in the 1920's," in Bender and Flemming Larsen (eds.), *Danish Emigration*, 125–45, especially 126–32.

16. "Canada som Indvandringsland: Beretning afgivet af den til Undersøgelse af Betingelserne for dansk Udvandring til Canada udsendte Delegation" *(Canada as a Land for Immigration. Report Submitted by the Delegation Sent out to Examine the Conditions for Danish Immigration to Canada), Udenrigsministeriets Tidsskrift* (3 Januar 1924).

17. Olaf Linck, *Kanada det store Fremtidsland (Canada the Great Land of the Future)* (Copenhagen: E. Jespersen, 1926).

18. Ibid., 99–100.

19. C. Mikkelsen, *Canada som Fremtidsland* (Copenhagen: Aschehoug, 1927).

20. A few people in Redvers recalled Mikkelsen's visit when I interviewed them in the fall of 1987. One of them, Arnold Olsen, in his 30s at the time, remembered being asked by Mikkelsen, "Why are you here?" to which Olsen replied, "If you tell me why you're here, I'll tell you why I'm here."

21. Aksel Sandemose, *Rejsedagbog (Travel Diary)*, The Royal Library, Copenhagen (September 29, 1927).

22. Aksel Sandemose, "Canada som Fremtidsland," *Hareskov Grundejerblad* (July 15, 1927).

23. See table of numbers of Danish immigrants to Canada between 1912 and 1931 in Olsen, "Emigration from Denmark to Canada," 140.

24. Olsen, ibid., 144, estimates that about 60% of them stayed in Canada.
25. There are three biographies of Aksel Sandemose on which much of the following is based: Espen Haavardsholm, *Mannen fra Jante. Et portrett av Aksel Sandemose (The Man from Jante. A Portrait of Aksel Sandemose)* (Oslo: Gyldendal, 1988); Carl-Eric Nordberg, *Sandemose. En biografi (Sandemose. A Biography)* (Oslo and Copenhagen: Schønbergske, 1967, Stockholm, 1968); Ole Storm, *Janteloven. Sandemose. En biografi (The Law of Jante. Sandemose. A Biography)* (Copenhagen: Gyldendal, 1989). In addition a number of articles and pamphlets, dealing in particular with Sandemose's early years, such as *Aksel Sandemose og Jante (Aksel Sandemose and Jante)* (Copenhagen: Vinten, 1965) have been published by Johannes Væth, who has done extensive research into Sandemose's life and possessed an extensive collection of copies of his personal papers which now are housed in The Royal Museum, Copenhagen. The only account in English until now is to be found in Randi Birn, "Aksel Sandemose—Exile in Search of a Home," in *Contributions to the Study of World Literature* 2, (Westport, CT and London, England: Greenwood Press, 1984), 1–9.
26. Another boy in the family, born in 1903, died at the age of 2.
27. Aksel Sandmose, "Barndom" *(Childhood), Arbeidets Jul* (1934).
28. Johannes Væth, "Om Sandemoses læreår" (Concerning Sandemose's Apprenticeship), in *Atlanten har så mange mil. Strejflys over Sandemose og hans forfatterskab* (Copenhagen: Aschehoug, Copenhagen, 1986), 10–11.
29. The house is still there, though it has been remodelled since Sandemose lived there. On the wall near the door is a plaque commemorating the author.
30. Exclusive interview with Anna Paris, June 1987, Erie, Pennsylvania. Recording housed at the Languages Resource Centre, University of Alberta, Edmonton, Alberta, Canada. There is a photograph dating from 1898 which shows the Danish flag flying from the window in the roof of Færkenstræde 12. See Væth, "Om Sandemoses læreår,"12.
31. Anna Paris interview.
32. See Aksel Sandemose, "Borgerkrig" *(Civil War), Arbeidets Jul* (1936).
33. See the discussion in Haavardsholm, *Mannen fra Jante*, 52–55.
34. Anna Paris interview.
35. Photocopy in Johannes Væth collection, but published in part in Johannes Væth, "Blade af Axel Nielsens dagbog" (Pages from Axel Nielsen's Diary), På sporet af Sandemose (Nykøbing: Forfatterforlaget ATTIKA): 37–41.
36. Haavardsholm, *Mannen fra Jante*, 94–96.
37. This street, in reality the Calle de la Aurora, just north of the main district, is now almost totally deserted and in ruins, though a few prostitutes still frequent the area. The main red light district has moved to the western side of the harbour since Sandemose's time.
38. Aksel Sandemose, translated by Eugene Gay-Tifft, *Horns for Our Adornment* (New York: Alfred A. Knopf, 1938), 3.
39. Estvad saved the letters he received from Sandemose and published them after the latter's death in *Aksel Sandemose først i 20'rne* (Copenhagen: Carit Andersen, 1967).
40. See, for example, the photomontage reproduced in Haavardsholm, *Mannen fra Jante*, 141, which shows a photograph of Sandemose trying to look like J.V. Jensen beside a painting of the latter author in a similar pose.
41. Transcriptions of this recommendation and other letters Jensen sent to Sandemose are to be found in Niels Birger Wamberg, "Johannes V. Jensen og Aksel Sandemose," in Niels Birger Wamberg (ed.), *Sandemoses ansikter* (Oslo: Aschehoug, 1969), 61–77, together with a tribute to him which Sandemose wrote shortly after Jensen's death.
42. Letter, Johannes V. Jensen to Aksel Sandmose, March 24, 1923, in ibid., 68.
43. For an account of the negotiations Sandemose carried on with the three publishing houses, see *Storm*, 125–27.
44. Jørgen Bukdahl (1896–1982) was a Danish author and literary critic whom Sandemose had met through J.V. Jensen. In 1925, Bukdahl moved to Norway where he lived and wrote until 1932.
45. Aksel Sandemose to Jørgen Bukdahl, Copenhagen, January 10, 1926, photocopy, Johannes Væth collection.
46. Ibid., January 12, 1926.
47. Ibid., March 10, 1926.
48. See, for example, letter from the attorney Axel Laursen, Copenhagen(?), January 14, 1926, photocopy, Johannes Væth collection, on behalf of the printing house of Pedersen and Carter, requesting payment of 1,000 kroner on the sum owed.
49. Aksel Sandemose to Jørgen Bukdahl, Copenhagen, August 5, 1926, photocopy, Johannes Væth collection.
50. Ibid., June 5–6, 1926, photocopy, Johannes Væth collection.
51. Letter from Jørgen Bukdahl to Aksel Sandemose, Oslo, no date, photocopy, Johannes Væth collection.

52. Letter from *Berlingske Tidende* to Aksel Sandemose, Copenhagen, November 6, 1926, photocopy, Johannes Væth collection.
53. See notice in *Berlingske Aftenavis*, November 20, 1926: "At the end of winter the author Aksel Sandemose will take up residence in South America."
54. See letter from Aksel Sandemose to H. Jerichow, Copenhagen, May 22, 1926 (?), Gyldendal Archives, where Sandemose mentions in passing that an unforeseen event put an end to his plans for going to South America.
55. Personally related to me by Johannes Væth.
56. Letter from P. Hess to Aksel Sandemose, Copenhagen, February 10, 1927, photocopy, Johannes Væth collection.
57. See letter from Gunnar Gunnarsson to Aksel Sandemose, Gentofte, January 8, 1927, photocopy, Johannes Væth collection.
58. Herbert P. A. Jerichow (1889–1967), manager at Gyldendal's publishing house 1925–31.
59. Letter from Aksel Sandemose to H. Jerichow, Copenhagen, February 11, 1927, Gyldendal Archives.
60. Aksel Sandemose to Jørgen Bukdahl, Copenhagen, April 20, 1927, photocopy, Johannes Væth collection.
61. Aksel Sandemose, "Den flyvende Hollænder," *Berlingske Tidende*, aftenudgave (August 23, 1928).
62. For further discussion of *lykkemand—nidding*, see Johannes Væth, "Lykkemand eller nidding" (Lykkemand or Nidding), *På sporet af Sandemose*: 66–70.
63. See, for example, Axel Broe, "Klabavtermanden," *København* (March 15, 1927); Henning Söderhjelm, "En ung dansk författare" (A Young Danish Author), *Göteborgs Handels-och Sjöfarts-Tidning* (March 28, 1927); Otto Gelsted, "En Søroman" (A Sea Novel), *Extra Bladet* (April 1, 1927); Kai Flor, "En Bog om Søen" (A Book About the Sea), *Berlingske Tidende* (April 22, 1927); Tom Kristensen, "Aksel Sandemose," *Politiken* (May 16, 1927), and Poul Levin, "Nord og Syd" (North and South), *Tilskueren* (May 1927): 355.
64. Letter from Jørgen Bukdahl to Aksel Sandemose, Oslo, no date, photocopy, Johannes Væth collection.
65. Hans Brix, "En Fortælling" *(A Story), Dagens Nyheder* (April 16, 1927).
66. In a letter to Jørgen Bukdahl (Copenhagen, June 5–6, 1926, photocopy, Johannes Væth collection), Sandemose rails at those who awarded Weltzer the grant and says such things as: "In regard to form, concept and consistency, Johannes Weltzer has no more conception of them than does a starling (a grey starling, if you like). I have always had a weakness for what is neat and well dressed, but here a man is presented to me about whom there is no doubt that sexually he has gone to pot."
67. See Tom Kristensen, "Aarets Humorist" (Humourist of the Year), *Politiken* (April 26, 1927).
68. Related to me personally by Johannes Væth who, in turn, got this information from Sandemose's friend Poul Munk-Madsen.
69. "Carl Møllers Legat," *Nationaltidende* (April 26, 1927).
70. Letter from Aksel Sandemose to M.K. Nørgaard, Copenhagen, April 28, 1927, Royal Museum, Copenhagen, NKS 2632 2°.
71. Diary fragment, Aksel Sandemose, 1929, handwritten copy, Johannes Væth collection.
72. Letter from Henning Söderhjelm to Aksel Sandemose, Göteborg, May 17, 1927, photocopy, Johannes Væth collection.
73. Letter of conveyance from Aksel Sandemose to Co-operative Housing Society "Paa Bjerget," Copenhagen, June 7, 1927, photocopy, Johannes Væth collection.
74. Aksel Sandemose to H. Jerichow, Copenhagen, May 22, 1927, Gyldendal Archives.
75. Aksel Sandemose to H. Jerichow, Copenhagen, May 23, 1927, Gyldendal Archives.
76. See, for example, letter from Aksel Sandemose to H. Jerichow, Blidstrup, July 29, 1927; letter from Gyldendal Publishers to Housing Co-operative *Paa Bjerget*, Copenhagen, August 11, 1927; letter from Aksel Sandemose to S. Schmidt, Erie, January 16, 1928, and S. Schmidt to Aksel Sandemose, Copenhagen, January 17, 1928, all in Gyldendal Archives.
77. M.B. Sorensen to Aksel Sandemose, Copenhagen, July 24, 1927, Gyldendal Archives.
78. Aksel Sandemose, *Rejsedagbog* (Travel Diary), Royal Library, Copenhagen, entry, August 23, 1927.
79. Aksel Sandemose to S. Schmidt, Father's Point, August 19, 1927, Gyldendal Archives.
80. Aksel Sandemose to Poul Munk-Madsen, Father's Point, August 20, 1927, photocopy, Johannes Væth collection.
81. Aksel Sandemose, "I Pennsylvanien" (In Pennsylvania), *Morsø Folkeblad* (October 14, 1927).
82. In his article, "Porten til Canada" (The Gateway to Canada), *Sorø Amtstidende* (June 5, 1928), a good part of which parallels "From Belle-Isle to Montreal," Sandemose talks about how horribly hot it was in Montreal. Upon hearing that this

heat wave was plaguing only Canada, and that the United States was quite cool, he decided to go south to Erie instead of waiting for four months as planned.

83. Interview with Anna Paris.
84. Sandemose mentions in his article, "Billeder fra en lang Rejse" (Pictures from a Long Journey), *Aschehougs Magasin* 7 (July 1935), that he made a trip to Chicago, Detroit, and several small towns in Pennsylvania at this time. The diary, however, makes no mention of any such extended journey, nor would the dates of his Erie stay have allowed him to have taken such a one.
85. Diary entry, September 9, 1927.
86. Ibid., September 10, 1927.
87. Martin Jensen, "Østergaard, Johannes and Sorine," *Across Border and Valley. The Story of Maryfield and Fairlight and Surrounding Districts*, Vol. 2 (Maryfield, SK: Maryfield and District Historical Society, 1984), 972.
88. See, for example, "Whisper of the Blood."
89. Diary entry, September 15, 1927.
90. Ibid., September 17, 1927.
91. Diary entries, September 12 and 15, 1927.
92. Diary entry, September 17, 1927.
93. Ibid.
94. Ibid.
95. Ibid.
96. See "The Last Duck Hunt."
97. Diary entry, September 27, 1927.
98. Diary entry, September 27, 1927.
99. The actual hotel Sandemose stayed in burned down in 1951, and a new building, which currently serves as one of the town's two guesthouses, was erected on the same site. I have been told by the local historian, Bill Murray, that the old hotel changed owners quite frequently and thus conditions there could vary considerably.
100. Diary entry, September 27, 1927.
101. During a stay in Redvers in the summer of 1984, when I talked to several of the older residents who recalled Mikkelsen's visit, I also inquired whether they remembered Sandemose. Several of them, including Ejner Larsen, recollected that he had been there but were not able to tell me much about him. Ejner Larsen, though, had read his novel *Ross Dane*, so a copy or two of the book had found its way to Canada.
102. Diary entry, September 29, 1927.
103. See Mikkelsen, *Canada som Fremtidsland*, 75.
104. Diary entry, September 30, 1927.
105. Related to me by Godtfred Madsen's grand-nephew, Ross Madsen.
106. Diary entry, October 1, 1927.
107. Diary entry, October 6, 1927.
108. Ibid.
109. Ibid., October 7, 1927.
110. Diary entry, October 8, 1927.
111. Ibid., October 9, 1927.
112. Diary entry, October 12, 1927.
113. Diary entry, October 18, 1927.
114. Interview with Christine Mikkelsen, Vancouver, BC, Fall 1987.
115. In Montreal he stayed at the Place Viger and later on at the Palliser Hotel in Calgary.
116. Diary entry, October 27, 1927.
117. Ibid., October 29, 1927.
118. Ibid., October 30, 1927.
119. Back pages of Part II of diary, no date.

120. Letter from Valdemar Henriksen, Vils, Denmark, to Johannes Væth, October 11, 1966, photocopy, Johannes Væth collection.
121. Diary entry, November 4, 1927.
122. Diary entry, November 4, 1927.
123. Ibid.
124. Ibid.
125. Ibid., November 6, 1927.
126. Ibid., November 5, 1927.
127. Ibid.
128. Ibid., November 8, 1927.
129. Ibid., November 12, 1927.
130. Ibid., November 17, 1927.
131. Ibid., November 18, 1927.
132. This is confirmed by Sandemose's article "A Canadian Pastor" and by an interview with Thora Jorgensen, née Rasmussen, November 1989, Langley BC.
133. Interview with Thora Jorgensen.
134. Diary entry, November 20, 1927.
135. One was not dedicated until 1936.
136. See *The History of Dalum*, 10.
137. See notes to "A Canadian Pastor" below.
138. Thora Jorgensen remarked that Pastor Juhl was considered to be long winded. Thora Jorgensen interview.
139. Diary entry, November 28, 1927.
140. For example the entry for December 11, where mention is made of a discussion the two of them together with Oscar Sørensen had about the fate of married women coming to the prairies.
141. Diary entry, November 29, 1927.
142. Ibid., December 3, 1927.
143. John Andersen wrote many books, according to his nephew, Axel Ostergaard. He had served in the same unit as the American critic Edmund Wilson during World War I, and they had gotten to know one another. Wilson was of the same opinion as Sandemose concerning Andersen's writings, but Wilson had to admit that he was a great talker. Andersen did, however, later get a book published under the name John Andersen Udmark, *The Road We Have Covered* (New York: Modern Age Books, 1940).
144. Diary entry, December 4, 1927. The safe is still there. No one in the area was able to tell me why on earth such an object was thrown down into the coulee.
145. "Naturangst" (Fear of Nature), he calls it in a diary entry, December 7, 1927.
146. Diary entry for December 14, 1927.
147. Ibid., December 15, 1927.
148. See Mikkelsen, *Canada som Fremtidsland*, 81–82 and Linck, *Kanada det store Fremtidsland*, 114–15.
149. The school was finally closed in 1935, due to the Great Depression. The house has since been torn down, and a large apartment block currently occupies the site.
150. See B.M. Greene (ed.), *Who's Who in Canada 1927* (Toronto: International Press, 1927), 542.
151. Diary entry, December 16, 1927.
152. Ibid.
153. Ibid., December 18, 1927.
154. Ibid., December 17, 1927.
155. Diary entry, December 18, 1927.
156. See diary entry, December 7, 1927, where he says, "Tomorrow or the day after tomorrow at the latest I have to take off from here to the school. There can now only be time for a quick visit to the Pacific."
157. Letter from Aksel Sandemose to S. Schmidt, Calgary, December 17, 1927, Gyldendal Archives.
158. Diary entry, December 18, 1927.

159. Ibid., December 19, 1927.
160. Ibid., December 21, 1927.
161. Diary entry, December 22, 1927.
162. For example, diary entries December 23 and December 25, 1927.
163. Interview with Anna Paris.
164. Ibid.
165. Letter from William Walter Ludlow to Aksel Sandemose, Joe Batt's Arm, March 7, 1928, photocopy, Johannes Væth collection.
166. *Social-Democraten* (December 24, 1928).
167. Interview with Anna Paris.
168. See diary entry, February 8, 1928.
169. "Danish Settlers in Prairie Provinces Terribly Sea-Sick," *Montreal Herald* (February 10, 1928).
170. "Danish Settlers on Western Farms Suffer Sea Thirst," *Free Press Weekly Prarie Farmer*, Winnipeg (March 7, 1928), and "Danish Settlers and Sea Thirst," *Weekely Manitoba Liberal*, Portage la Prairie (March 15, 1928).
171. Diary entry, February 10, 1928.
172. Diary entries, February 10, 15, 17, 19, 1928.
173. Ibid., February 17, 1928.
174. Ibid.
175. This account and other instances noted in the diary from his trip home are included, with some embellishments, in the article, "Hjem til Danmark!," *Dagens Nyheder* (June 10, 1928).
176. Diary entry, February 19, 1928.
177. Ibid., February 20, 1928.
178. Letter from Aksel Sandemose to H. Jerichow, Copenhagen, March 15, 1928, Gyldendal Archives.
179. Letter from S. Schmidt to Aksel Sandemose, Copenhagen, March 22, 1928, Gyldendal Archives.
180. Letter from Aksel Sandemose to S. Schmidt, Copenhagen, April 25, 1928, Gyldendal Archives.
181. Consulent Ludvig Holstein's assessment of *Folket paa Prærien* by Aksel Sandemose, Gyldendal Archives.
182. Letter from S. Schmidt to Aksel Sandemose, Copenhagen, July 7, 1928, Gyldendal Archives.
183. "Aksel Sandemoses Ny Bog. Ross Dane" (Aksel Sandemose's New Book. Ross Dane), *Morsø Folkeblad*, October 10, 1928.
184. Tom Kristensen, "Efteraarets Bøger" (Autumn Books), *Tilskueren* (November 1928), 323.
185. Otto Gelsted, "En Dansk-Amerikaner" (A Danish-American), *Ekstra Bladet* (December 12, 1928).
186. E.J., "En Roman fra Kanada" (A Novel from Canada), *Aalborg Amtstidende* (December 11, 1928).
187. Oscar Geismar, "Aksel Sandemose: Ross Dane," *Fyns Venstreblad* (October 13, 1928).
188. M.u., "Literatur," *Aalborg Stftstidende* (November 13, 1928).
189. Axel Broe, "Aksel Sandemose," *København* (October 2, 1928).
190. Povl Engelstoft, *Den nye Litteratur* (6. Aargang, 1928–29): 39.
191. Chr. R., "Ross Dane," *Politiken* (November 3, 1928).
192. Harald Bergstedt, "Aksel Sandemose: Ross Dane," *Social-Demokraten* (December 23, 1928).
193. Axel Broe, October 2, 1928.
194. Oscar Geismar, October 13, 1928.
195. M.B. Sorensen to J.S. Dennis, Copenhagen, April 14, 1928, Photocopy, Johannes Væth collection.
196. Letter Aksel Sandemose to S. Schmidt, Paa Bjerget, April 25, 1928, Gyldendal Archives.
197. Letter Aksel Sandemose to H. Jerichow, Paa Bjerget, October 28, 1928.
198. Letter from Aksel Sandemose to S. Schmidt, Paa Bjerget, October 29, 1928, Gyldendal Archives.
199. Letter from S. Schmidt to Aksel Sandemose, Copenhagen, November 11, 1928, Gyldendal Archives.
200. C. Houmark, "Det middelmaadige Geni" (The Mediocre Genius), *Berlingske Tidende* (November 24, 1928).
201. John Frimand, "Til Canada" (To Canada), *Aalborg Venstreblad* (January 1, 1929).
202. Aksel Sandemose, "Sandemose: Det er Arbejdsglæde" (Sandemose: It's Joy of Work), *Hjemmet* (December 18, 1928).

203. Letter Aksel Sandemose to Godtfred Madsen, Paa Bjerget, February 26, 1929, Udvandrerarkivet, Ålborg.
204. Diary entry, November 2, 1929, handwritten copy, Johannes Væth collection.
205. Ibid., November 6, 1929.
206. Ibid., November 8, 1929.
207. Letter from M.B. Sorensen to P.L. Sanford, Copenhagen, January 29, 1930, photocopy, Johannes Væth collection.
208. Aksel Sandemose to Department of Industries and Immigration, Halifax, Nova Scotia, Copenhagen, January 27, 1930, photocopy, Johannes Væth collection.
209. Letter H.H. Congdon to Aksel Sandemose, Halifax, February 15, 1930.

Notes to Sandemose's Canada Articles and Stories

Quite a few of Sandemose's Canada articles and stories were published in more than one version. Before he settled in Norway in 1930 he wrote the originals in Danish, but after his move the originals were written in Norwegian. Then Sandemose translated many of his previously printed works into Norwegian, publishing them in various newspapers and periodicals in Norway. Since the written forms of Norwegian and Danish are quite close, this meant that Sandemose could keep much of the same phraseology he had used in Danish when putting them into Norwegian. Later on these works might appear again in Norwegian publications, differing slightly in orthography and grammar. This is because in the 1930s, 1940s and 1950s the language was going through a series of spelling and grammar reforms and these are reflected in the written texts. Since Sandemose spent most of World War II in Sweden, a number of his shorter pieces came out in Swedish translation during this period. As he also had a readership in Denmark, quite a few of his Norwegian writings were translated into Danish and appeared in Danish publications.

A number of Sandemose's articles about Canada have not been incorporated in this collection. These include the Danish "Porten til Canada" (The Gateway to Canada), *Sorø Amtstidende* (June 5, 1928); "Danskeren i Canada" (The Dane in Canada), *Danmarksposten* 6 (June 1928); "I Canada skal du æde dit Brød i dit Ansigts Sved" (In Canada You Shall Eat Your Bread in the Sweat of Your Brow), *Hjemmet* 29 (Copenhagen) 29 (July 18, 1928); "Sandheden om Canada" (The Truth About Canada), *Aalborg Venstreblad* (January 24, 1929); and "Canada," Anglodania 12 (April 9, 1929); and in Norwegian "Da julebukken ble skutt" (When the Christmas Goat was Shot), *Arbeiderbladet, Lørdagskvelden* (December 24, 1932) and "Billeder fra en lang reise" (Pictures From a Long Journey), *Aschehougs Magasin* 7 (July 1935). This is because either much of the content of these is included in the articles already translated or because they are factual and statistical or have reference to cultural and topical material that would be difficult to understand for a reader not having intimate knowledge of Scandinavia during the 1920s.

In addition to those mentioned above, several other works include later versions or parts of the Canada articles and stories. These are the short story collections *Sandemose Forteller* (Sandemose Relates) (Oslo: Tiden, 1937), and *Dans, dans, Roselill* (Dance, Dance, Little Rose) (1965) and the periodical that Sandemose published himself, *Årstidene* (The Seasons) (Oslo: J. Chr. Gundersen, 1951–55), especially issue 9–10 (1954). Finally, the Canada novel *Ross Dane* (1928) included or was the source for several texts.

The translations have usually, though not always, been based on the original versions. Passages from other versions have been used when the text seems to flow better in English. At times Sandemose expresses himself better in the diary he kept while in Canada, and so occasionally passages from it have been utilized. A number of redundant passages have been omitted and, as with some of the texts mentioned above, passing references made to topical or cultural matters which would not be understood by a reader not having intimate knowledge of Denmark or Scandinavia in the 1920s. Under each title a more detailed history of the articles and stories and a description of what texts were used in the translation is given, along with other commentary where applicable.

FACTUAL ARTICLES

Prairie Women

I met her on her way home from Copenhagen to London. She was in her late thirties and always seemed to be freezing and tired, with a look of hopelessness in her eyes. A lonely woman nearing forty with all the expectations of youth behind her, without a home and without a job to fill the emptiness in her existence. All this stood so clearly written on her face that it was almost boring when she told me her life's story on the way from London to Liverpool.

She hadn't wholly cast off her illusions, but they seemed like dusty and dilapidated backdrops which she herself had become fed up with.

It's a shame that many women are so certain of marriage that they don't take employment for the sake of the job itself, a job that isn't just something to pass the time with until a man comes around, but a lifetime goal. An unmarried woman who bears a responsibility fills a genuine place, is ageless. One doesn't even think about whether she's forty or fifty, probably because she doesn't do so herself. But if a woman's main ambition for a dozen years or so has been to snare a husband, the words *Old Maid* are written prominently on her brow. She evokes sympathy; and is there any fate on this earth worse than being pitied?

The woman about whom I am speaking has perhaps felt something similar. Seven months later I read in a Danish-Canadian newspaper about her marriage to a farmer in Manitoba. What she could not attain in twenty years on the other side of the ocean became a reality on this side in six months. *That* is first and foremost the fate of women in Canada. They become helplessly married. There is no way around it.

Those women who most closely fit into the category of old maid usually get the most out of life by immigrating to a country where there's a lack of women. And there's nothing ridiculous or offensive in that. These disregarded creatures have a right to a place in the sun like everyone else, but human cruelty, true to form, only reluctantly allows a person who has suffered hardships to find happiness. Another side of the coin is that these older girls often become heavy crosses for their husbands to bear. They have lost the adaptability required for living with a spouse, and now he must pay for all her disappointments with regard to men. After three years of marriage he has forgotten how to laugh. After five years he lives only a shadowy existence on his farm. When ten years have passed it is he who resembles an old maid, while the woman has indefatigably extended her sphere of power to the whole of the colony, where by means of weddings and baptisms she determines what is good taste. She takes revenge. She makes the most of things but isn't happy. Her fate is better than she could have expected, but she complains year in and year out. Each day brings a new illness, a new injustice.

Poor old maid!

ຄງຜ

Young girls, though, get married quickly. They come from all levels of society in Denmark and emigrate for a great variety of reasons. Most frequently they say they are sick of the old country—a strange reason to give, since "Denmark" for the majority of both male and female emigrants means just their home parish. In most cases they have never seen anything else. It is indeed better here than in Denmark! And in order to show what advantages they can enjoy in Canada as opposed to Denmark, they rattle off things that are part of the daily drudgery in Odense and Maribo.

Almost all young girls have to take jobs as domestics, and they usually continue in this line of work after getting married, at least if they settle down in a city and have no children. On the whole, the Dane who keeps to the cities will belong to the lower classes and will remain there. Only very few exceptions prove this rule. All the talk about Canada's being a country without class distinctions is a happy delusion, most likely explained by the fact that the upper echelons keep themselves at a distance from the lower levels of society even more so than in Denmark.

The young, unmarried woman is indeed the one who manages best. Psychological phenomena such as intense homesickness and loathing of everything in the new land, which are otherwise common during the first year or two, affect her least of all. She will never know unemployment and will have a salary that translated into Danish money would be considered high. She is in demand both as a worker and as a life-long companion and will never have to feel lonely. It happens that Danish girls cannot bear to see what a privileged position a woman has on the other side of the Atlantic, where the variegated mixture of the population has necessitated almost draconian legislation for her protection. They wish to enjoy these rights but shrink away from the moral obligations that accompany them. That is not the fault of the country. It is merely a corroboration of the saying that it takes a broad back to bear good times.

They virtually always marry Danes, or at any rate Scandinavians, and exceptions to this are few. Canadians don't marry immigrants and don't open their doors to them. Many immigrants don't take this into account ahead of time, but the fact is they'll experience this like a slap in the face, if they're not prepared for it. For this reason immigrants should, more than ever before, move to the west where national feeling among the many foreign elements is least developed and where the conditions for a secure future are currently the best, regardless of how forbidding the prairie might seem. As for the Danish city dweller, Canada overall has no use for him, either in the east or the west.

There is much more to say regarding married women.

When a family has decided to emigrate it's usual that the man goes first. Often only enough money can be provided for his ticket, and he generally has some indistinct ideas about wanting to "look things over," and so forth. He comes to Canada, gets a job and begins sending money home. Almost everything he earns goes to Denmark where his family uses most of it to live on. The time of reuniting is pushed to an indefinite future date. One, two, three years pass and the man is no further ahead. Finally friends step in and give the now sullen and unapproachable man a loan so he can bring his family over the ocean.

Only at this point can he start. The intervening time has been wasted, but even that's not the whole story. I've seen sad things and have had them confirmed by well-informed men like Pastors Knudsen in Calgary and Damskov in Winnipeg. Simon Hjortnæs in Alida could tell about tragic cases. But should these really be necessary? Shouldn't it be immediately evident what a gamble it is to separate a man from his family for several years? There has long enough been silence about these things which in the midst of all the lyricism about America it has been considered improper to discuss.

A man who loves his wife and children goes to Canada with the idea of later sending his family tickets. They never see him again. Another manages to get his wife over; six months later they end up in divorce proceedings. A third one sends money for his wife's ticket: she never comes—another man has taken his place. In the vast country from Halifax to

Vancouver there is certainly not a single Dane who is not familiar with examples like these, and it's about time that this trifling with human happiness be stopped. It sounds so plausible, this travelling off to "look the land over," "see what it is," but the man should prepare himself for the fact that he has to be in Canada 15 years before he can know it even half as well as he knows Denmark.

The emigrants' own arguments will frequently make any warning ineffective. *My husband* or *my wife* would never do that! But they don't consider the fact that Canada is so far away, that the mind cannot conquer the distance. A bond is broken. Just look how quickly a large number of emigrants stop writing to their parents! Accounts of men who completely forget about what they would earlier have given their heart's blood for make up the blackest chapters in the history of emigration. Economically it involves in most cases a loss for the family as well that the man goes alone. When after a couple years have passed the wife and children come, they can begin right where they could have started two years before.

Let's look at a typical example: The man meets his family at the station and drives to where he has set up a home. The woman's disappointment is without bounds. She looks through Danish eyes at the hovel he has built on the prairie: a wooden shanty with a stove. It's miles to the nearest neighbour who's more likely to be a Russian, Dutchman or halfbreed than a Dane. Outside, the billowing prairie stretches for hundreds of miles. It's too much for her. She doesn't see what this has cost him in drudgery and constant toiling. She doesn't see that the climate makes this house habitable, that the land in many cases pays for itself with a single harvest. She breaks down and reproaches him for what he has done.

To him that blow can be almost fatal. If her disappointment is without bounds, then his is no less so. And those wounds which stem from that reunion can bleed for years. It could all have been avoided if they'd gone together. Other difficulties would of course have arisen, but none of them insurmountable. They both would have begun with their bare hands and would have seen how things gradually grew and increased for both of them. Then the woman would have wept for joy when they moved out into that cabin which has now become the bitterest discouragement of her life.

෩෬

There has been a lot of talk about the depression of women on the prairie. Great care should be taken in discussing that subject. When I mentioned what I'd seen to Consul Pallesen in Calgary he said with a smile, "Danish peasant women often have a tendency toward melancholy. And when they get here, the prairie is usually blamed for it."

That is partially true. The new land gets the blame for all adversity, and the farmer woman forgets that it could have been worse for her in Denmark. But the whole truth is so complex it would fill volumes. For example, there's the appearance of the country. This fruitful land, compared to Denmark, often resembles the Sahara Desert. It's a long way to the nearest neighbours, and often she doesn't understand their language. During a seven-month stay in Canada I have, except for those born in the country, met only one woman whose language did not grate in the ears of even another foreigner. The result, in many instances, is that the greatest service a husband can do for his wife, when there are visitors in the house, is to keep her in the background like a servant.

Later there is the tragedy with the children. English is soon their language of preference. They hear only a limited number of people speaking Danish and consequently their language of birth becomes impoverished and colourless. Their stock of Danish words and expressions diminishes. Standard Danish or another dialect is often unintelligible to them. They can read Danish only with difficulty and would prefer not do so at all. When the children are seven years old they are taken by the school, where they learn English, Canadian history, etc. They are indoctrinated with a patriotic feeling for Canada, pride in being part of the British Empire. They are to be sure Danish-Canadians, but mostly Canadians. This is a deadly blow to a Danish and Danish-speaking mother. She feels she is standing in her children's way. Whatever they are happy about she doesn't understand. They quarrel with her, that strange creature who can't speak the only proper language. Soon they move about in what for her is a distant haze. She is a helpless, strange bird to her children. She cannot assist them and doesn't know whether what's happening to them is good or evil.

It grows worse as the years pass. The children sit in the room with her and speak English if they don't want her to understand something. She thinks they're talking about her...

The new land has robbed her of everything. The first year she complains and suffers openly. Then she becomes silent. But anyone who denies the tragedy of the first generation woman is quite simply blind.

To Simon Hjortnæs in Alida, one of the finest Danes I have ever met, it never occurred to dispute that fact. A Danish newspaper one time gave him the nickname *King of the Danes*. This is in no way applicable in a material sense, but in character he is a prince who brings to mind those hard-necked heroes of Denmark's earlier history. I have heard him say things that could be attributed to George Bernard Shaw. He's fast thinking, quick to act and has a pair of hands which look as though they could twist the neck of an ox. He, who has come from the poorest of the poor in Denmark, once said, "Here the most wretched crofter can find happiness if he keeps a close watch on his wife. It's like a warning sign to me that the first woman who came to this colony went insane. But *that* tribute to the new land would be considered paid long ago if married immigrants would go to the Danish colonies. Here in Alida there's currently not much room for more, but there are a half dozen other places where a Danish cultural life exists. Many men say they can't stand the gossiping in the colony. Of course there's gossiping! That's the case everywhere in the country. But is it a manly thing to do to run away on account of stupid gossiping and encumber your wife with devastating depression?"

That's the way Hjortnæs talked, and that is the way all the old pioneers speak who came to Canada in the bad old days. And everybody knows what it means to a woman to be able to converse with others of her own sex—people who live under the same conditions as she—and she can be certain that in sickness, childbirth, etc., help will be near. Some of Canada's happiest women live in the Danish colonies.

Notes to "Prairie Women"

Appearing first as "Pæriens Kvinder" (Prairie Women) in *Aarhuus Stiftstidende* (March 22, 1928), Sandemose used a somewhat shortened and slightly rephrased version of the article in "Nybyggere i Canada" (Pioneers in Canada), *Morgenbladet* (July 18 and July 20, 1929).

The translation is essentially based on "Præriens Kvinder" except in a few places the phraseology of "Nybyggere i Canada" is used where it seems to flow better. Also several sentences and phrases are omitted which would make the translation a bit awkward or which contain topical or cultural references which would not be understood by someone who did not have intimate knowledge of Denmark in the 1920s. Several longer paragraphs have been divided into shorter ones.

For further discussion of Sandemose's opinions on prairie women, see Christopher Hale, "The Image of the Prairie Woman in Aksel Sandemose's Diary and Published Work," *Atlanten har så mange mil*: 139–49.

Christopher Hale

The Emigrant's Start

Not in all, but certainly in a lot of people, there lies hidden an urge for adventurous experience. In many it doesn't show up clearly, even though it is there. They fulfil their obligations in that position where they have been placed and are satisfied to experience the adventure second hand through, for example, reading. But everyone knows people whose need for adventure is so great that they have to give in to it. A large number of them go to sea—usually the worst possible thing they could do. Others seek out a new country.

Even in days long gone, it was clear that the one who chased after adventure chased after a will-o'-the-wisp. It is often very difficult for the lover of adventure to realize that he will drag all his physical requirements along with him, that he'll be plagued with bills, toothaches and poor digestion in the new land as well as in the old. Life has its joys and its prosaic annoyances in roughly the same measure wherever one resides on the globe.

To the one going to Canada, where of course currently the largest stream of emigrants is headed, it cannot be stressed too clearly and forcibly that he should not travel over there with his head full of romantic notions. Canada is the land of hard work, and he who does not work doesn't eat either. There is no other nobility than that of work, and it is written in fire over the vast land: Help thyself or perish. Even that is turned into romanticism by numerous young men before they leave. They understand the words but not the cold, hard reality behind them. They pride themselves secretly with the thought that they will go to this land of work and become really somebody and do the work of twelve. They flatter themselves with this beforehand—and find they cannot do the work of one when it comes down to it.

To adventuresome romantics there is only this to say: Remember that hard work is no more enjoyable just because it's being done on the other side of the ocean. Your arms don't get any stronger by travelling from Copenhagen to Quebec. In Canada you will work harder than in Denmark, and twelve hours are equally as long whether you're in Langeland or Manitoba. Try to face reality in the Kingdom of Denmark. If you cannot do so, you will be lost in Canada. Because there your determination has to be hurled out into the tips of your fingers and never slacken over months and years. It's of no use to be well dressed, have fancy handwriting or play the piano. If you have a good upbringing, there's no one but yourself to admire it. If your hands are nice and white, you're best off to hide them. If you have good references, you're suspected of not being able to show your abilities except on paper.

There is no other measure of a man than that which he can perform in physical labour. And that criterion he cannot escape from, however cunningly clever he may be.

But, when that is said, it must also be said that just such conditions are of course ideal for the sons of crofters and farm workers who in many instances have worked just as hard in Denmark as they are going to work in Canada. When they've gotten through the first often extremely difficult years, you see them in their true element. Here they reap recognition for what they were virtually looked down upon for at home. They feel as if they had been raised up into the nobility—and that is in reality exactly what has happened. You see in this new land what limitless reserves lie hidden in the Danish common people. The farmer's son throws off those restrictive bonds so that suddenly, straight across the centuries, you see the Viking again. Often you find a certain haughtiness in him—the self-contained haughtiness that comes with achievement. That is better, though, than the slave mentality, the penchant for envy and gossipy ridicule that's likely to flourish in the shadow of the poorhouse.

※

It is precisely the Viking you see again, not a reflection nor a replica of him, but the Viking himself with both his good and bad qualities. After all, who was the Viking? He was the Scandinavian emigrant around the year 800. And the races in Scandinavia are the same today as they were a millennium ago.

There has always been overpopulation in Scandinavia, for the most part in the south, in Denmark and Skåne. From the beginning of history, people have migrated from the north. The pressure outward was just as great in days gone by as it is today—perhaps even greater. The heather-covered and forest-clad north didn't offer good opportunities for a population which didn't possess science and technology. People now support themselves relatively easily on an area which a thousand years ago could not feed even one person.

Back then as well there lived in the minds of the people a dream of bright and happy kingdoms on the other side of the ocean. Youth could voyage to them, if there were no place for them at home. But these lands were not without owners. Fine. But if you could not persuade them to hand over a part of your land of dreams voluntarily, then you had to use force.

The entire structure of Europe at the time permitted the use of force. You needed only courage, boldness and skill in the handling of weapons. This very quickly led to the idealization of a certain type of man, that is, the man who was not afraid to die and was not afraid of killing others.

But ideals change as time passes. The warrior is no longer the ideal man. Many a young lieutenant laments that fact, and his successors will lament it even more.

The old ideal received its first wound when the monks came to the north. It received its second and most serious one when the way was opened to the new world on the other side of the Atlantic. The plough took the place of the sword. In the history of emigration, the warrior was replaced by the worker.

※

A rosy romanticism still floats over those lands yet to be conquered. The enormous distance means that the work does not become a reality in the mind of the emigrant until he is in the middle of it, just as it was surely one thing for the Viking to dream about the far-off land and something quite different for him actually to stand in it with weapon in hand. One should not let oneself be dazzled either by the battle poetry of old or the current worship of the hoe, shovel and spade. Behind both is a hard and uncompromising reality. The hoe, spade and shovel are not badges to be pinned on a hat. They require muscles and sweat, toil and relentless determination. And the sword which now graces a lieutenant's uniform was, in the hand of a Viking, a tool with which he killed and caused the greatest possible suffering.

※

Let us now follow a modern Viking. These days he almost always journeys to Canada. We will skip over the trip itself. It is unimportant. We meet him from that moment when he is standing on a farm out in the west in one of the prairie provinces—Manitoba, Saskatchewan or Alberta.

His disappointment is boundless. He would never have dreamed that a person could feel himself so helpless, merely because he did not know the language. He feels as though he were standing in front of a wall he could never climb over. He becomes half desperate in his helplessness. And the Dane, unlike other Scandinavians, gets an additional punch in the pit of his stomach. He has often been thinking, say, that the farmer would stand waving his hat in the air and shouting with joy because he has been so unbelievably fortunate as to get hold of a Dane. We are certainly not any more delighted with ourselves than people of other nations. On the other hand, we think that other nations are just as delighted with us as we ourselves are, and that is a sad misunderstanding which is naively based on the polite comments of visiting foreigners. The Canadian usually knows nothing about Denmark or Danes. Just like the Norwegians, we have to put up with being called Swedes. Danes are no more renowned than that, and in many cases this rankles in the soul of the immigrant.

Aside from those disappointments, the result of a series of delusions from the old country, there is the difficulty of getting used to conditions which in no way resemble those in Scandinavia. The farms are situated miles apart. Loneliness is so great that it weighs heavily on the mind. It combines with homesickness, which in the beginning can be somewhat painful, and the way people are treated here—coolly, mechanically. The man is left in no doubt about what is expected of him, nor what will happen if he doesn't fulfill expectations. People here don't mask their callousness and don't waste their time saying niceties. Lodging is generally poor, but the food on the other hand is always good and there's plenty of it, something which certainly is due in part to the machine-like way manpower is regarded. You've got to have lubrication!

The work is hard. The workday is seldom shorter than 12 hours, during the harvest often fourteen. Except for a lunch break in the middle of the day, you have to stand the whole time without a rest. It wouldn't be a bad idea for a Dane to realize what this means! After breakfast you're in the fields at six o'clock, and the tremendous pace which is immediately struck you have to continue in until twelve or one o'clock. You don't take notice of what is going on in nature. You don't study your watch. You don't stop to chat or daydream. As the sun rises, turning the prairie into a glowing oven, burning your face black and drying your sweat into crusty streaks, you tackle your work without a stop or rest or thought. Back home there was always time for a greeting or a talk with a neighbour. Here a man is at his place of work to work and for no other conceivable reason. When you have eaten lunch you go at it again where you left off—the whole live long day until seven, eight or nine o'clock without a chance to catch your breath for even five minutes. These people remind one of working machines, of whirring flywheels, in a changeless pace from the time the sun rises until it sets.

You need endurance, and you need determination! First and foremost determination! Because this is a merciless land which offers no other means of sustenance than work, work and more work. Work or perish! But on the other hand no work is too lowly not to be considered honourable. The concepts of work and honour are so closely tied to each other that they're almost considered one and the same. The worker is an aristocrat.

Among the Latins such a great value was attached to bravery that the word came to signify virtue. In Canada one can well imagine that some day work will become the term for honour.

For the one who is convinced he can manage and is not afraid of hard labour there is however a pressing question: Can I *get* work?

Yes, you can, but there are a few drawbacks. In the cities the opportunities are few and far between. They have no use for more people there. And if the emigrant has no knowledge of horses and machines, his chances are considerably reduced out in the country as well.

Those groups which manage best next to farmers are certain tradesmen, in particular carpenters and blacksmiths.

People who are able and who want to work (hard!) at farming will always have a job. The pay is good during the period from March to November. Wages vary from 30 to 60 dollars a month with room and board, depending on the place and a man's capability. From November to March the pay is little or nothing at all, except room and board.

At that time of year many prefer to go to the forests. The lumber companies pay between 25 and 35 dollars a month, including room and board. I have never heard of anyone's not finding a job there. Norwegians and Swedes fare better in the forests than Danes, but there are also numerous Danes who have spent one or more winters under these circumstances. Here too conditions are harsh. The working day is somewhat shorter, simply because there are fewer hours of sunlight at that time of year. The work is strenuous—absolutely not for weaklings.

The logging camp consists of a large log house. The entire crew sleeps on a shelf along one of the walls—a form of communism which means that no one gets the blame for being more lice-covered than anybody else. You live completely cut off from the world, hearing little or nothing from the outside. And in the spring when you leave, you often feel as though you were returning from a desert isle.

It is on the farms and in the forests that the Scandinavian in Canada builds his future. But it's a sad mistake for so many to go to Canada for "just" three or four years to earn a bit of capital to bring back home. That is rarely feasible. The surplus of the first year is put into machines, horses, etc., so that the second year will yield more. The same thing happens year after year. The undertaking itself absorbs the earnings. When a man is sitting on a farm which with buildings, land, machinery and horses can be valued at 50,000 dollars—and may be paying interest on this sum—he can seldom do anything but stick with it. It cannot be sold. There are no buyers. Even people with a lot of capital prefer to buy virgin prairie and build up a farm themselves from scratch. A farmer in Canada can earn money, sometimes lots of it, but at the same time he is forced to shackle himself to the land. He can say, I am well-to-do as long as I stay on my farm.

A man doesn't prosper just because he is independent. In order to make a go of it in the beginning, he will have to take on a job (preferably two) as a day labourer. He will have more to do than ever before, now that he also bears the risk. Everybody from householder to hired hand is subject to the same iron-clad law in Canada: He who does not want to work will not eat either. Help yourself, for no one else would dream of doing so.

For several years a not insignificant amount has been spoken and written about Canada, that country which has become a dream for so many in our land-without-colonies, since the U.S. for all intents and purposes has closed its gates.

There are opportunities over there. In places they are quite considerable. But he who goes to Canada in the belief that gold drips from every blade of grass makes a mistake, a frightful mistake. Can it be recommended after everything is taken into consideration that anyone go there—?

Another question must be answered first. Shouldn't Danes be kept for Denmark?

Conditions for farm workers here in Denamrk are hopeless. If you investigate them, you will see that they are no less than catastrophic. Resentment and hate grow more intense each day that passes. These people do not live like human beings.

Canada will pay them ten times the wages for a job that is essentially no different from the one they perform now. What then weighs heavier in the balance—these people's interests or the interests of Denmark in keeping them inside the country's borders?

It is my conviction that the good fortune of the individual rests with the good fortune of the country. We are better served both now and in the future with a thousand satisfied countrymen outside our borders than with the same number of dissatisfied ones inside them.

One doesn't usually say rash things which can influence the fate of large numbers of people. It is possible that I place too much significance in my own words, but even if they are of interest to only one person or even to no one, they have at least been well considered and come from the essence of everything I heard and saw in Canada. Landless sons of farmers and farm workers who believe they can do without Denmark and its social and cultural life, who are trained workers and who are dissatisfied here—they, for their own sakes and for the sakes of their children and Denmark, ought to give up their native country and go to Canada.

Unfortunately, so few of them can. The expensive journey keeps them behind in the daily grind.

Notes to "The Emigrant's Start"

"Emigrantens Start" (The Emigrant's Start) was originally published in two parts in *Sorø Amtstidende*, the first appearing on April 10, 1928 and the second on the following day. The first three paragraphs, in almost identical form, were used to begin "Danskeren i Canada" (The Dane in Canada), *Danmarksposten* 6 (June 1928). Finally, it reappeared in a considerably reworked form as "Emigrant-Immigrant," *Danmarksposten* 9 (September 1930) as one continuous article. This last version adds essentially no new information to the original article, though the phraseology in places is quite different, and sentences have been eliminated and some new ones added.

The translation is based primarily on "Emigrantens Start," combining both parts into one article, with the occasional use of phraseology from "Emigrant-Immigrant" when the latter flows more smoothly. Several phrases or short sentences have been eliminated, most of which either were felt not to add anything to the rest of the text or which have a topical or cultural reference which would not be understood by a reader who didn't have a close knowledge of Denmark in the 1920s. Some of the paragraph divisions have also been changed to make the text read better in English.

Life on Canada's Prairie

Introduction

The prairie districts of the United States and Canada form a geographical unit which fills up the whole middle part of the North American continent. The border between Canada and the U.S. follows a rather arbitrarily chosen parallel of longitude, and if the customs authorities did not inform people about it most firmly, it would be impossible for a traveller to know when he was on the northern side and when he was on the southern side. Everywhere on the prairie the climate is continental with cold winters and hot summers, but the further north you go, the longer and harsher the winters are.

Most people probably have some idea of what is meant by the word "prairie." Originally the word referred to naturally occurring meadows, but now it's used exclusively to signify somewhat flat, treeless tracts of land, covered with self-sown grass and other less conspicuous vegetation. Fire is the reason that forests haven't covered the prairie. Those groves of trees which are found are seldom very old. Only as humans cultivate the prairie are the trees protected from that wildfire which so often killed both animals and plants over hundreds of square miles in earlier times. Elderly farmers can relate what a catastrophe it was when fire ravaged the land, raging with a speed equal to that of the fleeing animals. Fortunately such fires are now virtually history, even though they can still occur in more remote districts.

In only a few areas is the Canadian prairie that completely flat land which a Dane imagines it to be. Absolutely level, pancake-flat stretches indeed exist, for example near Saskatoon in the province of Saskatchewan and other places. But the typical prairie country in Manitoba and Saskatchewan looks quite different. It is a billowing landscape with small woods around large and small lakes and sloughs which make extensive use of tractors difficult. The horse is still held in high regard on the prairie, even though tractors are naturally to be seen here and there in the countryside.

This billowing type of prairie extends over southern Manitoba, most of Saskatchewan and western Alberta, those three districts which are generally called the prairie provinces. North of the prairie, Manitoba is filled with enormous lakes and swamps reaching all the way up to the timber line, but in Saskatchewan and Alberta there is mixed forest and prairie in the north, until the forest takes over completely. These mixed regions are called parkland. They can resemble Denmark and possess absolutely the greatest natural beauty the otherwise seemingly lonely prairie displays. Toward the west, Canada's prairie is interrupted by the Rocky Mountains, and to the south, of course, by the United States border.

The climate, as said earlier, is continental. The regulating influence of the ocean on the weather is lacking. The winters are not grey and nondescript such as those we are familiar with, but real winters with frightful cold on occasion. In southern Alberta the thermometer at the end of November, 1927, measured between -35 and -39 degrees centigrade for one whole week. And people did not consider that unusual.

But a winter which is never interrupted by thawing also has its advantages. People seldom catch cold and never get wet from the snow. And it may sound strange, but is nevertheless true, that the harsh, uninterrupted winter makes it possible for poor settlers to inhabit primitive dwellings in which they would simply perish in Denmark's variable climate. And fuel is inexpensive on the prairie. Wood for heating can normally be had for nothing, and the nearest coal mine is rarely far away.

In only very few places does one experience mild periods during the winter. For example, in a particular part of Alberta there is occasionally a warm wind from the mountains called a "chinook" after the name of an Indian tribe which lived in the mountain pass through which the wind found its way. But exceptions confirm the rule; the winter is long and hard. Yet you can hear farmers complain that the frost isn't always exercising its valuable crumbling effect on the soil, since the snow with its insulating properties, if it comes early and remains high the whole winter, will prevent the soil from freezing.

After you have finally adjusted to the winter, you have to admit that it actually is marvellous. That time I spent in the prairie winter has given me some of my life's most beautiful memories, but I will leave that for inclusion in a description of the farmer's life later.

It is a similar situation when it comes to the summer, as there is seldom a happy middle way. It's scorchingly hot. But it happens that it agrees with Scandinavians, and now and then you get relief with a thunder shower. Everyone complains how mosquitoes are a plague during the first summer, but afterward people seem to be immune to their poison. When the prairie rose is in bloom and the wheat is tall enough to hide a man, it's not easy to dispel the thought that there is nothing more beautiful in the world.

ಸಿಂ

The climate of the prairie and indeed its whole character gives rise to a distinctive animal life. After the encroachments of man, the larger plant-eating animals have disappeared and are found only in the areas of mixed prairie and forest. The bison was completely eradicated but has later been reintroduced and is quite prolific in the north. In the parkland on the northern borders of the prairie can be found the large species of deer, of which in particular the colossal moose is a favourite quarry for sportsmen. Since hunters used to mistake each other for game a little too frequently, and negligent homicide occurred a bit too often, it is now required that hunting be carried on in white clothing. Once when I was out with a couple of farmers, I dressed in white pyjamas, while my companions walked around in the discarded nightgowns of their respective wives. It was not without comic effect, as we all looked far too scantily clad for the -30 degree weather.

Aside from the now very rare flocks of wild horses, the coyote is the largest of the prairie's wild animals. But the coyote is not dangerous. It is both cunning and cowardly, never occurring in sizable packs like the larger wolf in the forests. But it takes its toll on the farmers' chickens and is hunted with a passion. In many districts it is still numerous.

The large feline, the lynx, strays onto the prairie only occasionally. Otherwise the most common animals are small rodents, badgers, foxes, skunks—and legions of hares and rabbits which are such a nuisance that in most places there are bounties for killing them, such as we have for rats.

Duck hunting here is in a class by itself. There are swarms of unusual aquatic birds and a large selection of birds of prey. Hawks are constantly soaring over the countryside.

ಸಿಂ

If I have left the prairie's human inhabitants until last, it is just to familiarize the reader a little with the conditions under which they live.

Canada's prairie has only recently acquired culture, at least in those places where this has happened at all. Enormous tracts of land are still virgin territory, among others some in northern Alberta in the Peace River region and other places where the railroad hasn't yet reached.

The railroad is necessary for farming, and the settlers didn't begin coming in earnest until the Canadian Pacific Railway connected the Atlantic to the Pacific at the end of the last century, so the riches of the prairie could be transported to the coasts. People down in the States didn't immediately take this development seriously, but regarded it at the same time with a not completely inexplicable irritation, which in the American Senate gave rise to the sarcastic name for their neighbour to the north: "The Dominion of Canada on Wheels." But indeed the railroad was built at the last moment. Had it not been, there would scarcely exist any Canadian prairie today, and what has now become the main cornerstone in the British Empire would have had its western border drawn between Hudson Bay and Lake Superior.

The population in the new regions to the west doesn't form a solidly amalgamated mass but consists of colonies, formed by each ethnic group itself. In the beginning, the stream of immigrants came from the United States, but later and to a greater and greater degree from Europe out of which the numbers have increased considerably in recent years after the U.S. partially closed its doors to immigration. On the prairies there is absolutely no use for people who are not physically strong and who cannot work at farming. If they are able to do that, then they will also forge ahead, even if the conditions for doing so are not favourable. Though you still have to work hard, the circumstances are far less harsh than in the old days, when a man on the prairie could be as lonely and cut off from the rest of humanity as the man in the moon.

Those immigrants bound for the prairie all come via Winnipeg in Manitoba, the easternmost prairie province. From here they spread out over the west, and even though many bad things are said about the ethnic colonies, it is to them that most people go. The typical immigrant is one who starts out as a hired hand and travels from place to place getting work until he has earned enough money to be able to provide the down payment on a piece of land where he can begin on his own account. It is first and foremost wheat that's grown, secondly oats and flax. Only in the neighbourhood of the cities is there mixed farming.

Single crop farming requires a completely different approach from mixed farming, which keeps the work evenly distributed over the entire year. The growing of wheat demands a tremendous effort both in the spring and summer, so that farmers are completely unapproachable at these times of year. The work goes on at a furious pace, 13 to 14 hours a day. It is so busy that in strictly religious homes I have heard the head of the house make the morning prayer shorter and shorter as his fear grew that all the wheat would not get threshed.

It's no use for office people and others not brought up doing physical labour to let themselves be lulled by romantic self-deception concerning what they are capable of. Their disappointment is terrible, as they fail miserably. Their good upbringing, beautiful handwriting and splendid talents they can play with on Sundays. The weekdays require muscles of steel and scarcely anything else. Naturally there are others besides farmers in possession of endurance. But he who has handled horses from childhood has a great advantage, even if he also has a lot to learn.

The settlement in colonies means that an indefinite amount of time will pass before the inhabitants of the prairie are of one nationality. It's clear that the wish of the government is for them to become Canadians as soon as possible, but for practical reasons it seems to be working toward the completely opposite goal by giving certain nationalities first rights in the buying of land. Each group therefore is able to live according to its own character and customs, but since the school is English, already in the second generation there emerges a double culture, and the English element naturally becomes stronger with each succeeding generation. It is presumably only a question of time, even though it might be lengthy, when all the inhabitants of the country will speak, feel and think like the citizens of the British Empire.

Already fear is being expressed in Danish-American newspapers about the development of the situation in the U.S. They are afraid that with the decreased influx of immigrants, the Danish language will disappear from the United States within fifty years. I believe that Danes and other nationalities in *Canada* will eventually face the same fate—though considerably later than in the U.S.A. That question is currently not relevant.

The Danish Farmer

The first great Danish immigration to the prairies occurred in the nineties and immediately after the turn of the century. These immigrants were, however, almost exclusively Danish-Americans who came to Canada from the United States, where they had begun to find their circumstances strained. Free land was no longer to be had down there. In fact it was getting expensive, and the costly road construction created a bothersome burden of taxation for those farmers who had previously been far less fettered. The new land was for them no longer new enough, and they began then to emigrate for the second time, namely to the north, to Canada. Most of them settled in southern Saskatchewan and up through central Alberta, and they form still today the nucleus of the Danish colonies. The growing stream of emigrants from Denmark, though, has resulted in their now being a minority, in spite of the fact that Danish immigration *from the States* is still taking place.

A misunderstanding which many in Denmark are guilty of is that Danes make up a considerably large element of Canada's population. They are, unfortunately, not as renowned as they would often like to believe and frequently have to put up with being called Swedes, unless they go to one of the larger or smaller Danish colonies, to which most of them come anyway sooner or later.

ΣΟ∝

We will try to follow a young farmer from the moment he comes to Winnipeg—and disregard completely the person who knows nothing about farming and is accordingly always worse off.

Straight from the train he goes to the immigration office, where he is found temporary work on a farm. Generally after a few days' stay in Winnipeg, he travels further west to a given address, and before long he gets a chance to test himself in the field.

In the beginning, most are disappointed. The transition from Danish conditions is quite drastic for them. To many a newly arrived Dane it is inconceivable that anyone can feel at home on the prairie. It is no setting for a centuries-old culture with pleasant villages and scattered farms. The buildings on the desolate Canadian farm are without the charm of the Danish ones. In Canada the farm is like a factory, and that's exactly what it is—a factory for the utilization of the soil. The farmer isn't bound to the soil through generations of love. Farming is exploitation, and the owner is almost always prepared to negotiate, move or exchange.

Danes are so unused to this that a very large number of them have only one thought after a few weeks—to earn enough money so that they can head for home. In addition, almost everything a young man has learned to appreciate is lacking. There are no movies here. There are no parties. There are no other boys and girls around. The prairie stretches as far as he can see. To put it bluntly: here there is only work.

So he throws himself into it in order to earn enough for the trip home, and eventually he has the money—but—then, almost invariably he changes his mind. He becomes thoughtful as he looks at this money. He thinks about Denmark where he toiled for years before he had saved up enough money for the ticket—the same amount which he has put aside in one summer here. During the following days he walks around silent, and it's as though only now, after seven or eight months, that he has really arrived and begun to look at the country. Is it really so bad? To be sure, there haven't been many diversions. The prairie is no less lonely than it was when he came, rather more so, now that he knows it inside and out—but, ting-a-ling, listen to the money jingling, 300 good dollars—let me see—in three years, let's say four, I can buy my own farm—

And he stays on the prairie. Nothing goes as smoothly as he had hoped when he gave up the idea of returning home, but all the time he sees that he's further ahead than he could have been in the old country. He never goes back. And I remember here some words of Pastor Knudsen in Calgary. "Let's take things as they are. The majority of those who come over prefer Denmark in all other areas except precisely the economic, and more emigrants have been chased out of Denmark than have left voluntarily."

I believe Pastor Knudsen is right. Most emigrants are held back by the not-so-insignificant dollar. Here they have finally found a country where a worker is worth his pay, and a lot of other things are eclipsed by that fact. Our young man is also one of those who lets money weigh heaviest in the balance. He doesn't go home. But he no longer stays with the same farmer. He travels from place to place on the prairie until Denmark and what is Danish retreats further and further in his consciousness, even though he will never become a Canadian. The prairie penetrates his mind. As it is, that is the way his world has become as well, and only occasionally does it occur to him that it could have been quite different. He eventually acquires land and works hard on his own account as he has worked hard for others. Denmark drifts further and further away—for some it disappears entirely. His first wooden house becomes a bungalow. The small outhouses which he puts up at the start remain standing beside the enormous barn which has superseded them. One day he realizes that he is no longer poor. He thinks more closely about things and discovers that actually he's rich—but at the same time rheumatism nips at his back, telling him that he's no longer young either…

He has been so busy, this healthy example of the working Dane, that the years have passed without his really being aware of it. He has given all his years of manhood to work, but indeed he has done so with the certain conviction that he would reap the reward. He walks around on his property and sees what the result has been, at the same time thinking about all he has lost and all he has gained. And almost always he is in agreement that the books balance. The years and the rheumatism would have caught up with him in Denmark as well. And his farm here would be considered practically a landed estate in the old country—that country he abandoned…

Abandoned? He starts to consider whether he really *has* abandoned it. It's a typical trait in the middle-aged farmer, who has the prime of life behind him, to begin wanting to regain whatever has been completely or partially lost. He has had time to breathe and reflect—and farthest back he finds Denmark again. He sees that he is still a Dane and will never be anything else.

He begins to ponder this more and more. There is something to life other than earning money. Life among Danes begins to interest him. Gropingly, but with more and more assurance, he begins a new type of work, an effort to assemble Danes and what is Danish.

There is certainly not a single Danish-Canadian who doesn't know such a farmer between the ages of 50 and 60, sitting on his farm and pulling together the threads to help build a Denmark on the prairies. These grey haired and seasoned veterans, who bear hidden sores from the homelessness they have felt in the country, know where the shoe pinches, and they have even succeeded, in the past dozen years or so, in securing various patches of Danishness to the extent that individual Canadians go in for speaking Danish.

When that happens, you can talk about a Danish colony. It has formed not because of some previously laid plan, but because here lived a Dane to whom one did not turn in vain.

That's the way the colony of Dannevirke in the south-eastern corner of Saskatchewan was formed, and that's the way a new colony is being founded in central Alberta near Edmonton. And now these selfless leaders, who are trying to free their successors from the longings they themselves have suffered, are under fire from people who think they can go to Canada and gather up a fortune in a fortnight. That can't be done. From a purely occupational point of view, the difference between life in the ancient countryside of Denmark and on Canada's prairies is simply that in Canada you have to work harder.

In the Colonies

If you wish to imagine a Canadian prairie settlement, you must totally and completely rid yourself of any Danish preconceptions. And with the word "colony" you must least of all imagine a Danish village. The distances within the borders of a colony can be very great. Neighbours live 10 or more miles from each other, and only the general use of automobiles makes it possible for social intercourse to be lively—weather permitting. After rain, for example, the poor roads turn into dangerous strips of slick mud, and it's not much better when there's snow on the ground.

The building material is invariably wood. Colonists always provide housing for cattle and crops first, with the farmhouse itself always coming last. For many years this is often the least prominent building on the farm. A lot of farmers become so used to it that they never build a better farmhouse, but continue living under very primitive conditions their whole lives, even though they have become affluent.

This means that young people who come to the country are repulsed by the conditions. At the beginning it's very embarrassing for them to sleep in a bed together with other people. It's common for three farmhands to share a bed. The one who tries to look at things from all sides meanwhile submits to it, seeing that the head of the house doesn't consider himself too good to do the same. And he realizes further that if he himself ever gets ahead, he will probably offer his own people the same conditions. But it's embarrassing and uncomfortable in the beginning.

The first time I was shown a sleeping place in a double bed between an Indian and a Pole, my jaw dropped. You would think there should be limits as to what is democratic. But it's most surprising how quickly you get used to it, and after a month, you only have cause to complain when your sleep mate kicks a lot. On the whole you must always count on two things, compared to what you are used to in Denmark: Housing is invariably poor. On the other hand you live better. It's pure fiction that Danes in Denmark live so well. Once you have gotten used to the food a Canadian farmer gives his people, it's difficult to become satisfied again in Denmark. You eat far better than back home, because it has become a cardinal rule that if you want to get out of him all the work that is in a man, then three times a day you have to fill every nook and cranny in his stomach with good things to eat.

It is very difficult to describe how a farm is generally built, since there are so many different types, depending on the owner's predilection and financial means. The penniless beginner lives in a simple wooden shack and has no outbuildings. The property of the well-to-do farmer is often dominated by the large stable and barn structure which can resemble the nave of a church. In addition there's a machine shed, garage, meat house, chicken coop, etc., so that the whole place looks like an entire village. Round about the farm roam flocks of pigs, chickens, ducks and turkeys which during the summer have to fend for themselves.

There's a greater difference in the intensity of work on a prairie farm than we in Denmark are used to. From the time you can break the ground in April until you have threshed in the fall, the farm is a fulltime job every hour of the waking day. On the other hand, social life revives during the winter, when there's next to nothing to do. Then the minister becomes the main figure in the colony, and everybody gathers at the church on Sunday, afterward dividing up into smaller groups around friends and acquaintances. At that point the lack of space becomes acute. The women gather in the bedroom or they annex the kitchen. Sweethearts sit together in the automobiles, and the farmer and his friends share a jug of beer out in the garage. Young farmhands play cards in the hayloft, while others talk about horses in the stables or prowl around out on the prairie with their guns. Many a young man saddles his horse and rides off to hunt coyotes with the dogs, if the girl he has been waiting to see has not come or, even worse, is sitting in a car talking to someone else.

There is something very peculiar about such a get-together. Everything is foreign, but everybody speaks Danish. It can remind you of a meaningless dream, going about in a strange and foreign land and chatting in Danish about the most ordinary things under the sun. The bizarre impression is intensified by the fact that everyone is speaking the same Danish dialect. In Danevirke, where almost everybody is from Vendsyssel, the person from Copenhagen even begins speaking the Vendsyssel dialect—and I have heard a Norwegian woman speak the same dialect. It is Denmark, and yet it is not Denmark. Here you are neither a Dane nor a Canadian. You have a hyphen: Danish-Canadian.

One of the main impressions you get is that as the Danish colonies become built up with an established social life, our countrymen feel comfortable in Canada. In most cases they are not made of sentimental stuff, and economic matters take precedence over national and cultural ones. All in all, *men* have rarely been objects of pity. It has been worse with regard to women, especially in earlier times when they established a home on the open prairie and lost most of what used to mean most to them. The man, of course, could always find satisfaction in his work, and besides, it's generally less difficult to transplant men than women. They would be left to themselves, while the man would go out, learn the language and familiarize himself with the customs of the country. Danish women have wept a great deal in these regions, but a mighty bulwark against women's depression is the colony life which is led currently. Fortunately, an increasing number of men realize that they owe it to their wives to join a colony.

In the past half dozen years, attempts have been made to create colonies in a way different from before, when they grew up organically where the circumstances were favourable, and mostly because individual Danes wanted to organize an ethnic community in their district. Now attempts are made to establish the settlement before people arrive. This is what happened with *Dalum* in Alberta, founded in 1917 by the Danish People's Society, which as early as 1921 managed to obtain a minister. He currently runs the only Grundtvigian highschool in Canada.

It was in Dalum that I met a Danish farmer who I believe can be regarded as a symbol of some of the best qualities in the Danish people; and as a Jutlander myself, one who is fed up with the ridiculous idolization of Jutlanders now current, it gives me pleasure to note that this man is from Falster.

It makes no difference what his name is. Thirteen years ago he came to Calgary, Alberta, with his wife and two small children. He got a job in a factory, but after only three months, he had a severe accident. He lost one of his legs. A catastrophe like that can be distressing enough for a poor man even in his home country. But in Canada—well, I will leave it up to those who have been there themselves to imagine the extent of his misfortune. There was now for that little family a time of suffering, but it carried on. And the couple was only forged closer together during the bad times and kept each other's hopes up in spite of everything. When the man eventually got up from his bed, it was not to complain about his fortune but to grapple with it. No one came to help him, but if he had lost a leg, at any rate his arms were uninjured. Let us jump over the intervening 12 years. The invalid man from Falster is today considered one of the richest farmers in his district—a gifted man with the joy of life, whom the struggle year by year has made stronger.

Meeting such men makes one proud to be Danish.

Notes to "Life on Canada's Prairie"

"Livet paa Canadas Prærie I–III" (Life on Canada's Prairie I–III) appeared in three parts in A*arhuus Stiftstidende* (May 2, 3, 4, 1928). Sections of it were also reproduced, virtually word for word, in "Danskeren i Canada" (The Dane in Canada), *Danmarksposten* 6 (June 1928), except that the man from Falster in Part III of the original is said to come from Lolland in the latter. The first three and the last five paragraphs of "Life on Canada's Prairie I" are also found as the final part of "Canada," *Anglodania* 12 (April 9, 1929) with slight changes in wording and the omission of a few sentences and phrases.

The translation follows closely "Livet paa Canadas Prærie" except that a few phrases and some sentences have been omitted either as being redundant or to make the English version flow more smoothly.

Culture on the Prairie

Cultural life on the Canadian prairie revolves around the church. There is little room for anything else. Yet it cannot be said that a living intellectual life is not to be found outside the framework of the church.

For instance, in one Danish colony I came upon an entire little group of very engaging people of honest character through and through who had formed a society outside the church. Its leader was a highly gifted man, whose name it is superfluous to mention. He and his friends were unsympathetic toward religion but were generally popular nonetheless among the ultra-religious elements. Only the minister referred to them with reservation. Yet those people had their religion as well—they were faithful Communists and rich in illusions concerning the possibility of the betterment of man.

Their leader was one of those mild mannered, accommodating men who at least in theory defend the wildest excesses. He did not believe in a victory for Communism on the American continent, did not even regard such a victory as desirable, but felt it was imminent in Europe. Perhaps this feeling of his was due to the fact that his knowledge of Europe was far inferior to his familiarity with America.

Examples such as this are exceptions, however. Those Emigrants who are not completely indifferent to all intellectual life attach themselves to the church in practically all cases.

ഇരു

Little is read on the farm—perhaps a provincial newspaper from Denmark, otherwise devotional literature and a dime novel. There is seldom any time or desire for stronger fare. These people have come with one quite specific objective in view: to work their way up out of poverty. Everything else gives way. What we understand as culture will be created by future generations.

Even in places in Canada where one would expect to find it, there is scant or no understanding of literature. "Authors" who themselves have no idea of what literature is are placed on a throne. A Dane in Canada can say the same thing the Englishman said when he saw the translated English books in Denmark: "I never knew that we had so many authors in England."

The Dane often abandons Denmark in externals; for example, by introducing Canadian customs during holidays, etc. This does not mean any abandonment in reality. It's as though Danes would prefer not to be too conspicuous in company. For example, they almost always stop eating horse meat and rabbit, because Canadians are astonished at this custom.

It's different with people from Norway. They let it be known far and wide that "We are from Norway!," and they stick to their customs from the home country.

ഇരു

There's a distinct type of emigrant who is described in Danish literature dozens of times—the homeless one who doesn't know whether he wants to be in Denmark or in America and therefore is constantly travelling from the one country to the other. I think there is more literature than reality in this "tragedy of the emigrant." Only once have I met a man who could qualify for one's discussing such a case at all—and then it was a question of a sick person who was regarded by his neighbours as a strange bird.

There are often the worst possible conditions for family life on the prairie. The husband frequently sleeps in bed with the farmhand and the wife with the servant girl. Single beds are rare. Whenever people come to the house, two, three, or four men sleep in the same bed—people who have perhaps never seen one another before—without regard for cleanliness or race. Here the work is everything. You don't live in the house, but go in there to eat or sleep. You get food, warmth and sleep there just like you get the horse from the stable or the plow from the machine shed.

If on a Sunday guests come to the farm, and that is a common occurrence when the weather permits it, the need for company makes itself felt. People gather in groups out in the cars, smoke and converse. The sons or young daughters of the house appropriate a car with their girlfriend or boyfriend and have a prim and proper date there at the steering wheel, close the door and dwell in a house of glass. You see them sitting nicely beside each other; the fathers look over at them from *their* cars and have a little smile in their eyes. A jug of wine in some places may be passed from car to car. If there's somebody around who doesn't like it, the farmer goes by the cars winking, so those wanting a swig can gather in the garage. It happens now and then that the jug gets heavier to lift the lighter it becomes, but that usually happens only when the wife is on a visit to Denmark.

෴

That the needs of the country are turned exclusively toward muscle power leads to a suspicion of anyone who does not earn his bread by physical labour. Doctors, ministers, dentists, office workers, druggists—they are objects of a backbiting which in Denmark is found only on a rudimentary level. It's as if the Dane deep down has more of a slave-like mentality than people from his neighbouring countries such as Norway. If a Norwegian "does well" in Canada, his countrymen refer to him with pride. As soon as someone mentions his name, you find the Norwegians boasting, "You see, Norwegians can do it!"

The Dane backbites his kinsman. And there is hardly anything to do about it. For if you talk about gossiping and the plague it is in the country, the fact is every single Dane smugly agrees with you, and the greater a gossipmonger he is, the more quickly you gain his support. It's worst of all in the cities, second worst on the solitary farms among those who in bitterness have withdrawn from the colonies. Although the colonies always get the blame for being downright hotbeds of gossip, still gossiping is least prevalent there, probably because of the presence of a group of elderly, stalwart people who have a generation of experience in the country behind them.

෴

Against the background of what was previously mentioned and hinted at here and there, must be seen the vigorous life centred around the church. The church stands there with its ancient ritual, inherited from its forefathers. It is the fixed point in the loosely woven society on the prairie. It is the centre without which human life can hardly be led. And the difficult conditions allow the church to have a relatively easy time of it, even though it is true that the ministers still do not complain any less there than elsewhere about poor church attendance, declining virtue, easy morals, etc. That comes with the job. On the other hand they don't complain so loudly about the poor economic conditions under which they live. It's a strenuous life being a minister in Canada, and you cannot have anything but respect for those who want to lead it. They meet with teasing from all sides, their small private shortcomings are discussed orally and in print, their income is suspiciously large or just suspicious in itself. They are supposed to exercise extreme patience, though it would only be human for them now and then to smack the congregation in the head with a hymnal.

On the other hand, here the minister has all nuances represented in the church. Here there are types who in Denmark would never come to church except for confirmation. And thus it can be said that the Canadian ministers now and in coming years have their opportunities—in more than one sense. If they have as much understanding of human beings as of theology, the Lutheran Church in the new land can obtain power in circles where in the old country it can scarcely dream of being heard.

გა

The large patronage of prairie churches certainly has its origin in the desire for a unifying centre, something which doesn't belong to the everyday, but precisely to the day of rest. Only secondarily does it satisfy the need for expressing religious feeling, unless one does not take the position of connecting everything over and above the everyday with religion.

It can seem like a meagre result that on the whole only the weekly attendance at church is an evidence of cultural life. But it must be remembered that in this country people work so hard and long that there is only a *small* empty space left for filling in the soul. On the prairie a man's thoughts revolve first and foremost around the struggle for survival, and *that* in itself is a value when you live in a country where the struggle almost always bears rewards. Can culture really lift us any higher than to the joy of work?

Notes to "Culture on the Prairie"
"Kulturen paa Prærien" (Culture on the Prairie) was published in *Aarhuus Stiftstidende* (June 11, 1928).

A number of sections of this article have been omitted in the translation which are either redundant or which for the reader to understand would require an intimate knowledge of Danish history, culture and literature of the 1920s. The paragraphing has also been changed. The anecdote about visitors coming to the farms has been taken directly from Sandemose's diary as it is more immediate and fresh than the similar version in the article.

Canada's Horse

Pulling power has undergone tremendous changes in Canada since the colonists lawfully took possession of the land. In those days there were some really peculiar teams to be seen. People did not respect the Law of Moses which says that animals of different kinds must not pull together; they had to let the law and the prophets sleep. Teams of four sometimes might consist of a horse, a cow, a donkey and a mule, and that required a person to be a farmer by the grace of God, if one were to have any benefit from it. A thorough knowledge of the nature of each individual animal was necessary, and you had to be a wizard and Jack of all trades as well—for what got the mule to run caused the horse to stop, and the shout that stopped the cow set the donkey into a gallop. The harness had to be a marvel of invention, and the driver the same. Whenever old farmers started talking about those days, a smile would come into their eyes. "Oh, yes, back then—in the wild old days."

※

There are many stories from that time. Some of them are tragic, some of them quite burlesque. A certain farmer who wanted to get home quickly with his team of oxen knew about the animals' desire to run off, and he used this knowledge to get them to pick up speed. He hid himself in the bottom of his wagon and peeped out through a knothole as he shouted the signal you give when you want the animals to stop. They then turned their heads, and when they saw that he wasn't on the wagon, but must have lagged behind, thus wanting them to stop, they started galloping. Each time when they thought they were far away from him, he shouted out his stop signal so that they started off again like wild horses.

The same farmer once came to a place where the owners had eight oxen which they couldn't break in. Our man offered to do it for twenty dollars and a load of hay. This was agreed upon. He hitched them to the wagon two at a time, and they immediately tried to run the cart to pieces. But the farmer just let them run until they were far out on the prairie. Before he set out he hadn't let on to having any weapon other than a long branch with a piece of twine fluttering from the end, and the owner of the oxen asked, surprised, if he could manage with that. Indeed, he thought so, he said. But he didn't mention a six-foot long chain he had in his pocket. When the oxen out on the prairie changed tactics and lay down, he took out the chain and lashed it at them in such a way that the blow struck from head to tail. It took him fourteen turbulent days to break in the wild animals, but in the end he had the load of hay which he really needed, and twenty dollars.

※

Those days are gone. Oxen are no longer used for pulling, and the horse is put into the background many places as well. Tractors go rumbling in front of the plough, though not nearly so often as one imagines when it comes to the prairies. The diverse natural conditions make running a tractor difficult. In one place it's too hilly, in another there are too many sloughs, marshes or lakes. The horse is still held in honour on the prairie.

※

Everywhere on the prairies the horses are outside during the winter. You see horses in flocks on the white stretches, carrying their customary snowdrifts on their backs. They are outside from the middle of November until around May. There's a lot of discussion on the part of those who haven't seen this before as to whether or not horses suffer a lot from being out and having to feed themselves through the long, harsh winter. Of course they suffer to a certain degree, but not very much. All creation suffers, including people. And when one winter day you meet a flock of woolly horses playing in the snow, you don't take the talk about their suffering too seriously any more. You see that the animals are just being allowed to follow their own nature. And one thing you must of course remember: horses aren't harnessed up to anything until spring comes. There's a lot of food on the stubble fields. They keep themselves close to the straw stacks, especially those with straw from oats which they wear down vertically by nibbling off them and rubbing against them. This leads to the stacks' resembling some sort of domed shed during the course of the winter.

ଈଔ

Horses are far more to be pitied during the summer. They work hard, but that doesn't matter. Insects pursue them to the point where frequently they don't have a chance to graze. There's a certain kind of fly which is particularly hard on them. It gets into their nostrils, and the sting is so painful that the horses go wild when they sense the fly is around—and that's often all day. While they are working it's all right, since they're protected around the muzzle by a wire netting. Without it the animals are impossible to work with. When they are grazing they're ready to run at any moment. They stand with their muzzles in a hole in the ground but then suddenly rush away crazed. At other times they can come running and thrust their heads into an open window, some times a closed one, where they stand looking helplessly around in the room. You see by their large, dewy eyes how the animals are suffering. Even though they're outside the whole long, harsh winter, I certainly believe that they prefer it to summer. And anyone who has the habit of giving horses bread out of the window has a couple of nodding horses' heads in at each window the whole day long.

When you consider Canada as a whole, horses are on the average not treated well. The Scandinavians are kind toward animals, but otherwise the creatures are often maltreated with too little feed and a lot of beating.

ଈଔ

There is one thing that's said so often and in the same way that there must be something to it: almost all farmers are agreed that the horses in Canada are more manageable than those in Denmark. For all intents and purposes you never need to be afraid of their kicking, biting or having the fixed ideas you hear so much about in Denmark. On the other hand there's no agreement as to the explanation for this. The first farmer who tried to explain the situation to me thought that horses' manageability came from their having fewer demands made on them. They were left so much to themselves that they didn't pick up the bad habits they always learned from people, he maintained. If he were right in the latter—and to a certain extent he certainly must have been—then his explanation could be reasonable. But I gradually began to have doubts, for many farmers said exactly the opposite, namely that horses became manageable because people occupied themselves *more* with them there than in Denmark. I frequently heard both interpretations and drew the conclusion that in Canada there are both farmers who have a lot to do with their horses and others who don't. Secondly I saw that horses didn't get ideas into their heads. There can scarcely be any question either that Canadian ones are no different from Danish ones.

෴

Out on the prairies you hear farmers complaining that a farmhand from Denmark sometimes believes that he knows everything about horses since he has used horses in Denmark. A lot of friction arises on farms when the hand doesn't want to learn and the farmer on the other hand doesn't want his horses spoiled. It is, of course, a considerable advantage for the man if he has driven two horses, but that gives him absolutely no right to think he can, as a matter of course, drive with twelve. That demands a month-long study of animals and harnesses. A hand who is driving eight horses often has only four pulling, although the job requires the full strength of all eight. No farmer will be in any doubt about the result. The four cheaters are taught to shirk their work, and the other four, as each month passes, look a year older, until the hand has to give up or is stopped by his employer.

෴

It seems there's a general conception that a horse in Canada can be got for virtually nothing. And there is of course some place where one little feather has become five hens, but usually the farmer is in no doubt that he will be allowed to pay for his animals. For example, it can be stated that in 1927 a farmer in southern Saskatchewan had paid from 90 to 135 dollars for twelve working horses of average quality. In the fall the price of horses can decline somewhat, on the average twenty percent, since there are only a very few which are used during the winter for transport of grain to the station or for pulling the family's sleigh. A horse which has just been caught on a ranch in Alberta can be had for a price varying from fifteen to forty-five dollars, but in the long run it hasn't much value as a working animal, and if it's sent east, there's the cost of transport and dealer's commission to be considered.

Riding horses can be obtained cheaply, or for what one in Denmark would call cheaply, but whether they're cheap for young farmhands in the long run is still a question. Distances are too enormous for one to keep a horse continually, and if a hand wants to continue to have one, horse dealing soon becomes a side occupation. Of course farmers often will require payment for a horse's feed (oats), since naturally not all have the means to show any greater generosity either to farmhands or to other people. The necessary saddle often costs more than the horse, and it frequently turns out that both horse and saddle become a millstone around the neck of the young man. The case is naturally somewhat different for somebody who stays for a long time in one place.

෴

There are various rules for how horses may move around during the winter. These are generally decided by the counties, so that the same rules apply for large, continuous areas of a province. In certain districts, as in Denmark, you're responsible for your horses not going on to another person's land; and the consequence of this is a sea of barbed wire which is hated by the male youth during winter because it is a significant hindrance to coyote hunting. But in other districts people have to fence in their land if they don't want to have other people's horses there, because the owner of the animals bears no responsibility. The consequence is that most fencing comes down in the spring.

It is expected that a horse in the fall, before it's set loose, is to be in the condition one desires it to be in when it's brought home in the spring. But if there's a thaw after a large snowfall, the frost causes a crust to form on the snow, and then come hard times for the horses which cut their legs trying to break through it. Older or weaker animals can lose weight, or even perish. Nevertheless, even the animal of average endowments manages somehow and gains back its strength summer after summer for thirty years. It must be remembered that the form of existence horses are offered also is very close to their natural one.

But animals should preferably not be put in harness after they are let loose, unless they are given additional fodder somewhat beforehand.

There are still flocks of wild horses in the northern parts of Saskatchewan and Alberta outside of inhabited areas. Now and then a few of the horses are captured, and if they have no brands, are put up for auction. They often are not suited for work and it's generally too much trouble to deal with them. They're not hunted as game. People make a point of chasing them far away from their land since they eat the seed, and what's worse lure the tame horses with them, so that it's impossible to catch them again. Wild flocks of horses are, however, rare everywhere.

Horse meat is not consumed in Canada. Even Danish immigrants usually stop eating it.

෨෮

Horses don't seem to have much enjoyment from their existence, but I think that if a horse could choose between Denmark and the Canadian prairie, it would still choose the latter. Freedom during the long winter months agrees with it, in spite of the hazards that accompany this liberty. It moves about on the wide plains where in the dawn of time it came from, has enough food and adjusts quickly.

But it ends tragically. A worn-out horse may be led out into the prairie and shot, to lie there until the coyotes have eaten their share and the rest has become earth. Well, it has at any rate ended up in its old home, on the plains.

Often the end is worse, though at this point the horse could not care less: the farmer carves it up for his pigs.

Notes to "Canada's Horse"

"Canadas Hest" (Canada's Horse) was published in *Aarhuus Stiftstidende* (June 27, 1928). A number of points mentioned in the article are also noted in "Danskeren i Canada" (The Dane in Canada), *Danmarksposten* 6 (June 1928) but differently worded. In addition a couple of anecdotes, in particular the one about driving a team consisting of several different animals and the story of the man breaking in the eight oxen, were incorporated into the novel *Ross Dane*, though in a different form.

The translation is based on "Canadas Hest" with a few lines taken from "Danskeren i Canada" which were not included in the former. Some phrases and short sentences have been left out to make the text flow more easily and half of one paragraph was omitted as being redundant.

On the Rails

There are a multitude of ways for a poor man to get a cheap train trip, if he's familiar with conditions in Canada. Walk through a smoking car and ask the passengers how they got their tickets. You'll get the strangest replies. Some travel cheaply or for free, others pay through the nose.

It's quite common to take a chance on a train carrying livestock from one town to another. And then there are of course the large numbers who out of principle travel only by freight train, hanging down under the cars, crawling on top of them, sitting between them or lying inside them—all in a never-ending battle with the train employees. That mode of travel can be dangerous, but there's sport in it. When the long freight trains pass a curve on their way out of town, the ditches come alive, and the vagabonds board the train like cats. During one single raid carried out on a freight train in 1927 outside Regina, 185 vagabonds were caught, sitting unconcerned in groups in the open cars playing poker for the meagre belongings even a vagabond can have.

The "blind passenger" is a chapter in itself in the history of Canada, indeed in that of almost all of America.

The railroad employees handle the matter in very different ways. Some of them pursue the "blind" passengers, others pose as "blind" ones themselves and facilitate boarding by decreasing speed at the outskirts of the city. Direct help is not extended, of course. Occasionally the train personnel won't give chase until the train is in motion, though that rarely happens. The passengers place themselves on top of the cars, hang under them on a steel rod or on a three-to-four-inch wide board on the end of the car to which they tie their upper bodies with a rope. They can be found hanging there unconscious when the weather is poorly suited for that form of travel, and the employees put them usually into a waiting room by the stove without doing anything more about it. Sometimes when the train stops people run along the backside of it to find an empty car, and the one who finds one shows the whole group the way.

Naturally the employees do not want to take any responsibility, so if they see a man jumping onto a train, they keep quiet in many instances and throw him off again, often with a quite open-hearted declaration that he should act more wisely. No tramp with any respect for himself lets it stay at that. It is a matter of honour for him to be on precisely that train he has been thrown off of; consequently he is often thrown off two or three times.

Even if a starving group gets the chance to steal food on the train, it does so only very exceptionally. The tramp's unwritten law says, "You must not steal on the train, because you have already put yourself at risk by jumping onto it!"

The problem with the "blind" passengers is not as simple as one might think. The fact is, it's an open question whether this mode of travel doesn't also have its good points for precisely the railway companies. The railways, which in Canada are a very great power, exist obviously on the transporting of goods and people, but chiefly on the former. They are interested most in getting people spread across the thinly populated country. And the blind passengers are often excellent workers. They are just people who don't have any money and thus would never have bought a ticket anyway. It is said that the railways' administration of justice is purely formal. In reality they have nothing against stowaways in their freight cars. Still it's wisest not to take their indifferent attitude completely for granted.

One day on the way from Regina to Winnipeg I sat in the smoking car talking with a tall, husky worker who had come in from the harvest. He was of Nordic race and spoke poor English, but I didn't ask him where he was originally from. When I came back after having been in the dining car, he had begun conversing with four other workers, and I sat down a short distance from them. A little later they got up, all five of them, and went out. I thought they had left the train together at the next station, since they didn't show themselves again. But at Cypress River the following story went through the train: The four had lured the fifth one out on the car's platform and demanded from him his earnings from the harvest. But the man was wiser than average. He became quickly aware that the minute he paid, they would throw him off the train. Therefore his first action was to cast himself like a tiger over all four of them at once, and the result was a bloody battle. The weakest of the four bandits was knocked half senseless, but the other three at last brought their victim to the floor and emptied his pockets, after which they threw him off the train that was travelling thirty miles an hour. At the next stop they disappeared.

It happened in the meantime that some linesmen found the victim almost immediately, and a half hour later the police were at work. Already the next day the gang was captured, and the following week judgment was pronounced in Winnipeg. The youngest one who was eighteen years old got off with three months in the work house, two got one and a half years in prison each, and the leader got three years and twenty strokes of the cane. Since ten strokes is all a man can take and costs him six to seven weeks in bed, he gets ten immediately and the other ten on his release as a reminder. It almost seems too much that a man is to speculate for three years about a torture which will come to pass just as certainly as if he had already received it.

The victim got all his money back.

ຮດເບ

People travelling in trains don't stand on ceremony and etiquette. They go around making acquaintances, play cards or improvise an orchestra with accordion, mandolin, Jew's harp, comb-and-paper and boot stomping. The whole car sings along. Wrestling matches are arranged, people tease the conductor who teases back, they stand on their heads if they feel like it and wear their hats as they like. Let somebody look so strange that the eyes of everyone in a Danish town would be popping out at the sight of him—here it makes no difference. If someone had a tall top-hat, sea boots and a naked chest—yeah, well, funny way of dressing, but people wouldn't be discussing taste, because it can't be discussed. That's the man's own business.

Life is never comfortable on a train. The distances are too great. Most passengers will, of course, be of the opinion that a place to sleep is a necessity. If you're going to travel six or seven days without interruption and don't have one, it is enough to rob you of your reason. Nevertheless, it's quite common for those who have no money to travel without sleeping accommodations.

It is customary for a man to carry his train ticket in his hat band where the conductor himself places it or removes it at the appropriate times. When I first got on an American train, the conductor surprised me by taking my hat off my head and looking at it from all angles. Afterward he asked where I was going. Somewhat confused I showed him my ticket. Irritated, he grabbed it out of my hand and put it in my hat. I looked at him for a moment, and then I took the ticket and put it back in my pocket. Now it was his turn to look at me, but he didn't do anything except say nasty things about me with a derisive smile as he went through the rest of the car.

Even though there is only one class on the trains and only one ticket price, there is nevertheless a difference in the cars. In the smokers the seats are covered with leather or painted wickerwork, in the others most often with plush. In a smoker you never see women or children and rarely better dressed people. This in reality causes the formation of two classes between which the difference is greater than between Danish second and third class.

The smoking cars are always occupied by people in working clothes. People often put on working clothes when they travel in Canada since this is both practical and sensible. I always sat in the smokers, because it is there you hear and see most of what interested me. They are magnificent fellows you meet there, and you always come to concern yourself with them, whether or not you feel any desire to do so. It's much too deadly depressing to look out of the windows for days on end, especially when passing through prairie land, and you can't read the whole time without eventually going half crazy in the lurching train. Outside is the endless, flat lowland without trees. It's miles between human habitation. Here the world, life and time come to a halt when the snow comes.

A glowing strip of smoke stands here and there in the sharp sunlight. It looks as though they aren't burning as many stacks here as elsewhere. The eye catches sight of them and tries to rest on them in the far-reaching, flat landscape. A cosy atmosphere has come to the sleeping car, where the lower bunks during the day become seats and the upper ones an inwardly slanting attic. The car takes on an unusual appearance at this. I am sitting here thinking about where I have seen something like this before. It suddenly occurs to me that it was in Cartagena. There was a Norwegian steamer docked there which had a hold in exactly this shape. The name of the steamer was *Guernsey*. Well, that was then—. I am looking out over the land where the straw fires are burning. Then the conductor comes through the car rattling off names. Just opposite me he stops and says curtly, as if addressing me, "The next station is Guernsey."

For a moment I looked at him surprised. Then I laughed in his face. He kept on staring at me during his whole way through the car.

Notes to "On the Rails"

The Danish title of "On the Rails" is "Fattige Folk paa Rejse" (Poor People Traveling). It appeared originally in *Sorø Amtstidende* (July 4, 1928) and in a second version on April 7, 1930 in *Aarhuus Stiftstidende* called "Paa Billig-Billet" (On a Cheap Ticket). The latter article is shorter than the former and ends just before the anecdote about the farmer who was robbed. It has some minor word changes and several additions, but they don't add anything to the content of "Fattige Folk paa Rejse."

Neither of the Danish titles seemed really satisfactory in English, so I called it "On the Rails." The translation otherwise follows very closely that of "Fattige Folk paa Rejse" with an occasional change of paragraphing and the omission of the odd phrase or short sentence to make the text flow more easily in English. One paragraph was added about the placing of train tickets in men's hatbands from an entry in the Canada diary, September 17, which Sandemose wrote on his way back to Winnipeg from Maryfield.

ANECDOTAL ARTICLES

From Belle-Isle to Montreal

Late that night it became foggy. The huge ocean liner rounded the northernmost point of Newfoundland at half speed, piercing the air with its horn every three minutes. It was bitterly cold, even though it was the middle of August. Icebergs appeared out of the fog in all their white majesty. Looming up like floating cathedrals, the surf pounding at their feet, these towering giants remained seemingly motionless.

The night passed. When the sun came up, the fog was still thick, but directly above us was blue sky. Now and again the mist parted, and we looked out over the sea through enormous corridors.

Toward noon we could see the foot of Belle-Isle under the fog. The sea stormed against the cliffs. Whales swam close by the surf, sending clouds of spray into the air. It became colder. The mist began falling like ice-cold rain. I stood alone on the upper boat deck staring toward the land, a desolate, god-forsaken rocky coast.

Now the shores of Labrador emerge out there. The low mountains lie grey and sombre just as Norsemen lost at sea saw them a thousand years ago—this pale and tranquil land with icebergs like a string of pearls along its shores.

It suddenly occurs to me that Newfoundland must now be visible off the port side. There it is, even more low-lying than Labrador. The great island rests there, naked and drab, splitting the Polar Current in two.

Hour after hour I walk from port to starboard, staring first at one coast then at the other as the ship steams southward through the Straits of Belle-Isle. For the past ten years I have longed for these places in the same way that I undoubtedly will soon long for Denmark from this side of the Atlantic. I feel at home in two places. It has been called the "emigrant's tragedy", but that is just a label, pasted on by people who have seen the situation from the outside. Who but the one involved knows whether or not there is any tragedy.

The following night is full of stars. Of the two coasts, the one I discern the longest is that of Newfoundland, lying there like a blue shadow in the night until again we are in open water.

A day and a night and then it can be seen that the water bears greetings from the St. Lawrence River. I have never seen phosphorescence flare up as in the Gulf of St. Lawrence east of Father Point. It is a cold and windy night with thin strips of cloud propelling the stars, which rush across the sky in a hailstorm of fire. To the west is the lighthouse on Father Point. Every three seconds it emits four rapid flashes, four cones of light pursuing each other in over the low, forest-clad mountains shaped like the face of a sleeping person as seen in the light of a flickering candle. The phosphorescence lies on the water like hammered silver. Seabirds flap into the air, leaving a rain of fire behind them, and a tongue of flame licks upward where each drop falls. Over the glowing gulf the Milky Way is a fiery sea in the sky.

Never the same, yet forever the same, the St. Lawrence receives the stranger. When at night you follow this artery from the heart of America, a breath from the New World blows into your face. America! For centuries that name has been ablaze in the Old World, and every skipper who has come to these shores has sailed home with more wood for the fire.

Trees, tangled in each other, their roots reaching out of the water come sailing with the current. Some have no bark, others are shattered, logs churned around in Niagara and now on their way to the ocean, all the way from Michigan, Ontario or Ohio. In a few months perhaps one of them will be hauled on board by a schooner in the middle of the Atlantic and be burned in the galley.

The river still resembles the open sea, but the water is yellow. Soon shorelines rise on both sides of the ship, and ahead stand the towers of Quebec.

A feeling of uneasiness spreads among the emigrants. They drag out suitcases and chests. Soon they will be in the promised land, though some look as though they would rather return home.

It's early morning when the ship docks in Quebec. It has suddenly become quite warm; a dry, hot breath of air moves out from the St. Lawrence. Overburdened with clothes, lugging baggage and children, ten nations go ashore in order to become one. The agents are busy, it doesn't take many minutes before the whole crowd is inside Quebec's large immigration building. There are a number of ugly rumours around about Ellis Island, where emigrants are screened before getting in to the U.S. Canada receives her new citizens quite differently. Mothers get their children into bed, nurses lend them a hand. You see frightened women from Finland or Estonia sink down in a chair and breathe a sigh of relief—the whole thing wasn't really that bad! What difference does it make if the nurse doesn't speak Finnish, the child smiles in its own international language. No offensive examination, nothing but kindness and helpfulness. The men fill their pipes, "speaker" English as best they can and turn over in their minds the apprehension that wasn't necessary. May their future in the country match their reception.

The sun sets as the ship sails on toward Montreal. Strips of light from the now densely settled shore creep over the river, which has become quite narrow. A procession of steamers, magnificently illuminated, parade past us carrying Canada's treasure, grain, out from Montreal. It is dark, a mist veils the sky. The stillness of the night becomes great and profound because you can measure it by the small sounds from the land—a dog barking, a mother calling to her child.

All at once a streamer of Northern Lights shoots out into the sky, arching from bank to bank, a gigantic luminous portal to the Dominion of Canada. Ahead shine the lights of Montreal.

Notes to "From Belle-Isle to Montreal"

Sandemose published this article five different times. Under the title "Fra Belle-Isle til Montreal" (From Belle-Isle to Montreal) it appeared first in *Berlingske Tidende*, Aftenudgave (October 8, 1927) in Danish. The second and last time it was printed in Danish was as "Porten til Canada (Gateway to Canada)" in *Sorø Amtstidende* (June 5, 1928). Its first Norwegian appearance was as part of the rather lengthy article "Bilder fra en lang reise" (Pictures from a Long Journey), *Aschehougs Magasin* 7 (July 1935), which describes a number of Sandemose's experiences in Canada. The last two times it was published was under the title "Gjensyn" (Meeting Again) in *Sandemose Forteller* (1937) and as "Tilbakekomst" (Return) in Sandemose's own periodical *Årstidene* 9–10 (1954).

These articles are in essentially two different variants, a Danish one and a Norwegian one. "Fra Belle-Isle til Montreal" and "Porten til Canada" are basically the same except that in the former Sandemose has inserted, just after he tells about sailing past Belle-Isle, a short story about a fisherman who lived on that island and whom Sandemose claims he met on his first trip to North America in 1916. This story is not found in the latter. The reason for this is that "Porten til Canada" begins with a brief historical overview of the St. Lawrence and the areas around it, and the part that is similar to "Fra Belle-Isle til Montreal" doesn't start until the ship Sandemose is sailing on enters the river itself. Also "Porten til Canada" concludes with a description of Sandemose's short stay in Montreal, consisting mainly of his complaining how hot it was there. The text in "Bilder fra en lang reise" leaves out a number of passages, such as the description of the immigrants' arrival in Quebec City and the story about the fisherman. In addition the language has been streamlined with somewhat more concise phraseology, and the narrative is more flowing. It is obvious, however, that this text is an edited version of the Danish ones and shortened to fit into the larger article. The final two texts are almost identical to the one in "Bilder fra en lang reise" with only minor differences.

The translation is based on "Fra Belle-Isle til Montreal," but makes extensive use of the wording in "Bilder fra en lang reise" As is the case with all the later versions, the story of the fisherman from Belle-Isle has been omitted. In spots I have kept sections, like the description of the immigrants in Quebec City, sentences or phrases that the latter has eliminated. In all the versions Sandemose alternates between using the present and past tense, but I have used present tense throughout, since I feel by doing so the text flows better and is made more immediate in English.

Harvest Time in Canada

Many big, strong men of all nationalities had stopped me in the streets of Winnipeg to beg. On the surface this gave me the impression that unemployment there was greater than in Denmark. However, I quickly became suspicious. On the windows of employment offices were numerous notices of available jobs, and they could hang there unchanged day after day. Occasionally there were jobs that anyone, no matter who, could take on. They weren't particularly lucrative, but at any rate they were better than begging. I asked a Dane why these jobs were not snapped up right away. "Because," he answered, "we're now in the middle of harvest time and that work is better paid."

"But the beggars?"

He shook his head and said, "Over here we get all those Europeans who want to spin gold. Some of them are willing to work for it, others want to discover it ... but if there's gold here, you won't get it until you've paid for it with sweat."

Even before I arrived in Winnipeg, I realized that this country should be viewed in overalls. An empty space is formed around the well-dressed man, and no one can preserve his fundamental character if it is discovered that he came here for any reason other than to make money. If you have eyes in your head you quickly see that it's a waste of time to "do" Canada in a sleeping car, talking to the odd person waiting at stations. You can get a certain picture of Canada doing that, but it can never be more than half the truth—its sunny side. Naturally it's a pleasure to be welcomed by the rich Dane who made his start over here a generation ago and worked his way up. But what about his contemporary who acquired neither a name nor gold?

It would be of interest to meet those who are working themselves up right now or who are desperately struggling to keep above water—the one who has a future and the one who in a generation will go to ruin. If you tell the young people of Denmark about Canada—and perhaps willingly or unwillingly cause them to come here—it's not right to relate to them the legends of the past. You have to go out into the line of fire, into the frontline trenches where people in 1927 are either triumphant or defeated, without giving a thought to the victors or the dead of 1890.

I put most of my baggage in storage, got some workclothes and started out west one morning without any money. The smoking car was full of harvest workers, seasoned labourers discussing clothes, food and tobacco, but never uttering a word about why they were on the train. At every station veritable orgies were celebrated. The farmers came on board begging and threatening, trying to persuade us to go with them. It was funny to see how the workers enjoyed the situation. They inquired with a haughty tone in their voices about the working conditions, meals, the pay and how many blankets they would have over them at night. Then they would phlegmatically roll a cigarette and say they wanted to go further west, after which the farmer would curse and go on to the next man where the result as often as not would be the same. If a man were recruited, he was led off the train in triumph, the farmer not leaving his side. At stations where the train stopped for just a short time, it was literally stormed, the farmers fighting to be first down the narrow aisle where the workers held their audiences. Who wants a nice job? Who wants a good, steady job, 5 dollars a day, wonderful food, marvellous bedroom, easy work, free tobacco? Who wants to work for an all right fellow and get lunch both morning and afternoon—*how about you?* And before you have a chance to consider, you're in for a cross-examination: *You don't?* There's a world of contempt in that question. You break down under that icy look which doesn't creep up on you in a roundabout way but strikes you in the face like a snowstorm, these cold, sterile American eyes that slash you from top to toe. My God, how little you have become after he has given you his farewell glance. There you sit, a lazy, stupid, slow-witted and contemptible bum without a shred of self-respect. When the next farmer chooses a man to sacrifice, that one surrenders and slinks off the train with him like a whipped dog.

I took work with a farmer up toward Regina. As soon as he had lured me off the train, he began singing a different tune. I was loaded into a rigid box wagon and transported ten miles into a prairie apparently devoid of both gods and human beings to the benefit of howling coyotes and silent crows. It was dark when we reached the farmer's wooden house standing in the middle of the plains. I went in and was presented to his wife who exhibited no enthusiasm. Her husband answered her nasty looks with a shrug of his shoulders as if to say: He's not worth much, but there wasn't anyone better.

After a simple, but solid and good meal, I was shown my sleeping quarters in a shed. The roof was leaky, you couldn't close the door, and boards were missing all over the place. Already several people were lying on the floor sleeping, and I lay down carefully among them, staring out at the moon rising fiery red and five times larger than I had ever seen it. I couldn't sleep. The strange sounds of the prairie kept me awake—the cries of birds, the howling of foxes and coyotes, the wailing bleat of rabbits in the claws of some predator. It was 3 or 4 o'clock when I fell asleep at last, and at 5 o'clock we were waked up.

It was still before sunrise when we sat eating breakfast: oatmeal, eggs, bread and tea. Good food for someone who's going to do some work, if only it were possible to get such nourishment down at that time of day. At 6 o'clock we were in the fields putting sheaves together behind the harvester.

Those first days on the farm haunt me like a repulsive and senseless nightmare. Up at five o'clock, breakfast, in the field before six—work at lightning speed without rest or pause until 12:00. An hour for lunch, then at it again until seven. Already after three hours work, I was staggering around blindly that first morning. The stubble field reared up, the sheaves became hateful creatures plotting my destruction, those man-high, enormous objects never did what I wanted them to. Go ahead! The field was bumpy and full of holes and I fell down over and over again. There was a nasty wind as well. By noon I would have had enough if I hadn't by nature been as stubborn as a mule. I ate as if there were no tomorrow and then started in again. The strangest insects conspired to chew me alive; chaff and seeds dug into me as though I were being stung by a legion of wasps. At last I had no idea whether I was standing on my head or my feet. I was conscious of nothing except for a silent but frightening feeling that I couldn't keep up with the others. When finally at seven o'clock the day was at an end, quitting time held no joy, everything was irrelevant. Sun, moon and stars, let them fall out of the sky… I ate, crept out into the leaky shed where a couple of men were already asleep, flopped down before I had taken off all my clothes and passed out. The next morning at five o'clock: Come along! When I had been in that orgy of work for a week, I was no longer a man, just an emasculated, mechanical creature, mumbling awake and asleep: Go ahead, go ahead, go ahead. I'd bet that if somebody had come up and put a revolver to my head, I would have said the same thing. Are you going to shoot me? For God's sake! Go ahead!

Not a thought was given to anything to do with cleanliness. The only thing to wet your face was a thunder shower or nosebleed. Your hair never saw a comb. If I ever managed to strip off enough clothes in the evening, I would see my limbs for a second like strange things, red and blue appendages, coated in grey, but before I could realize where I was, I would fall down between a snoring Finn and a lice-covered fellow of indeterminate race.

And then I was fired, in so many words, because I didn't work enough. A more mind-boggling experience I have rarely had. I took up a mirror and said to the black, swollen, bearded head in it: Oh, so you don't work enough. I'd certainly like to see you when you've learned that lesson. Right now you look strikingly as though you've been through a stone crusher and have skin like a crocodile's.

Out in the prairie by a slough I rinsed my hair in gasoline, groomed myself mercilessly and took a bath. I packed up my dirty clothes tightly so they could do no damage before they had been boiled.

My next employer was a Dane. Here I was the only hand and could keep myself clean. The working day was one hour shorter, but still it was backbreaking labour. After four days had passed he didn't want to have anything to do with me any more. "It would take a year and a day," he said, "before it would pay a farmer to hire you. You work like a horse, but we can get elephants for the same price."

I gritted my teeth and went to a German at the next station with the firm intention of working like an elephant. Those twelve days I was with him I would not go through again for three times the pay. I left voluntarily. The man would have liked to keep me, even though he freely admitted he found me somewhat below average. On the other hand the work there had been more strenuous. We were into the threshing which takes place in the open. I had loaded 15 wagons a day and driven them to the threshing machine, but another fellow had managed 22 wagons—a fantastic performance.

On the train I met the Danish farmer I had previously worked for. He was travelling to another station to recruit people. I told him about the outcome of my last job. "Can you keep it up?" he asked.

"Yes," I answered, "but I don't want to."

A dangerous look appeared in his bright eyes. I heard the anger working in his throat: "You're one of those who will go into Winnipeg and ruin the good reputation we Danes have had in Canada. You're one of those who can learn, but who don't want to. It's us farmers who reap the trash you sow. What the hell are we going to do with you lazy bums in a country that only has use for strong hired girls and trained farmers?"

He swore at me and got up. I had listened to him let off steam with great interest and could have heard more, but he had already left the train.

I rode on all the way to Winnipeg, where I stayed for a while. Now that I've tried harvest work, I'll have a go at whatever there is to do during the winter.

There is certainly a lot here to occupy the Danish farmer. However, only those who take the trouble to inform themselves about Canadian conditions will avoid mixing up what is Danish with what is Canadian. A while ago I was travelling with a Danish visitor. He pointed out of the window and said, "Look at that wonderful, black soil! You can buy it for seven dollars an acre. That would be the very thing for a Danish farmer. If only I were twenty years younger!"

I will ignore the fact that this last sentence sounded very much like a quotation. Yet in that wonderful black earth is grown much too much straw, which of course can be made into a beautiful bonfire, but that's it. Straw makes an awful lot of work without giving any yield. And those seven dollars an acre he mentioned (incidentally land is more expensive in Canada) would be considered cheap if the land were in Sjælland and were to be used in mixed Danish farming. Unfortunately, though, the land is in the middle of the Dominion of Canada and is to be used for growing wheat!—and with *that* fact in mind it would be wisest to consider the purchase price. Later on we can discuss to what extent the price is high or low.

I sit in the train in a comfortable state of lethargy, constantly turning over in my mind the idea that I'm not going to take on any more work. It's a cold, windy day and the heat is on in the car—something that doesn't happen at a certain date or time, but when it's chilly. Later in the afternoon it gets darker and darker on the horizon, black as night, while up in the sky the storm lashes the clouds. On the station platforms people stand shivering and round-shouldered, the constantly drooping American trouser seat hanging down more dejectedly than usual. Toward evening the clouds sink lower, and the wind gets colder, lashing the stiff prairie grass. Way in the front of the car sits a worker. He takes out his harmonica and begins sadly and with a contemplative look to blow on it. Round about in the long car several people begin to whistle along plaintively. Is there anything more melancholy than harmonicas and barrel organs? I close my eyes as the prairie lives on in my heart. Now many are singing along softly as the train rushes on through the wintry day:

> Oh, I wish I had someone to love me,
> > And had someone to call me their own,
> > Oh, I wish I had someone to live with,
> I am tired of living alone…

The tune continues on sadly, accompanied by the clacking of the wheels on the rails:

> Oh, please meet me to-night in the moonlight,
> Oh, please meet me to-night all alone…

ഓര

After it has got dark, we go into cold, pelting rain mixed with clumps of sticky snow. A week ago the sun scorched the earth, and by night there were swarms of mosquitoes. But already then there was a foreboding in the air that winter was on its way from the north. The storm surges around the train as if trying to lift it off the rails. Then there appear scattered strips of light through the rain-streaked window panes—ever more light, a world of light: *Winnipeg*.

Notes to "Harvest Time in Canada"

Sandemose published this article only once as "Høst i Canada," *Berlingske Tidende*, Aftenudgave (December 23, 1927). However, paragraphs 4–5 are found in quite a different version in the Norwegian article "Bilder fra en lang Reise," and in "Hesten" (The Horse) in *Sandemose Forteller* (1937). Sandemose tells a somewhat different version of the same story in "I Canada skal du æde dit Brød i dit Ansigts Sved" (In Canada You Will Eat Your Bread in the Sweat of Your Brow), *Hjemmet* (July 18, 1928).

The translation is based on "Høst i Canada" except that several sentences have been omitted from the original as it was felt they didn't add anything to the text. Paragraphs 7–8 are taken from Sandemose's Canada diary with a few additional short sentences and phrases, and the tense is changed from the present in the diary to the past in the article. The paragraphing has been altered in places to make the text flow more smoothly in English.

The veracity of Sandemose's experiences described in this article is highly suspect, and it is very unlikely he actually worked as a farm hand in Canada. On December 17, 1927 he wrote a letter from Calgary to Office Manager Schmidt at Gyldendal's Publishing House in Copenhagen. In it he asks for money and among other things states, "It's naturally been a very enriching trip, probably especially because I have continually had to take work in the various districts." (Letter, Aksel

Sandemose to S. Schmidt, Calgary, Alberta, December 17, 1927, Gyldendal Archives.) Three months before he had written a letter from Maryfield, Saskatchewan to his friend Hans Helge Jensen where he says, "I had to take off again, am travelling to Winnipeg after having done harvest work in Alberta and Saskatchewan, hellishly hard work and not very well paid, from 5 in the morning till 7 in the evening at a deadly pace." (Letter, Aksel Sandemose to Hans Helge Jensen, Maryfield, Saskatchewan, September 18, 1927, Johannes Væth collection). When he wrote this letter he hadn't yet been in Alberta, and the truthfulness of his statement is thus open to doubt.

On September 17, the day before he had written to Jensen, Sandemose had made an entry in his diary which is almost word for word the same as paragraphs 10 and 11 in the article, except that the tense has been changed from the present in the diary to the past. Just above the diary entry is written, "John Østergaard Experiences". Sandemose had probably heard about harvest work from John Østergaard, whom he stayed with in Maryfield, written down his experiences and eventually made them his own. For two of the days he was in Maryfield, Sandemose made no entries in his diary. The first day was rainy and the second day there was a storm. While he was in Redvers and Alida he wrote in his diary every day. The only other days he didn't make entries he was in Winnipeg. After he left Winnipeg in November there was snow on the ground the whole time.

One would think that such an unforgettable experience as working as a hired man during the Canadian harvest would have left further traces in his diary. Therefore, I think it safe to say that Sandemose never did such work in Canada. His letter to Schmidt was likely merely an attempt to convince him that Sandemose had tried to earn money, but is not true. Sandemose, though, went even farther when he described how he worked as a logger in the article "Paa Skovarbejde i Vest-Canada" (Working as a logger in Western Canada), *Hjemmet* (August 15, 1928) which is definitely not the truth.

Winnipeg

When you are used to walking about on a planet the movement of which at least is not noticeable, it quickly becomes a torture to sit on a train. The first day is all right. The next one you get tired. The third day you have an intense longing for the end of it, and on the fourth one your brain has become a dried-up walnut. On the fifth you have aged twenty years. That was the condition I was in when I got off the train in Winnipeg, Manitoba.

Until now the place had been only a name to me, and it was not much more than that for the first couple of hours. A quarter hour after my arrival found me in a bathtub, and if I had immediately travelled on, I would always have thought of a bath whenever someone mentioned Winnipeg. Afterward I went out, seeing nothing, just walking and feeling firm ground under my feet. Before I knew it, I was standing in a churchyard surrounding St. John's Cathedral. By the back wall of the church was a wooden beam, so I sat down and looked out over the gravestones. I closed my eyes and felt a wonderful peace, the likes of which I had not experienced for years.

The exhausting trip up through the United States, the difficulties with the customs and immigration officials, the trip itself with the heat, dust and dirt—all had been forgotten. In the distance, behind the trees of the churchyard I could hear an organ grinder. It became a summer in my childhood, one of those days when the hourglass had stopped running.

I do not know how long I was with the dead. Perhaps just that sort of half hour that in coming years will have seemed an eternity. Yet when I left the churchyard of St. John's Cathedral I was prepared to meet Winnipeg.

Slowly I walked back to the station to arrange for a hotel. Later, as I was standing out on the steps looking around, it occurred to me that the only thing I had heard about Winnipeg before was that it had a monument in a park consisting of a locomotive. That was something I really did want to see—for there are certain things one has difficulty believing in spite of what reliable people say. At that moment there was nobody on the steps except a Negro in red livery. He had both hands in his mouth and was biting his nails while glowering at me with his prune-like eyes.

I said, "How do I go about seeing that locomotive in a park you have here?"

He took one hand out of his mouth and answered, "How? Well, Mister, by turning around of course. Because I guess you don't have eyes in the back of your head." Then he put his hand back in his mouth, glowered, and tried with his mouth full of fingers to say, "Stupid idiot."

I turned around. There it was.

Cautiously I stepped closer and pinched my arm. Then I accepted the fact. The machine stood on a lovely lawn, newly mown and surrounded by trees. It was painted and as splendid as if it still had not yet left the factory. Except for a peculiar funnel on its smokestack, which I had at first thought was intended to catch birds, the engine appeared modern and would signify enormous progress on some of Denmark's railways. In front of it hung a sign proclaiming that this was the first locomotive to operate in western Canada—between Emerson and St. Boniface. Bought in the United States 1877. On its sides was painted in large letters: *Countess of Dufferin*. Both on the engine and its tender hung large boxes with geraniums and other greenery in them. A bit of track had been laid on the green grass. At first sight I only had eyes for the comical—a freshly painted and brightly shined locomotive, its purpose to

Aksel Sandemose, 1927, at the time of his visit to Canada.

Courtesy: Goldie Decterow
Simon Hjortnaes (second from left) and three brothers, as well as their mother, 1920s.

Simon Hjortnæs's farm near Alida, Saskatchewan, as it looked in the 1980s.

Redvers, Saskatchewan, 1920s. The hotel in which Sandemose stayed appears to the right.

Buffalo skull which Sandemose brought home with him, and which was the subject of the article "Winter and Spring."

John Anderson (with arm in sling), standing by the shack he had dragged into East Coulee as fancifully described in "Moving Day." Anderson also figures in "East Coulee." The photo was taken in the 1920s. The other people in the photo are probably Anderson's neighbours.

The Sorensen family of Holden, Alberta, summer 1926. Left to right: Carl, Ebba, Peter, Esben.

Manitoba Archives.
The "Countess of Dufferin," as described in the story "Winnipeg."

Sandemose's drawings in diary entry, Calgary, Sunday, December 18, 1927. The caption, "Stemninger fra Calgary" translates as "moods from Calgary." These drawings are mentioned on p. 35.

Home coulee, Dalum, Alberta, near Pastor Peter Rasmussen's farm, 1980s.

overcome distances, decorated with flowers among green trees. But as I stood staring, my smile gradually disappeared, and I began to feel ill at ease. Was I distressed over the tastelessness of it all?

This feeling of despondency came over me several times during the day, but it was especially strong that evening as I was passing a church and heard a hymn being sung. I stopped and tried to grasp the connection between a hymn and a decorated locomotive—there *was* a connection, but I couldn't make it. So I went back to the park to take one more look at the machine. It stood there in the twilight, lit up by streetlamps around it, and under them were 25 or 30 men in their shirtsleeves bowling on the grass with balls about the size of coconuts. There were balls all over the lawn, and the men walked back and forth quietly rolling them. No one said a word. It was as though they were performing a holy mystery in front of the *Countess of Dufferin*. I walked closer to the locomotive, but stopped all of sudden in the middle of a clear, sharp vision. Somewhere in Jutland I was in the funeral procession of a close relative. I was standing beside the tall black hearse hung with wreathes, and we were singing a hymn. Again I stared at the *Countess of Dufferin*. It was a depraved caricature of a hearse.

※

You can see on the map how the Canadian railway net is drawn together in central Canada until all lines meet in Winnipeg. Toward the Pacific and the Atlantic they spread out like thunderbolts from the hand of the sky god. Where his hand grasped the bundle, there Winnipeg arose, Canada's restless heart, the city of contradictions, gateway to the land of work in the west. In this melting pot the people of the world encounter each other; the south confronts the north, east and west. Here the Indian meets the Malay, the Chinese the Negro, while the white man realizes his dreams in stone and steel—churches and banks that take one's breath away. Towering over a run-down section of town full of second-hand stores and populated by the diverse races of the south and the Orient, is Hudson's Bay Company's huge building—a city within a city. This ancient firm, established in 1670, stands in the maelstrom of Winnipeg's business life like a rock of distinction and tradition, unshakeable as Mount Everest. Its window displays are works of art. You circle the building transfixed, looking and looking, forgetting everything around you. In the middle of the hustle and bustle a certain sense of peace comes over you. Once more you walk the long way around the building, touch the polished wall in parting and come to a stop down the street for a final look as newsboys and beggars step all over your toes. And suddenly I feel sympathy for a poor Italian who cheated me out of half a dollar this morning…

The picture of Winnipeg is violent and rugged. Just a couple of snapshots from Portage Avenue where the large and splendid post office is located a short distance from Hudson's Bay Co.

The traffic noise thunders in the air. Evening is approaching. A sea of street lamps and neon lights. I come out of the telegraph office and approach the post office. All at once there is a commotion on the steps. My curiosity is aroused, but before I can get there, a police car with its siren shrieking rushes up to the building. Four constables run out into the middle of the scuffle, and I hear the dull thud of billy clubs. I go over and see two men lying lifeless and bleeding on the sidewalk as the police write up their report: the two had been caught as they were running off with a lady's purse.

"Are they dead?" I ask breathlessly.

My question evokes shouts of laughter. Why? I become angry but remain silent.

One of the officers looks over his shoulder at me and says with a smile, "Well, they aren't going anywhere. Safety first!"

Anyway, you don't have to be long in Winnipeg before you understand why the constables carry a long billy club in their hand and a revolver sticking out of their pants pocket. A civilized city to be sure, but loose at the seams and with a constantly shifting population. The number of Danes alone can vary by 100 a day. Murder and robbery are daily occurrences, and you understand as time goes by what nonsense it is when in Danish newspapers you now and then run across stories about the brutality of American policemen. Indeed they would be considered brutal in a calm old city like Copenhagen where you have so much room to breathe that you can discuss whether or not the abolished death penalty ought to be abolished.

The two poor fellows are put into a car, but before the crowd disperses, its attention is drawn to a peculiar vehicle—a couple of men dressed in oilskins pulling an old Ford on a rope. A sign announces that they have been walking with the car from Halifax and are planning to go to Vancouver. Its name is *Spirit of Blue Nose*. It has no motor, and it looks as though it had fallen from the city hall tower into a crate of eggs. In the middle of the crowd it stops. Picture postcards sell like hotcakes. A card is dipped in the robbers' blood and tacked on to the car's body: Souvenir from Winnipeg! Then something new takes place in the street. 20 or 30 cars come driving in a line honking madly. A half dozen or so have old fenders, pots and pans rattling behind them. The stuff flies into the air every time in hits a bump in the road. All cross-traffic stops.

I go out into the street and interview the grinning policeman. "What is that?"

He looks sympathetically at me and replies, "That's somebody getting married."

"Married?"

"Well, today's Saturday."

"I know, but…"

"We marry off a bunch every Saturday. Isn't Saturday a nice wedding day?" he adds laughing.

Over in the street a car has stopped and a man jumps out. On his back is written, "Just married."

The emigrant has stamped Winnipeg. You meet him everywhere—on the streets, in the stations, in shops, often preposterously and gaudily dressed, speaking broken English, with sun-burned face and keenly observant eyes. Whole sections of town are populated with the sharks who live by robbing him. Also among them is found the Dane, and the misused dogma that one should stay away from his countrymen when abroad is a sad truth here. The great stream of emigrants who travel out into the west from the Maritime provinces have to go through Winnipeg, and at this crossroads the weak fall away or return when they have suffered their defeat. Down in the States in Buffalo I met one of my old, harried countrymen who had lived many years in Canada.

"Oh, you're going to Winnipeg," he said. "There you will meet the fallen Dane."

And I have met him, not once but twenty times. The first time was when a pale, sharp-nosed and beady-eyed fellow in a store wrote me out a bill and said four dollars and seventy cents. I had bought a number of small items and was about to pay, when I looked over at the piece of paper. The total was $4.69.

"Why did you say one cent more than is written there?"

"Oh, just to round it off," he answered, without batting an eye.

Now I took the bill and added it up. It came to $3.30. He accepted the money without saying a word.

Then a husky voice in the back of the store said softly in Danish, "He's got something in his outside pocket."

At that moment I met the eyes of the storekeeper. We both turned white, for when it dawned on me that he was a Dane, I recognized him and he recognized me. He cast down his eyes and wet his lips. I was unable to say a word. I hurried out and got far away from the place before I overcame my shock. Those are not exactly the circumstances under which one wants to run into old acquaintances again.

Here at the gateway to the land of work, the weak one falls away and becomes a parasite. He never got any further, he recoiled at the first decisive leap. Nevertheless, he has his illusion, he talks loudly, he is abused, he will not, by God, stand for this and that, over here they only wanted him to work himself to death! He came over here as a *Dane*, he thought they would blow him a fanfare when he came ashore, that all of Canada's farmers would fight over him. And then someone has the audacity to ask him, "Denmark? A city in Sweden maybe?" He failed precisely because he was a Dane, one of the most capable and enlightened people on earth—something which I learned in school and which my children will presumably learn.

But thank heavens, by far the most of them buckle up, become productive, create a future for themselves and forget how perfect they are. In Winnipeg, as in all of Canada, there is a group of sturdy Danes who by toiling for themselves have benefited both Denmark and Canada. On the other hand, the person who comes here without a will of steel commits an offence first against himself and secondly against others. There is no use here for the lazy incompetent who "is sent" over. At home he can keep afloat on his own illusions and those of others, but here he will immediately sink mercilessly to the bottom. Over here a human wreck is regarded differently. A man who cannot keep up or who shows a weak side, either moral or physical, is looked on as a horse which has an irregular gait or a machine that doesn't function properly. Get rid of him. In that respect Canada is after all like the U.S.A., the nation of the dollar and the land without pity.

Those conditions can precipitate a man's rapid undoing. But they also build men the likes of which we seldom see on the other side of the ocean—short-tempered, tough and unbending, with faces like masks and fists like shovel blades, no time to waste on talk! Many a time when I have met that sort of person on the street here a voice inside me has inquired whether this might be a Dane. The first day I was here I encountered a man at the immigration office. He was carrying an enormous load on his shoulders and was bent over almost into a right angle. From a distance I thought he was a Negro, but when he came just in front of me, he put his burden down and took a breath. They were white man's eyes looking out at me from the black, discoloured face. He let a Danish word fall as he asked me for a light, and we spoke to each other for a minute. He had been here one year, had just come in from the harvest and today was finally able to send money for the tickets so that his wife and children could join him.

"That crate's heavy", I said. "You should have hired a porter."

"Costs 50 cents," he answered and began loading it on his back again.

As we parted, I hastily asked, "What were you in Denmark?"

"Unemployed cobbler."

Indeed, it's not merely an ocean that is in between, it's not just another part of the world, it is another world. It was brought home to me one evening here in Winnipeg that I was on another planet against which one is profoundly unjust, if he tries to judge it by European or Asiatic standards. America must be judged by American standards. It has its own beliefs, its own ways of life. Sometimes it turns out comical and at other times tragic when Europe raises her moral forefinger toward America. The last time it happened, that finger killed Sacco and Vanzetti. At any rate it's the general opinion in Canada that the two Italians, guilty or innocent, were irrevocably lost when the protest came from Europe.

It wasn't specific evidence I found nor things I saw which convinced me that Canada cannot be judged by a European. Rather many small events pieced together became a whole one evening as I walked through Winnipeg. I was standing by the Parliament buildings around midnight. Its tower stretched toward the sky, dazzling white under the full moon, a sight so moving that I felt close to God. It's a different sky over this vast continent—distant and wild like a vision of the Atlantic Ocean. My feelings, which from hour to hour had changed during my meeting with Winnipeg, immediately settled into place. I knew that however long I might live, I would always be a stranger in this land.

ଽଠଓ

In 1954, Sandemose wrote the following postscript after the Norwegian version of "Winnipeg" in the periodical *Årstidene*:

It was in the summer of 1927 I stood looking at the locomotive which had become a lawn decoration. I was later attacked for my description in a way I found hysterical at the time. After all I was right—so I thought. I didn't understand that I was thinking like a young man, unhistorically, and was therefore a bit egocentric. I was in another part of the world and was gauging things from a European point of view.

This doesn't change the fact that I still have a hard time taking it seriously when someone sets up threshing machines, canons and locomotives in public places and decorates them with geraniums. They belong in their own special museums without flowers and other greenery.

What I at that time forgot was the background behind the *Countess of Dufferin*'s standing where she was. I didn't take into consideration the pioneers who had come there in their prairie schooners with children and animals, homeless, with a responsibility to the future, with anxious mothers and children who had to have food. *Food* was the number one concern. I didn't envision that day of joy when they opened their first railroad, that day of joy when their isolation was ended, that day of joy when these hard toilers could finally dispose of their produce. *Until then this was all they had dreamed about*. They felt a direct and unswerving gratitude to old *Countess* when she had served out her time.

They hadn't even thought about raising a work of art. They didn't understand such things and didn't really have the opportunity to do so. But they couldn't bear to lose her, and it would be sacrilege to send her to a scrap dealer. So they placed her in the middle of their city, and decorated her with flowers. And geraniums are beautiful flowers.

Several years ago, when I had matured further in my ideas, I came across a coloured postcard with a picture of the locomotive on the lawn in Winnipeg. Now I could see the matter from another point of view. Then I also saw that basically the whole thing was not that unappealing, and I remembered the verse that

Each land has its gods
And each its holy stone,
A thousand clouds pass the sky,
but the sky itself's alone.

Notes to "Winnipeg"

Only one version of the article "Winnipeg" appeared in Danish in *Berlingske Tidende*, Aftenudgaven, December 30, 1927, but four versions appeared later in Norwegian. The first is included as part of "Billeder fra en lang reise" and the other three, all under the name "Winnipeg" in *Sandemose Forteller* (1937); *Årstidene* 9–/10 (1954); and *Dans, dans, Roselill* (Dance, Dance, Roselill) (1965). These Norwegian versions are almost identical and differ from the Danish one in being more streamlined. Sentences have often been rephrased in the former and also small sections have been omitted.

The translation is based on "Winnipeg." Some of the phraseology from "Bilder fra en lang reise," where it parallels "Winnipeg," has been substituted for that in "Winnipeg" where the former seems to flow more easily. At at least one point a phrase was substituted with one taken out of the diary. Otherwise several short sentences and phrases in "Winnipeg" are omitted, primarily ones that have topical or cultural reference that would not be understood by one not having a close knowledge of Denmark in the 1920s.

According to his diary, Sandemose had completed writing "Winnipeg" on September 11, two days after he arrived in the city. In his Canada diary, he mentions sitting outside St. John's cathedral, seeing the Countess of Dufferin, walking through the streets of Winnipeg, witnessing the wedding cars and the men towing the car from Halifax to Vancouver often with the same or similar wording that he uses in the articles. Indeed, the passage about how the Dane is greeted in Canada is taken almost word for word out of the diary. On the other hand, no mention is made of the robbers nor of his being cheated by a Danish storekeeper acquaintance. Thus these incidents were probably fabricated, since they would likely have made enough impression on Sandemose for him to have noted them in the diary. After searching the Winnipeg newspapers that came out during his first stay in Winnipeg, I found no mention of the police beating up or the arresting of any pickpockets or thieves, unless at the time such incidents would have seemed too trivial or even too common to be mentioned in the press.

The *Countess of Dufferin* was situated in Sir William Whyte Park when Sandemose visited Winnipeg. Currently it is located in the Winnipeg Railway Museum.

The death penalty was actually not abolished in Denmark until 1930.

According to an article in the *Winnipeg Free Press* of September 17, 1927 ("Fun and Frolic Being Towed across Canada in Motorless Car") the two "men dressed in oilskins pulling an old Ford on a rope" were George A. Scott and Frank J. Elliott of Amhurst, Nova Scotia. They were attempting to cross the country by begging for tows from passing motorists. As far as Winnipeg they had had no difficulties, but the article speculates that they will have trouble farther west, as the roads are muddy, and cars have enough problems moving without pulling extra weight. There is a photograph of the car accompanying the article.

Nicolo Sacco and Bartolomeo Vanzetti were two Italian immigrants to the United States. In 1920 they became suspects in a murder, were later found guilty and finally executed in August 1927, shortly before Sandemose left Denmark. Already in 1925, however, another man had confessed to the crime. The trial was widely publicized, and it led to many protests both in America and in Europe, primarily because the two had been anarchists, and the action against them was regarded by many as terrorism against the workers' movement.

The Prairie Night

For a week I lived with a Norwegian farmer west of Moose Jaw. One morning I saw an animal out in the snow, thought at first it was a dog, but then I recognized the nervous and hungry movements of the coyote. I knew that the farmer's rifle was in Moose Jaw for repairs, but I got hold of his shotgun and went over to a hollow near the animal. Then it saw me and rushed off. It presented a good target as it ran from me in a straight line. I fired. It did a summersault, quickly got up and laboriously pulled itself along. I went after it, bringing it down with the next shot. It got up again and limped off with great difficulty, but when it saw that it couldn't escape, it threw itself down in the snow and awaited my arrival with its fiery tongue palpitating between its dagger-like teeth. Ten feet away I fired once more. It rolled around a while before it died. The pelt had been badly damaged by the buckshot.

I thought I had performed something of a feat by shooting a coyote with duck-shot. Of course it only happens under special conditions when you can get close to the animal, as in thick snow or during a prairie fire.

The same day I rode to Moose Jaw and picked up the Norwegian's rifle—a large pump gun with nine shots. In the afternoon it stopped snowing and became still. I practised my shooting a short distance from the farm where I had placed tin cans on a row of fence posts and attempted to find out what the rifle could do. On closer acquaintance the weapon revealed no great surprises.

The following night I got up at 2:00, dressed myself as for an Arctic expedition and turned my sheepskin coat inside out. It's difficult to distinguish that side from the snow and besides, it's a well-known fact that you see no ghosts when you've gotten into your clothes the wrong way. Slowly I walked through the house and out on to the veranda. The prairie lay in a white stillness, shiveringly cold. The waning moon was sailing high in the sky. It looked as if it had lost its missing part by a straight, well-carried stroke of an axe. I caught myself letting my eyes go searching the sky for the amputated piece.

The tall, barrel-vaulted stalls became clear in the lines between the snow and the moon. By the southern end of the barn stood a dozen horses which began carrying on a grumbling conversation when I stepped out on to the farmyard. You think yourself able to see a long way by the light of the moon, but I had not gone very far from the farm before the buildings simultaneously were dimmed and became transparent, while in a ravine between the prairie hills, down to which no moon ray reached, things could be viewed without resistance. The light from the snow wrestled under the sky with the light of the moon and dispersed the lines of vision. A bridge of darkness shot through the air, and on it went the northern lights, wavering from one horizon to another. It was as if in the moonlight nature too had put its fur on backward so that the darkness unveiled and the light concealed.

Soon it struck me that I was alone. It was not the usual feeling of loneliness which is independent of the presence of other people, but another, a certainty that here I moved, I alone. Everybody else was asleep. What I was doing would remain unknown by everyone as long as I wished. Here no mask needed to be worn. It was with a feeling of satisfaction, I maintained, that I was still the same as before. I wasn't doing anything extraordinary, I was walking quite naturally on my own two legs. I was out to shoot coyotes, the tracks of which stood in the snow each morning in a bog toward the northwest. They had been seen there several times at daybreak. It was so natural and simple out here. The world became whiter. The prairie spread out like a pale, sleeping face, the northern lights climbed higher. It was the last third of the night when the cold digs in its teeth. The snow puffed up like dust where I stepped. The northern lights sloped downward and formed a golden way right across the sky. On it hung the Big Dipper.

Out on the frozen bog I crept into a bush, rolled my blanket around my legs and sat quietly. Somewhat later the northern lights left the sky, the moon went away, and it grew dark. But the white snow kept the darkness from the earth. The night hung down toward the whiteness like the stalactite formations in a cave. And it was as if the white prairie hills began to breathe, to rise and fall like the breast of a sleeping person. I closed my eyes and felt how still the night was.

Like down an owl floated past me. It had surely seen me but went about its business without taking notice. And when it had been forgotten that a human being had come to the place, I discovered how full of hares the prairie is. You don't see them so much until the snow levels out the land, but now I had two, three or four regularly in sight. Then they were gone. I didn't see whether they ran, hid themselves or what happened. It was as if they just explained themselves away. They were gone, and only the owl silently kept me company.

A quarter hour after the hares' disappearance the coyotes ran into the hollow in front of me, one large one and two smaller ones. My shots could not fail to hit them, and therefore I waited, wanting to use the opportunity to observe the nocturnal howlers at close range. A moment later they stood still, the smaller ones on either side of the larger one. They held their heads in the air so that the white underside from the throat to the nose showed itself as three light triangles. They stood without moving a hair—and a thought occurred to me: At last a sculpture that fitted into the prairie.

With an embarrassing feeling as though I myself were making a blunder, I had looked at those white figures they have in many prairie towns in memory of the ones who fell in the Great War. They are so dreadful, that even the reason for their erection cannot shed a redeeming light on them—these copies of the same Tommy standing with his hands awkwardly holding his rifle. There's no doubt that he gets a weekly bath of soapy water so that he'll be clean and nice. If only he weren't so shriekingly white...

I have grieved over that monument they've set up in memory of the prairie Tommy. After all you don't create art by taking up a collection and converting the 49 dollars and 17 cents received into marble—and putting it up. But—what do I know? These hard-bitten fellows out here think this cleanly washed figure both nice and—pretty—I guess, and he in heaven above maybe thinks the same. Something similar once stood hidden in a corner of a museum in Copenhagen, and I heard a respectable man say, "It's too bad how little understanding the curator has of art that he can hide away the prettiest figure of all."

That was a long leap from three coyotes on Canada's prairie, but that was my train of thought as the barrel of my pump-gun was pointing at the white throat of the animal in the middle. It was the little one on the left that broke the motionlessness. Moving quickly three or four yards diagonally forward, it turned and looked back, pivoted around, stood still again and slowly moved its head in almost a complete revolution. The others walked forward and did the same. Then they began restlessly searching the hollow. A moment later I saw a remarkable sight: when the coyotes were in the middle of the little valley something began moving over from where they had come. It glided slowly up along the slope, on the top of which it appeared for a moment more sharply and then disappeared. It was a hare! The coyote had never stood high in my esteem, but after seeing this it fell abysmally. I shot just as much out of indignation and contempt as in an effort to hit the animals. The old one fell under the first shot, one of the young ones under the second. The third coyote took off. When I got to my feet I saw something streak over a hillcrest further away. I shot, but hit nothing.

I slung the coyotes over my shoulder and walked toward the farm. In the light of dawn it began clouding over, threatening snow. A flock of crows flew past me morning-low; the winter made them fearless. Their arrogant voices still rang after me as I came into the farmyard. There I put the coyotes on the steps while I made myself free of my heavy outer clothing. I'd become extremely hungry and was wondering what might be offered for breakfast. A dog came running and looked at its fallen cousins. It bared its teeth in a ferocious grin but kept itself a couple of paces away. Then it came over to me, wagged its tail and cast a sidelong glance at the dead. I hadn't seen that dog with such an expressive look before and didn't really like it afterward.

The farm wife stepped out onto the veranda and greeted me good morning.

"Here you can see," I said. "It was a cold night, but it paid off. Coyote meat's all right to eat, if you're hungry enough."

She looked at the pile and cringed.

"Take it away," she said vehemently.

I took the animals over into the barn and didn't think any further about her testiness. There are of course people who can't bear to see a dead fly. But a little later I saw her standing staring out into the prairie. There was a haunted look in her eyes. Something dawned on me. In the farmyard I met the husband, standing as if unsure. He wanted to say something, but was searching for words.

"Here … here we are in the habit of … when we've caught an animal, we go into the barn with it from the south, you know. And leave it there.

"Your wife can't stand…? I asked carefully.

"She can slaughter a bull."

I stood silent.

"But you see … when we came here … she of course longed to go home to Bergen. There was water there, you know. Here there's only prairie. And all the strange things we can get in from out there…"

He stopped resignedly, couldn't get his ideas sheathed by words.

"Is she afraid of the prairie?"

His eyes glinted.

"Yes, exactly, that's just it. *She's afraid of the prairie*. We men of course don't understand that sort of thing, do we? But she is, however much we talk … afraid of the prairie…"

He left, and I remained standing, strangely affected. Slowly I strolled over into the barn and looked a while at the dead coyotes which lay senselessly gaping with a fixed look of hate and hunger in their glazed eyes. I wanted to shake something oppressive off myself but could not and hardly knew what it was…"

A hawk circled over the farm as the night retreated from the land.

Notes to "The Prairie Night"

"Præriens Nat" (The Prairie Night) was published in *Berlingske Tidende, Søndagsnummer* (March 25, 1928). An almost identical version of it from the fourth paragraph on is found in the novel *Ross Dane*. There it is written in the third person singular instead of the first person singular, as it is the main character Ross Dane who is doing the hunting. The description of the soldier's statue is not in *Ross Dane*, nor is a passage near the end of the article.

The translation is based on the article except that a few sentences and phrases, and especially several sentences in the next to last paragraph have been left out, either to improve the flow of the narrative or because they contain topical or cultural references which would not be understood by some one who did not have intimate knowledge of Denmark in the 1920s.

A Canadian Pastor

East of Edmonton in the province of Alberta is a small Danish colony of 10 to 12 families. The Norwegians were the first ones to take land here, but later on a few Danes and a large number of Ukrainians came. The Norwegians and the Ukrainians have each led a stable community life with churches, schools, ministers and teachers. But the Danes have been too few, and this has meant that they have associated themselves closely with the Norwegians. Here, as virtually everywhere Scandinavians meet abroad, they almost regard each other as countrymen, though it seems as though Danes attach themselves more easily to Norwegians than the other way around.

Those Danes who during the years since 1905 have farmed here around the station town of Holden have felt closest to the Grundtvigian movement, and it was thus natural that several years ago they gladly accepted an offer from Pastor P. Rasmussen to hold services several times a year in the colony. Rasmussen is the minister and highschool principal in the colony of Dalum near Wayne, Alberta, and in a moment I will get to a description of his work there.

In November while I was staying in Holden with a farmer, Peter Sorensen, I drove with him to Camrose, 26 miles away, to pick up the pastor. He reminded me of a Danish minister—and of Denmark itself. In a country like Canada, where a Dane has to speak English every day, he often comes to regard English as his true language after a few years and mixes his Danish up terribly with fragments of English into a language which frequently is harder to understand than pure English. But Pastor Rasmussen spoke a beautiful and pure Danish, though he has been in America virtually all his life. One quickly learns to appreciate that when travelling abroad. Many a time I have caught myself wishing that the Danish Canadian would immediately give up his Danish rather than maltreating it first. Not that it is necessary to give it up. I remember Simon Hjortness in Alida. He spoke pure Vendsyssel dialect without a trace of English. And he has been here since the age of eleven.

The humour of the Dane from Fyn was also alive in the pastor. On the way from Camrose to Holden we were hit by a Ford, so Peter Sorensen's new Chevrolet suddenly looked like a used car. He jumped out and demanded 15 dollars from the offender. The man grumbled but paid—that is he wanted to pay, but after checking, he found he had only 14 dollars and 90 cents. Sorensen was content with that.

"You have a keen eye for what people are worth", laughed the pastor. "You just figured the 10 cents out wrong. Those 10 cents the man paid in kind."

"In kind? What do you mean?" asked Sorensen.

Rasmussen pointed over to the hood. There the unfortunate motorist had put his mittens while he was paying. And they were still there.

"The poor fellow fell into the hands of robbers," said Rasmussen regrettably. "Present were the robber, the priest, the Levite and the unfortunate one who was fleeced. The Samaritan wasn't there."

He turned around to me and said, "For there aren't many Good Samaritans in Canada."

In various homes the pastor baptized children who had come to Canada without tickets since the last time he had been in Holden. On Sunday there was a service at one of the farms. The doors were opened up between the rooms and every seat made use of. People sat on chairs and the edges of tables, four placed themselves on the end of a bed, two took their boots off and lay down behind them. Men sat with their wives on their knees and they in turn held a child or two. A blanket transformed a sewing machine into an altar, and then things got going.

It was all primitive, but necessity dictated that that was the way it had to be, and it was beautiful to see this group of people from many regions of Denmark gathered around what to them was something of common value. You forgot the sewing machine under the altar covering, forgot the funny sight of an old farmer with a young girl on each knee, forgot that you yourself were the sixth man in a double bed. Still it was not really Danish, for outside a snow storm was raging across a boundless prairie which gave no rest to the eye in any direction. And of what use was it to speak Danish here when you were sitting and looking out over a land so incomprehensibly different from the one you were familiar with—a land on which only a few years ago no white man had set foot.

೫೦೧૩

I will give a short résumé of Pastor Rasmussen. He was born in 1877 in Brænderup on Fyn, where his parents were smallholders. At the age of 17 he came to Cleveland, Ohio, and worked as a gardener there for three years. Afterward, he was in Denmark for a year before enrolling in the seminary in Des Moines, Iowa. He graduated from there in 1903 and began teaching at Danebod Highschool in Minnesota. In 1904 he married Catrine Appel, from a branch of the famous Appel family, but born in Detroit of parents from Southern Jutland. As a minister, Rasmussen started first in Sheffield, Illinois, and was there for three years. After a visit to Denmark in 1907 he went the same year to California, where he was a pastor for six years. In 1913 he became principal of Ashland Highschool in Michigan and was there until 1920 when he became minister in Dalum near Wayne, Alberta, Canada, a colony which was founded in 1917 by the Danish People's Society.

A minister who is called to a "post" in Canada does not go to a parish farm, is not guaranteed anything at all, but generally gets something like promises that people will support him according to their ability. If it's a question of a newly founded colony like Dalum, the ability of the congregation to do so during the first difficult years will frequently be close to zero. It is expected that the minister will start out on something like an equal par with the rest of the colonists, run a farm and so on. When Pastor Rasmussen came to Dalum with his family—there are now nine children—it was to a piece of raw, bald prairie land. Here he was supposed to build a home, find the means of subsistence and form a congregation. The struggle was a hard one, and victory would not have been won had he not had his wife, a tireless worker who lost her health during the battle—and another helper who today understands the running of the farm, a Danish seminarian from the area of Løgstør, Oscar Sørensen. These three share the honour for what Dalum Highschool is today. The first years the harvest was bad and the whole colony was poverty-stricken. Subsequently the people worked themselves upward. The farmers no longer fight with their backs to the wall but have, as it were, had time to take a breath and look back. The minister and those with him had to accept the same circumstances as the others, not merely because they wanted to, but because there was no other choice.

It would be tempting to give a description of the first hard days in a new colony, but considerations of space prevent me from doing so here. The struggle can be so hard that generally the participants are reluctant to go into details, and you can see in their eyes when they speak that they shrink back at the thought of having to do it over again. And the consciousness of what it has cost them to make progress causes them to safeguard their property zealously. You do not see people who eat or drink themselves to the poorhouse; the price of money has been too high for that. In the meantime I should speak less here about the colony than about the school and those who built it, and most about what it is today.

After having been invited by Pastor Rasmussen, I came to Dalum in the middle of November. The name Dalum is not an official one, though perhaps in the future it will be.

It was a bitterly cold day when Oscar Sørensen met me with his sled in Wayne. A large snowfall had made all automobile traffic impossible in these parts, which differ considerably from the prairie further east in Saskatchewan and Manitoba. Alberta is distinct in many ways compared with the other prairie provinces. Large parts of it consist of foothills to the mountains which you can see from high ground in clear weather.

Wayne is a little mining town situated at the bottom of the deep bed of an old river, and a sled trip at night up over the slopes until the horses are dashing on to the plateau 3000 feet above is not soon forgotten. Already the first night gave strong impressions of life here. When we were a short distance from the school, which is six miles from the station, we met the principal on foot. At that time of year—as well as at other times—to see a person walking in Canada is somewhat of an experience, but then Rasmussen was out on unusual business. The fact was that there was a young Dane in Wayne, a mere boy of seventeen, who couldn't make himself understood to anyone, and since everything was now closed it was absolutely necessary to pick him up, since it's no fun to spend a winter night under the open sky in this country. The unusual thing was that there were no fresh horses on the farm, and Pastor Rasmussen was intending to walk to Wayne to get him. Oscar Sørensen in the meantime ordered the pastor back home and went himself to the nearest farm, where he borrowed horses and sledded to Wayne. He came back around midnight but hadn't found the boy, who, it must be presumed, had walked out into the prairie. The light was left on all night in the windows of the school, but he didn't come. Not until the next day did he appear—in the best of health. As we had hoped, somebody had taken him in; but anything could have happened. I myself one evening took a wrong turn and was lost within five minutes.

The school sits on a hill. Behind it stretches one of the large valleys, and in front is the far-reaching prairie. It was only after a number of years that Pastor Rasmussen decided to have a school, and since then there have been between 10 and 30 pupils each year.

Dalum is the only Grundtvigian highschool in Canada, and it's hard to imagine a finer life than is led there. I know that if I had come as a young worker to Canada I would have spent my first winter there. Though my discussions with Pastor Rasmussen were of such a nature that we had to take turns going outside to cool off, and though three quarters of what is called Grundtvigianism is Greek to me, I would not think twice about sending my son to him. Quite apart from what always floats on the surface in a highschool in the way of religious and political ideas, which are worthless as far as I'm concerned, Pastor Rasmussen knew how a home should be, and he has created a haven for more or less homeless Danish young people in Canada.

And he didn't spare himself. At five o'clock in the morning he was grappling with the central heating system, and afterward spent the whole day in unbroken activity until between nine and ten in the evening he closed his book after having given a reading on some rather light topic or other.

Dalum is not exactly the same as a Danish highschool. The most conspicuous thing naturally is that the school sits isolated in the middle of the Canadian prairie, but inwardly it must also be different. There has to be thorough instruction in English and in many conditions relating to the new country, where after all these people are living. This of course pushes aside a lot of what otherwise a Danish highschool is occupied with, and that hardly does any harm. In spite of this, Dalum Highschool resembles perhaps more the original highschool in Denmark than those now existing within the borders of the country do. It sounds like a contradiction, and an explanation could be in order.

Several years ago in Denmark I spoke with the principal of the Danish highschool in Cascallares, Argentina, Reinhold Rasmussen. He agreed with me that one ought to be very careful taking seriously the liberal-mindedness that the Dane abroad bandies about. It's only an outer veneer. Life among foreigners makes him in reality more conservative about Denmark when it comes to intellectual matters. The way he remembers it from his youth, that's the way it should be and keep on being.

Reinhold Rasmussen of Cascallares had carefully tried to break through some of this conservatism which is obviously not always of a desirable sort, as it can mean a stubborn adherence to an abandoned stage of development. But he himself understood this circumstance, because he came from Denmark with his extensive education and his many years of experience. Pastor Rasmussen in Dalum is in a different situation. His experience of Denmark and Danish schools occurred at the turn of the century while he was a teenager. The connection was suddenly severed, but became all the more fixed and unchanging in his mind. If he were to come to Denmark today he would be isolated in those circles which he should belong to. Pastor Rasmussen's school most closely resembles the essence of the Danish highschool around 1890, though certainly 38 years cannot have passed without leaving traces on the school he remembers in his homeland.

It is the lot of the immigrant that there is an abyss in his life. It has been called a tragedy, but that is surely just a convenient label. His intimate relationship with intellectual currents in his native country is cut off, and he continues to think of Denmark as remaining the same as it was before he left. It cannot be any other way, and naturally the one who wants to continue being Danish has to cling almost desperately to whatever influenced him while he was at home. It cannot be any other way, and it's better to recognize a reality and make the best of it than to complain about it. It is an open question whether this conservatism of the Danes living abroad ought to give occasion for joy.

ඝාභ

As yet Dalum has no church. A meeting house is used, and there seems to have been no talk till now of making anything better. But the house is decorated as circumstances permit, and a couple of small wheat sheaves above the simple altar probably speak more to the farmer than would an expensive altarpiece.

Here people go to church every Sunday, and the attendance is always large. It is undoubtedly the case here as in the other colonies that a full church is as much due to a need for social intercourse after a week's isolation on the prairie, as it is to precisely a need to go to church. Already early in the morning people begin to come—the younger ones riding on horseback, the older ones in sleds. The former go to the student rooms, the latter to the pastor's office. In both places feelings can run high. Upstairs the discussion turns to horses, then horses and again horses—horse illnesses, harnesses, saddles, spurs, riding boots. That night dreams are of horses, being trampled by horses and dealing in horses. Here you should keep your mouth shut if you're not a horse trader or veterinarian. Downstairs the conversation can vary somewhat more, perhaps in deference to the pastor. News is exchanged, good advice is given, etc. until the bell rings for the church service at 11 o'clock. Aside from the surroundings, it's just as it is in Denmark. Afterward the young people go back up to the student rooms and passionately continue their horse talk from where they left off.

Dalum was not quite as it usually is while I was there. Mrs. Rasmussen was in the hospital in Drumheller, where she was awaiting a not exactly minor operation. That, of course, meant no one really felt quite as usual. She has since come home in good health. But it was almost as though just her absence gave the stranger more opportunity to look behind things. It was like a house with one wall missing, so that from outside you could see all the details inside. All conversation turned sooner or later to her, and one understood how much she means to this place.

I hope many more Danes may find their way to Dalum.

Notes to "A Canadian Pastor"

"En kanadisk Præst" (A Canadian Pastor) appeared in only one version in *Fyns Venstreblad* (April 15, 1928).

The translation follows the original except a few phrases have been omitted and the paragraphing has been altered to make the English flow better. Also a section has been omitted which has a cultural reference which would not be understood by someone who did not have intimate knowledge of Denmark in the 1920s.

"Grundtvigianism" is the term used to describe the teachings of the Lutheran minister and theologian N.F.S. Grundtvig (1783–1872). For further discussion of Grundtvig and his movement see Introduction. Pastor Rasmussen's school in Dalum was based on the concept of the Grundtvigian folk highschool.

In 1887 F.L. Grundtvig (1854–1903), the son of N.F.S. Grundtvig founded the "Dansk Folkesamfund" (Danish People's Society) which was designed to preserve the Danish language and traditions in America and to establish colonies of Danish immigrants in a Grundtvigian setting where a Danish cultural life could flourish. During the 19th century a number of such colonies had been founded in the United States under its auspices.

Medicine Men

There is no more horribly depressing place than a farm on the prairie when the weather holds up the work and keeps people inside. The houses are almost always very primitive with thin wooden walls, often full of cracks. Inside are two rooms—a bedroom for women and one for men in which food is also prepared. The beds are almost always double, and as many as possible sleep in them—often five or six people in each during the busy seasons in the spring and fall. Conditions for family life are poor. There are naturally farmers who have arranged things more comfortably for themselves, but that presupposes both that the man has been in the country for a long time and that during the first hard years he did not completely lose his sense for some of the nicer things in life.

Rain began to fall early in the morning, turning into a heavy slushy snow toward noon. The water stood in clear puddles. Chickens and pigs walked around dripping wet and cold out in the mud. Where there was no water the snow lay in a thin layer. It rained and snowed, soaking everything both outside and in. The air was like thick, cloudy glass in the darkness. In the stall the farmer sat with a sagacious expression in an empty manger, calculating his annual accounts with chalk on the backside of a shovel blade. He alternately sighed and grunted approvingly. Eventually with two fingers he collected the plug of tobacco out of his mouth and threw it over to a pig which ate it with relish. Then the man lowered his head, placed his elbows on his knees and started tearing at his hair. The rain drummed monotonously onto the domed roof of the stall.

The weather didn't manage to keep everybody indoors. Some young people ventured out onto the muddy roads in their battered old Ford cars. Around noon came a man who was looking at land. His car made a terrible racket, out-of-stroke like a steam threshing machine. Its whole body shook and its wheels dug broad grooves into the ground where it stood. When he drove off, the muck spurted up behind the car like a mud volcano. Now and then it slid half sideways or came to a stop with its wheels spinning around in the mire as we stood in a row by the farmhouse laughing.

Before leaving, the man had told us that a travelling doctor was on his way to the farm. We kept an eye out for him, and a couple of hours later he appeared out on the prairie with his one-horse wagon. The horse was a lean, unshod nag, and the wagon sank up to its axles in the road. But it didn't occur to the doctor to get off; he was sitting raised up high above the whole world on the roof of the closed wagon saying, "Gee up!" Now and then without any warning he would explode into a shower of curses and whip lashes, each time causing the horse to stand still until he was finished. When he lowered the whip and became silent, the skeleton horse weighed the situation for a while before continuing on its way.

"I must say that did the trick," shouted the man of science triumphantly.

When he came into the middle of the farmyard he stopped and looked around probingly. Nobody bothered to come out. Remaining seated for a bit, the doctor cast a sidelong glance at the house, but since an invitation still wasn't forthcoming, he let go of the reins, climbed down and went to the door. He waited for a moment, then coughed in preparation and went in. He said hello, got a hello in return and looked fixedly at each one of us. Then he took off three or four layers of clothing and hung them on the back of a chair by the stove.

"Wet today," said the farmer.

"Beastly wet today," confirmed the doctor.

With that the conversation stopped momentarily while the doctor rolled a cigarette and stared searchingly at every person in the room.

"Anybody sick here?"

"No, esteemed sir."

The doctor lit his cigarette and addressed the farmer in a serious tone.

"You know I can tell you for sure that your daughter has anemia."

"No, she doesn't."

"You shouldn't say that," came the answer. "It's clear enough."

"No, it isn't."

"How do you know your daughter doesn't have anemia?"

"I don't have any daughter."

The doctor remained unperturbed.

"Perhaps this young lady is not your daughter, but she has anemia."

"No I haven't," answered the aforesaid lady. "You're not going to make me believe something's wrong with me. I'm not as stupid as that Mrs. Hughes who you said had gallstones!"

"Mrs. Hughes did have gallstones, and I cured her," the doctor said emphatically.

He suddenly turned toward me.

"You're looking poorly, mister."

"Oh," said the farmer peevishly. "That man is on the point of dying."

"I can see that," said the doctor.

"That is, from laughing," continued the farmer.

Those present let loose a howl of laughter. The doctor went over to the stove and warmed his hands.

"Everybody has something secretly wrong with him," he said composedly, "which sooner or later will cause difficulties if an experienced man doesn't take care of it in time. This young lady's anemia perhaps doesn't inconvenience her now. But in four or five years it could be her death if it isn't cured soon. In ten years it will be her death. Because anemia comes from a lack of veins in the blood."

He lifted a finger pontifically.

"The veins are the flowing ones, the arteries are fixed. When there aren't enough veins then the arteries can't flow, and they fill up the veins until you die of a heart attack without any warning. Like a thief in the night!"

The passage from the scriptures made an impression on my host.

"It's really bad," he said and looked searchingly at the girl, as if he expected her to topple over at any moment—like a thief in the night.

But the girl didn't let herself be upset.

"My blood is flowing quickly enough. I cut my finger yesterday and it downright squirted out. A little anemia wouldn't have been amiss then."

"May I see that finger? Look after that sort of thing! Out here where there are so many water holes, germs thrive in the air, and an open sore is a dangerous thing both for you and for those you prepare food for. Come here…"

"Go away," she answered.

"You should bear in mind…"

"Do you want a wash rag in your face?"

The medicine man sat down distressed. While he continued deploring the health of those present, I stood by the window studying his wagon, which was painted with advertisements and accounts of miraculous cures. There were solemn exhortations concerning the stomach, eyes, corns, nervousness and bad breath which bespoke internal defects and turned the heart of a beloved one cold. I went out and peeked into the wagon. It was full of strange things and reeked of sulfur.

The doctor left the farm after having contributed to its provisions with a bottle of American oil and a can of axle grease.

Travelling doctors in most cases come under the heading "quacks," and their noblest task consists of making people believe they are sick. This seems on the whole to be easy. If you tell a man he looks poorly, it may not be true, but he will soon come to believe it. In the country regions of Canada with its diversified population from all over Europe and Asia, the quack doctor has an easy time of it.

Normally every small town has its qualified doctor, but you have to send for him yourself, and he doesn't exercise as much mysticism. He makes no theatrical production out of a swollen finger. He doesn't cry with compassion, discovering the most interesting and remarkable cases ever encountered in the history of medicine on every visit. He is, in short, far behind.

So is his country. It is loose at the seams, and you can't really talk about a Canadian state, as it is only now being formed. In almost all areas, Canada lags far behind the European countries. Of course it's worse outside the larger cities, and for that reason doctors cringe at the thought of leaving them. The result is that there are far too many of them in the cities. They outbid each other in advertizing and gimmicks—and, as far as the most inferior ones are concerned, in humbug.

From Regina comes the authentic story of the doctor who found a miraculous cure for rheumatism. The idea was to take ten medicinal concoctions prescribed by him during the course of ten consecutive days at a cost of 100 dollars. Afterward, if you could produce a certificate that stated you still had rheumatism, you got 200 dollars back. The trick was that no one made it further than to the third or fourth concoction, and so they went away 100 dollars poorer. The first concoction was bad, and the second one was awful. The third was like being sprayed in the throat by a skunk. The fourth resembled musk mixed with sulphur, dissolved in boot black with an admixture of gunpowder. Nobody tried the fifth one. But it is said that one night one of the patients broke into the doctor's house and gave him a double dose of concoction number nine which resulted in his being unable to continue in his humane undertaking.

I myself had an unpleasant experience in Toronto. I was suffering from bronchitis and decided finally to go see a doctor. Passing one of the signs that looked least ostentatious, I found myself in a waiting room. After sitting there for some time, I had my turn at last. The doctor was charm personified as he asked me to take off my collar. All right, I took off my collar. He placed me in a chair, went behind me, put his thumbs on the back of my neck, while chattering away in very learned double-talk. Without any advance warning, he gave me a blow on the head, making me imagine myself swimming over a sea of steaming blood. I jumped up with a yelp, and before either the doctor or I was able to reflect on the situation, he was lying curled up over in a corner. Then I began to realize that this could probably lead to one thing or another, and it took only a short time for me to surface in another street.

The heavy and necessary protection women enjoy in America, which has the world's greatest crime rate and a more variegated population than any other country, often leads to tragi-comic consequences. A woman doesn't always understand that those laws which place a man in prison if she merely suspects him of making advances do not rest on the proposition that she is a superior creature, but are due to a plain and straightforward necessity. She becomes spoiled. Even doctors must take this into consideration.

In one of the western cities, a young girl came to a dentist and wanted to have "a couple of teeth" pulled. He examined her and declared that all her teeth were healthy. Yes, she knew well enough that there was nothing wrong with her teeth as such. But she had a job which had to be done standing, and she suffered a great deal from tiredness in her legs. The doctor she had been to had examined her thoroughly and given a learned diagnosis which she believed in but didn't understand. She was supposed to go to a dentist and have him extract a couple of teeth.

Only a fleeting glance at her feet told the dentist the whole story. The girl was pigeon-toed. And he imagined the situation: The doctor had simply not dared to say "pigeon-toed." Even if the girl well knew beforehand that she was, it was very likely that she would have been furious. And the dentist didn't have the nerve to do so either. He tried first to convince the girl to leave her teeth where they were, but after having it pointed out to him that there were other dentists in town, he pulled the teeth. A few weeks later, he met her and asked her how things were going. Yes, everything was better. He thought to himself that to a certain extent she believed this but that also the holes in her mouth gave her something else to think about. Three months later he heard that things were bad again. The comedy had repeated itself. She had gone to a new doctor who had taken out her tonsils. That too helped for a while, but then she went to doctor number three. He removed her appendix.

After the dentist had told me this story, I was reminded of what a Danish-Canadian craftsman had told me. Over here difficulties with the tonsils and the appendix are much more common than in Denmark. At the time I wondered casually why that should be true. Now I understood better. And it must also be conceded that people in all likelihood don't get more pigeon-toed by losing their teeth, tonsils or appendix.

It's not strange that medical books are so common in Canada. When absolute confidence in the doctor is lacking, people often don't follow his instructions and would rather "study" a bit on their own when it comes to the more familiar illnesses—and put themselves in God's hands, if they get seriously ill.

ഇൟ

All of this of course will change with time. People are always ending their arguments by saying that this country is still new. In a modern, closely packed population like that of Denmark a doctor's profession is of the greatest importance; and we feel quite secure there where a doctor's name is scrupulously protected, and where doctors themselves keep discipline in the ranks—a country where a doctor is so strong and valued that it causes him no difficulty whatsoever to tell a young girl she is pigeon-toed.

Notes to "Medicine Men"
"Medicinmænd" (Medicine Men) was first published in Danish in *Berlingske Tidende*, Søndagsnummer (April 15, 1928). The episode about the travelling medicine man was used in the novel *Ross Dane* in only a very slightly different version. Here the main character, Ross Dane, has been given the role of the "I-person" in the article. The same episode, Sandemose's remarks about doctors in Canada and the anecdote about the ten potions, appeared in Norwegian in the article "Jeg har vondt

både her og der, og selv er jeg ikke frisk heller" (I've Got a Pain Here and There, and I'm not Really Well Myself), *Arbeiderkvinnen* 2 (February 1937). Here the introduction is quite a bit longer than in the original, and quite different phraseology is used, but nothing really new is added. Sandemose's general statements about doctors in Canada, which follow the medicine man story in the original, are contained in this section. This is followed by the anecdote about the ten potions. The content of the next section of "Jeg har..." is, except for a few minor differences, essentially the same as the original but completely rewritten and somewhat rearranged.

The translation follows the original except for minor omissions which make the English text flow more smoothly. Two small passages have been eliminated that have a cultural reference which would not be understood by someone not having an intimate knowledge of Denmark in the 1920s. One sentence in the first paragraph has been taken from "Jeg har...," and some changes in paragraphing have also been made.

According to Petra Jørgensen of Virden, Manitoba, who as a young girl in the 1920's worked on Godtfred Madsen's farm where Sandemose stayed, Madsen lived in what was basically a small two-room house with a kitchen. This situation was not necessarily typical of living conditions everywhere on the Canadian prairie (Interview with Petra Jørgensen, Virden, Manitoba, Fall 1986).

See for Yourself

When I came to Canada I quickly discovered how hopeless it was to ask about things. Getting to talk with people was so extremely difficult. It was amazing how seldom they were able to understand that I only wanted some information. Whether this would be positive or negative was of secondary importance to me. Yet every single person insisted that this is the way it is. The next day you were told the exact opposite along with some gossip about the person you had talked with the day before. If you expressed your doubts about something or other, the opposite party would jump up like a jack-in-the-box. It was hopeless.

But it was precisely the *young people* I did not want to forego speaking with. After all they were in the midst of the struggle right now. But you had to be necessarily critical whenever two people did not express at least somewhat similar opinions. The explanation is probably that many young people often feel like bigshots, just because they have undertaken a journey about which there is no longer anything particularly exceptional. Also it's as if the difference among Danes has become sharper in Canada. Indeed most class distinction disappears, but under the hard conditions the gifted man grows bigger both inwardly and outwardly, while the one who is poorly equipped psychologically, and for whom in reality the class distinctions of Denmark were a protection, sinks even deeper into gossiping and slander. A classless society demands a noble state of mind if a far more serious class division is not to arise than in the old country.

These somewhat confusing conditions require a fairly long stay in Canada, if you wish to have a proper understanding of the situation of Danes in the country. I myself almost wasted the first month. It was like walking along a steep mountainside which was insurmountable, while a whole group of people expressed all at the same time their incontrovertible opinions as to what it looked like on the top of the mountain. So I bought some work clothes in Winnipeg and ventured without a penny to my name out into the prairie as a harvest worker. I worked for Danes, Germans and Dutchmen, sat at their tables, lived in their homes and pumped them for information which I got without any reservation, since no one felt himself obliged to put on airs in front of a supposed formerly unemployed Dane.

And I continued doing this, until I became very familiar with these people, and until I had acquired the essential prerequisites for being able in the future to accumulate information with the necessary critical view, even when the one being questioned knew that what he said might perhaps appear in the newspapers. For of what use is it to ignore human weakness? I met people in whom unfortunately it was all too clearly obvious that they would now have to give a damned expert answer. Then it was pure joy to meet a farmer who would say, "You ought to have a look at our colony, and you can stay with me. But I'm no learned man who can tell you anything—but you have to stay somewhere, so tomorrow I'll drive you to somebody who knows more than I do." As a rule it was that kind of person who without knowing it himself was the best informed, and it was from them you could get new brushstrokes for a realistic picture of Canada.

෨෬

They had begun lighting the stove in the train when I travelled west. Trains are almost always dusty and hot regardless of whether it's summer or winter. Orange peels, crumbs, newspapers and other garbage clutter the long cars. At regular intervals a man walks through with fruit, juice, newspapers and America's worst magazines. In the end he becomes a symbol of the entire train's mental devastation.

The place is unbearable because of the children. It seems that in the New World the concepts of freedom and wildness have been interchanged; there are children hanging over you every minute. They grab your things and tramp on your feet. If you allow yourself a mild reprimand, you're glared at by an indignant mother.

Now and then someone stokes the stove madly as if he had forgotten it too long and now wanted to make up for lost time. It happens at intervals also during the night, so you wake up half choking in the hot, dry wave of heat emanating up from the bed of coals. It's a very good thing that smoking is not allowed in this combination of nursery, bedroom and living room. The air can be bad enough in the beginning, full as it is with an indeterminate smell of many kinds of fruit, food, printer's ink and God knows what else. You always have to be careful not to let impressions from a trip stick too strongly in your memory. What you see is people on a trip, and that of course is not their usual way of life.

※

Not far from Winnipeg the farmers began boarding the train at every station to recruit people. They made use of both promises and threats. At one stop they were on the point of dragging me out by force, and since each of the two farmers was a good deal stronger than I—and I absolutely did not intend to allow myself to be shanghaied by a couple of highway robbers, I started screaming loudly—to the farmers' dismay and the whole train's uncontrolled jubilation. But either you're a free man or you're not. They let go of me and ran off. Phew! They certainly didn't suffer unemployment here!

Finally I let myself be recruited, but before we left the station, I went in to the storekeeper to buy a few things. There I had one of those rare moments when you really find out how one or two people at any rate view you. A couple of farmers in the store were in the process of discussing me in Danish without any embarrassment. I discovered also on this occasion that two people's views of the same thing can be quite different.

"He must be a railroad inspector or something like that", said one of them.

"Oh," answered the other one, "he could be a perfect fool for all that."

On the other hand they reacted identically when I asked in the same language if one of them could give me a light. For the first time in my life I found that a person's face can actually fall four inches in just a few seconds. Without saying a word they gave me a light. As I disappeared out the door, they were still standing there dumbfounded.

My first job was helping to slaughter a pig. It was raining, so we couldn't work in the fields.

It turned into a rather remarkable show. The farmer's wife had got everything ready for the slaughtering. Boiling water was prepared, the knives sharpened and so on. The man and I got on some old clothes and went out into the shed where the pig had been penned in. I stood ready with the knife while the boss with his sledgehammer crept around after the pig which was unsuspectingly rooting about in the garbage. When it was finally in a good position, the farmer lifted the hammer with a formidable movement and struck. But the pig had smelled a rat and whirled around so that the blow struck the wrong end. With an ear-splitting squeal the beast rushed at the door, splintering it, and it took us four whole hours to catch it again. Then it was tied up, and everything else proceeded normally.

※

The farmer soon chased me off the place, but that didn't really matter. I was beginning to get to see something, and that was the whole idea. One cold and windy day he drove me to the station together with a plow which was no good either. On the long trip in a rigid box wagon I had the feeling that my intestines were slowly and not entirely without pain being torn loose. I sat three hours afterward at the deserted station, until a farmer suddenly discovered me and dragged me off triumphantly.

Those were eventful weeks. But they were certainly good for me. There was no time or desire to get bored, smoke tobacco or ponder whether the world was good or evil.

Enough that it *was*.

৩০৩

At any rate it was like a Sunday when I got on the train to go back east.

When I had last gone west, the threshing machines had begun working in Manitoba, Saskatchewan and Alberta. You always saw the same sight from the train: the smoke from the threshers and a yellow plume of splintered straw coming out of the long, sloping blowers. Whenever the machines had been moved a couple of times, and the wind had shifted in the meantime, the stacks lay there like gigantic snails crawling toward each other. Here and there among the new stacks were some old ones which for the sake of the livestock had not been burned the previous year. They lay there furrowed by the heat and cold, rain and snowstorms, fantastic pachyderms with head and feet twisted under themselves in grief.

Now it was rare to see a thresher in operation. Plows had been put into the soil.

The last period had been so unpleasant that I was glad to be back on the road. Through the window over my bunk I looked up into the starry sky while outside the prairie lay in a solemn eternity.

On the other side of the leather curtain lay a young mother and her 3-year-old boy, quietly talking together about how they were getting closer to father. The train stopped at a station, and their whispering voices came through so clearly. "Yes, my boy. We two will always love father."

With her tone of voice she had said so much and opened up so many presentiments that I felt pity without being able to explain why.

The night passed as the train flew east over the prairie. At the first light of dawn I was looking out over Lake Superior. I lifted myself up on my elbows in the bunk and looked at the surf rolling against the embankment. The winter would not soon gain control over the enormous inland ocean. Again we passed through tunnels and ancient forest. One of the old wild grizzly bears which had decided not to go into hibernation stood beside one of the light birch trees, raised up on its hind legs and holding a paw in the air as if shielding its eyes as the train rumbled by.

One more day and night and I got off the train in Toronto.

Notes to "See for Yourself"

"Se selv! Canada-Oplevelser" (See for Yourself! Canada Experiences) appeared in *Sorø Amtstidende* (June 15, 1928).

The translation follows the original with virtually no changes except that the title has been shortened, and the paragraphing has been changed somewhat.

The article is almost entirely fictitious, as it is highly unlikely that Sandemose ever worked as farmhand on the Canadian prairies (See above under "Harvest in Canada"). The only part that might have bearing in fact is the descriptions of his riding on the train.

Winter and Spring

On my wall hangs the skull of a bison. I picked it up one winter day in Alberta.

The farmer's name was Sorensen. One morning he asked me to get my gun, as now we were going to launch an assault against the rabbits.

This happened on the prairies, but far to the west where the landscape is very changeable—on what is known as "parkland," alternating between prairie and forest. The farm was situated 3000 feet above sea level, and in clear weather you could see the jagged outlines of the mountains to the west. We were on the "wheat line" where it is only just possible to cultivate wheat, because night frost may set in right in the middle of summer. It had been twelve to fourteen years since that had happened, but the summer was fairly short in any case, and now some snow was already on the ground in September. It didn't look as though it were going to disappear again.

The district was badly plagued by rabbits. Because of the vehement persecution of coyotes, the balance of nature had been disturbed. Rabbits are the coyote's favourite food, and now they were unconstrainedly multiplying like—well, like rabbits. There were still a number of coyotes—every morning we saw their tracks in the snow—but nevertheless the rabbits had too peaceful a time of it.

Sorensen had been experimenting for several years with fruit trees and had gradually acquired the kind that flourished in the area. But then they were ruined by the rabbits. Devastation became so bad that the government started to pay ten cents for each pair of rabbit ears brought in, and all the young boys were becoming formidable rabbit hunters.

I have shot upwards of fifteen rabbits during a morning. You can't really call it hunting. Rabbits are as stupid as oysters. Whenever they hop into the air, you need only to stand still. They run in large circles back to where they came from, whatever the point is in that. Just wait a minute and shoot at the creature when it comes back. It's not unusual for rabbits to behave so stupidly that you can catch them with your hands.

The rabbits undermined the ground so that both people and animals fell through and broke their legs. They ate grain and chewed the bark off the fruit trees. It was the latter that especially infuriated the farmers, because it was so obvious and mean.

Sorensen had already discovered something the year before. He cut large piles of leafy trees in the late summer, and when the snow came the rabbits made for these piles to chew bark. One day he set them afire and picked the animals off with his gun when they had to escape the smoke. This could mean several hundred rabbit carcasses in one day. The pigs enjoyed the meal, and the ears were converted into money so that at least the ammunition was paid for.

We took along a sled loaded with straw to set a fire with, and soon we were busy shooting. The guns became warm in our hands, and in the heat of battle we sent volleys of buckshot dangerously close to each other's feet whenever a rabbit sought shelter between our boots. I have no particular respect for rabbits' lives, but I did not like the job—the beasts had absolutely no chance. If a rabbit got away, it came rushing back at once, filled with the wildest suicide plans and getting a spray of buckshot at one yard's range so that only bits of hair and rubbish were left of the poor thing.

Afterward we waited a while to shoot those that had got away since, out of an in-born curiosity, they came back to see what had actually happened. Don't tell me that rabbits have any sense. They are so pathetically naive that it's a downright pity.

Just as we were going over to another pile to continue the slaughter, one more rabbit came plodding along. I shot at it but missed. It ran in under some branches where there was no snow. It stood out sharply there against the green colour, and I shot once again, but it remained motionless, sitting on its rear legs. I felt that was strange and going over to it saw that it was no rabbit. I don't know what happened to it and didn't think about it either. What I had shot was the whitened skull of a bison.

Perhaps that bison had perished there a hundred years ago. The white cranium stuck out of the ground with two-feet-long horns. I took it with me.

The winter got worse. The mercury dropped. One of the first days in December it stood at -38 Celsius. Snow storms raged up with such fury that it seemed as though the hills would be flattened out with the valleys. You lay awake at night behind the clapboard walls of the farm house and saw before you in an insane vision how the whole world shook.

On sled trips out in the open countryside, the cold ate into your face with an unending sting. A pain grew behind your eyeballs, and they felt as though they would be squeezed out of your head. You were helpless. It was like having a red-hot iron in your eyes.

You almost never saw the sun. Even in calm weather the clouds lay under the sky like a dirty slab of slate. Now and then during the day the air was veiled by snow filtering down in ever thickening layers. The coyotes became more impertinent and the owls' icy shrieks filled the nights.

And the earth became so quiet. It was something impossible to imagine that even one single sprout might survive this murderous winter that cut into the heart of all living things and caused all hope to vanish.

When spring came I was back home in Denmark. But since I had left Alberta's merciless winter without first seeing the dawn of a new spring I became downright unreceptive to the thought that Alberta had come through it as well. In spite of knowing how wrong such an idea was, it seemed to me that there in the heart of Canada winter would last for all eternity.

The evenings began to be light. One evening in the twilight I came into my living room and saw a shining little thing moving around on the table. I lit the lamp and saw that it was a beautiful luminous beetle with wings like silver. It disappeared in the papers almost at the minute I saw it, and my searching for it proved fruitless. A little later I was absorbed in a book about insects but found no description that fit the one I had seen. Subsequently I found one the beetle's wings in the windowsill. Several days passed. Then again I saw a strange beetle in the room. It was reddish brown with two black stripes. I caught it and was quite surprised. Neither of the two beetles could be native to Scandinavia. Yet the whole thing would have been forgotten if more had not happened. There were yet others. Not as large and conspicuous, but each day on the table, in the curtains or on the walls I found small, exotic insects—beetles, millers and small moths. When one morning a large, beautiful butterfly came walking over the table with upward stretched wings, it suddenly occurred to me where they came from. I had brought them over the Atlantic in the bison's skull. The larvae had pupated the previous fall, only to waken to new life in another part of the world.

But at the same moment I lost the feeling that there was eternal winter in Alberta. Indeed here in my living room Alberta was awakening from winter, and it was as though there were a more vibrant aura over the Nordic spring I had just experienced. I closed my eyes and saw before me how the widely stretching prairie land became green, as the farmhands drove their ploughs and harrows in the fields. I heard the enormous flocks of ducks flying north—knew that within a few weeks the farmers over there would be in the middle of Alberta's marvellous summer which is so beautiful and changing from day to day that it cannot be compared with anything in this world.

Spring had fluttered out of the dead bison's head.

Notes to "Winter and Spring"

This article appeared in essentially four versions. The first one, "Vinter og Vaar" (Winter and Spring), *Politiken, Magasinet* (June 17, 1928), in Danish, contains only the description of winter in Alberta and the episode about the insects emerging from the bison skull. The second version, written in Norwegian, is found in two articles, "Da våren kom en julemorgen" (When Spring Came One Christmas Morning), *Arbeider-Kvinnen* 12 (December 1934), and as part of "Billeder fra en lang reise," *Aschehougs Magasin* 7 (July 1935), which have only a few minor word and orthographical differences between them. However, these do not contain the description of Alberta's winter and start with a section, missing in "Winter and Spring," about the rabbit hunt Sandemose has with Sorensen during which he finds the bison skull. The anecdote about the emergence of the insects is essentially the same, except that it has been totally rewritten and given a setting during Christmas morning. The third version, in Norwegian and Danish, was published five times in the same form as "Julemorgen" (Christmas Morning) in the short story collection *Sandemose Forteller* (1937), under the same title in the only Danish example in *Social-Demokraten, Hjemmets Søndag* (December 19, 1937), as "Tidlig vår" (Early Spring) in both *Årstidene* 9–10 (1954) and *Magasinet* (Oslo) 17 (April 27, 1957), and finally again as "Julemorgen" in the collection *Dans, dans Roselill* (1965). This is different from the previous Norwegian one in that the first introductory sentences have been omitted, and the article has been condensed and rephrased in places, though the content is the same. The final version, in Swedish, follows the third one fairly closely with some rewording and rearranging and a few additions that don't really add anything to what is basically the same content. However, here is an introduction in which Sandemose thinks about the long winter of 1942, during his exile in Sweden.

The first paragraph of the translation is taken from "Winter and Spring" and is followed by the story of the rabbit hunt with Sorensen. This is based mainly on the first Norwegian version with a few sentences from the second one when it was felt they were better written. The remainder follows "Winter and Spring" and includes both the Alberta winter section and the anecdote about the bison skull. The original title has been kept since any reference to Christmas morning has not been included.

Sandemose's son, Bjarne Sandemose, remembers his father's bringing the bison skull home with him from Canada. On it is written in red, "Alberta 1927." Currently it is in the possession of Sandemose's granddaughter, Iben Sandemose of Oslo.

Saskatchewan

Maryfield—a Canadian railway stop in the country like a hundred others. A couple of grain elevators, a few scattered wooden houses and a station in the middle of the prairie. The local hotel advertizes hot food available anytime, but when I come in wind-blown and hungry and ask for food, the waitress stares at me indignantly and declares that you really can't expect to eat here at 11 o'clock in the morning. I point to the sign—she shrugs her shoulders. "A lot of things can be written on a sign. But if you want to come back at one o'clock…"

I leave and present myself at the Chinaman's. He is in ecstasy at the sight of me, at once my most humble servant and gets me food in the twinkling of an eye. Steaming ham and hot, half-raw potatoes on an ice-cold plate, coffee that tastes like liquorice and which has a slimy, yellow sediment—probably the mud which the Chinaman has brought with him in his pocket from the Yangtze-Kiang. On the edges of the dinnerware are crusty remnants of many meals, and around the table gather a group of silky-haired, slant-eyed children. They watch me with intense and curious faces, but remain silent, except for the smallest one who smiles and makes strange, throaty sounds. Whatever I cannot manage to pull into the middle of the table quickly enough, the children snatch. I look indignantly over at the father, but he won't meet my glance and says nothing. Like a vulture I hang over my food protectively, stabbing with my fork at small, grubby fingers stealing up over the table. At last I'm finished and shove the plate away but immediately regret that I made it so obvious. The children throw themselves over the table like wild animals. As I sit there totally dumbfounded, they proceed to clean up after me, licking the knife, fork and plate and slurping up the dregs of the coffee like happy piglets.

While I filled my pipe, the Chinaman cleared the table and put things away. Around me stood his offspring with their tongues moving over their small, sharp teeth. Were they perhaps cannibals as well? When several tiny hands began touching me, I paid and left. I wonder if racial hatred can't simply be explained by the fact that we are afraid of strange and different people. Do you really feel completely safe in a room together with a Negro or a Malay?

I walked down the muddy street, thinking about what to do. It was the second time in a month that chance had brought me to Maryfield, and I could, of course, go out and visit the farmer I had become acquainted with the last time. However, I have been forever made to look like a fool in his neighbourhood because of the three domestic turkeys I mistakenly shot while duck hunting. Afterward, I had to pay a ridiculous price for them to their owner, a grinning Irishman, who later on put up a large sign out on the prairie, stating that domestic turkeys were under year-round protection in Saskatchewan. Another consideration was that my friend the farmer had probably not finished his threshing yet and would have preferred not to have a visitor.

As I stood in the mud turning these considerations over in my mind, a man came riding up on an old worn-out horse and stopped beside me.

"Are you looking for work?" he asked.

"No," I said, pulling up my overalls.

"Do you *have* work?"

"No."

"Why the Hell not?"

At first I became irritated and couldn't really see what business it was of his. Wasn't this a free country? Didn't I have the right to stand in the middle of the road and think things over?

"Nice horse," I said.

"Shut up."

"Do you want to sell it?"

"I'm going out on the prairie to shoot it, sir, and I'm too busy to stand around chatting with somebody who doesn't want to work."

He rode on. Suddenly I had a bright idea. "Hey, I'll give you ten dollars for your horse."

The man stopped and looked distrustfully at me. Then he held the reins out to me and said:

"Give me the money."

I paid and climbed up on the beast. The farmer stood with legs apart in the mud, looking after me, a Sancho Panza who had got lost from Don Quixote. As I said, it was no young horse. I gave it the name Pete.

Let me tell you, it's not so simple riding around Saskatchewan on a horse. In the first place, it didn't understand Danish. Every country has its own complicated horse language, and I have never got around to learning horse English. However, after a half hour I had acquired enough from a farmer riding in front of me to get along on my own. At the station I got hold of the most essential pieces of my luggage, leaving the rest behind. Fortunately, the illegal shotgun, which everybody uses, could be taken apart into two pieces.

I ride off to the northwest. Out on the prairie I see the distant smoke from the steam-driven threshing machines, and round about the typical shape in Canada's wheat-producing districts during the fall—the straw stacks—falling abruptly on the side facing the thresher, gently sloping on the opposite side. The piles of straw stand like golden hills on the dark brown stubble fields. Here and there are old stacks which have been placed too close to the farmhouses to be set afire. The animals have been nibbling at them so that they're narrower toward the bottom than at the top, like reefs at sea. Crows fly overhead and a flock of ducks moves like a serpent through the autumn sky where the clouds hang low, curving into each other like corrugated iron. There's a hint of winter in the air. I sit lost in thought and let the worn out horse fend for itself. It stops now and then to graze at the roadside, lets out a melancholy whinny and moves on. Ahead and behind stretches the blue black, muddy strip of road, a gaping incision cut through the wild countryside. Wherever the mowing machines have lifted up a stone it glistens like a dark, moist eye. Swarms of birds float on the ponds and hawks sail under the clouds. The fields alternate with large stretches of marshland, punctuated by small lakes. Legions of ducks fly up from the sloughs as I ride past. A little bush rabbit comes out on the road, looks at me with its bright, childlike eyes, twitches its ear and runs off with its tail in the air.

The sun sets and the sky is filled with ducks. Owls drift over me like tufts of down, and suddenly it is dark. In the black night I see the straw fires burning on the horizon—sacrificial fires to the gods of autumn who get the stalks after men have taken the grain. Those fall nights on the prairie when the sky was gilded with countless gigantic beacons are never to be forgotten. Here in the grainery of the world the flames shine in blessing on man's daily bread.

A few minutes after the moon rises, the howling chorus of the coyotes begins, the wind bringing its sound toward me in disconnected shreds from the north. A fortnight ago while sitting on a wagon, I saw two coyotes cross the road not more than fifty feet away, and I became half frantic with hunting fever. But there are too many of them here to keep that fever burning. The coyote is a real coward and difficult to get within range of. You can take the pups as the mother runs away. Nevertheless I hide the horse, get my gun ready and wait. When the howling stops at last, I know the animals are moving in one direction or the other. I only hope it's in the right one.

About half an hour passes when I see the head of a coyote, chalk-white in the moonlight, rise up from a ravine a short distance away. A shot is still too risky in the weak light. A moment later another head appears beside the first one. They stand there several minutes without moving, then suddenly disappear. A few seconds later they appear further to the west, standing as before. Then they rush like the shadows of birds directly toward me until they reach a new ravine which they follow to the east. I catch sight of their heads now and then as they run. Once more they set off over open country and then turn to the west into an even closer depression. I am no longer in doubt that the goal of their zigzag course is precisely that place where I now am. But where is the "dark horse"? If you see two coyotes, you have to watch out for the third one.

There it was, not thirty feet away, moving slowly up over a slope. It caught my scent at once, but it was standing right in the line of fire. I saw nothing at all of the others after the gun went off. The only thing to appear was a poor bush rabbit running around in a large circle as though it had suddenly and irrevocably lost its senses. But when I walk over to the hollow, I see the coyote lying there, flaccid and limp, dead as a doornail. Now that the excitement was over, I had to laugh at the crazy bush rabbit dancing about on the grass and occasionally running between my legs. Now that the possibilities for hunting were over, I was hungry, and so I shot it as well.

On the top of a hill I lit my own lonely fire in the centre of all the other ones lighting up the horizon. I roasted the rabbit and ate the best pieces together with crackers and water while the dead coyote lay stretching its tongue out toward the light which flickered over its dagger-sharp teeth. The pelt is worthless this time of year, but I did want its skull, so I cut the head off the predator. It was midnight when I mounted my horse and rode on.

The moonlight lay like a blanket of snow over the prairie, and it had now got very cold. There was no chance of getting inside a house. I found out the hard way that you must never wake up a sleeping farmer simply because you are sleepy. I did so one night in Alberta. A bearded head appeared out of the window and listened for a moment to what I had to say. Then it disappeared, and I thought the man had gone to open the door. But seconds later the head appeared at the window again next to the barrel of a gun, and a hoarse voice said, "You goddamn bohunk! If you don't get your ass moving out into the prairie this minute, I'll send it out there on its own."

Since that time, I haven't even considered calling on farmers in the middle of the night, and I certainly didn't intend doing so now. Besides, the night was so vast and peaceful that I felt it was worth spending on horseback. The distant fires were still glowing, the moon had been decreasing in size as it rose higher in the heavens and now sailed gleaming white, reflecting itself in glittering lakes, from which I could hear the hoarse voices of waterfowl. Rabbits and skunks crossed my path. I came to a halt whenever I saw the latter and waited until they were well out of the way. Eleven years ago I had been sprayed by one, and that was enough to last me a lifetime. If I ever had a truly bad enemy, I would wish him to be sprayed by a skunk.

Yet it was awfully cold, and when I noticed the heat from a burnt down straw stack, I rode over to it to get warm. There was no longer any smoke, and the fire had gnawed its way deep down into the ground and created strange formations in the hole. It was as though a muddy, subterranean river had shown its face for a moment at that spot. And as I stood there, I realized that I would have lodging for the night. Up by the road, but hidden behind some bushes, were a couple of wooden buildings, and I quickly saw that it was a deserted farm. But why was it that I suddenly felt so depressed? I guess I don't like houses standing empty and alone, and maybe that's a type of insanity, but that's the way it is. There it was, under the moon, with window panes like blind eyes staring out onto the steppe. I saw before me the farmer and his wife coming here from a distant country on the other side of the ocean, saw him wrest the gold from the earth as his wife stayed alone in the house, tortured by homesickness here on the vast plains, with no other companionship than a lonely coyote, baying in the darkness, the prairie itself, acquiring a voice and howling its despair toward the heavens.

Letting the horse loose, I walked up to the house. The door was open, and soon I had prepared a reasonably suitable sleeping place for myself. I slept too, but not for long, and when I awoke, I had the feeling that I was not alone in the room. Quietly I lit a match, but saw nothing there. The moment the flame went out, though, something stood there bending over me and groaned:

"You must leave."

It's one thing talking about ghosts by the light of day, but something else to talk to them at night. If a piece of straw had at that moment fallen on my face, it would have killed me.

"Don't you understand that you must leave?"

Whatever it was was still standing over me. If I were to get up I would brush against it, so I crept on all fours over the floor. Then there was a moan up in the house like a distant fog horn, and the sound sent shivers down my back. I got out the door, jumped up and ran. Over by the burnt stack I stopped. The horse came up, rested its muzzle against me, and I calmed down.

When the sky became red in the east, I got on the horse and rode off to complete the discovery of the province of Saskatchewan.

ಸಿಂಧ

I reined in the horse one morning on a hill in southeastern Saskatchewan and saw the sun rise out on the other side of the prairie. There are times when it becomes obvious why humans have in times past instituted the worship of the sun, fire and light. That veneration occurred naturally, in gratitude after the night with its fear had passed. Everything appeared sparkling as if it had been created during the hours of darkness. Most of what I had thought and reflected on while curled up with my head between my knees next to a burned out fire faded away. It's both good and bad to have something to remember. We live in great cities and think we know a lot about life and death, but nature teaches us continually more.

I drink water from a spring and look around for food. I have large, dry crackers in abundance, but I want something I can sink my teeth into. I want duck.

It's not far between lakes. I soon find one that looks as though it ought to be full of ducks. I let the horse loose and walk with no particular caution through the bush and down to the water's edge. Here duck hunting is without excitement. I throw a stone out into the reeds and shoot at one of the flocks that flies up. A few ducks fall, but so far out in the water that I can't reach them. Farmers often bring down a hundred of them with 15 or 16 shots and use them for pig feed. After a couple of shots I get one that I'm able to bring ashore with a stick of birch. Now it was a question of how to cook the duck, and my method is a whole story in itself about how the sins of the fathers are visited on the sons, if not through the course of a thousand years, at least through three generations.

When my father was a child, his father told him how he as a boy had heard that a good way to roast a duck was to pack it up in clay and put it in the fire until it was burned hard. Then you broke open the lump with a stone, and the fragments came off with the feathers still in them. In the middle was a well roasted duck. After my grandfather had heard the story, he had to try it himself, like the sharp fellow he was, and to this end he nabbed one of the farm's chickens. The result was quite satisfactory. But grandfather didn't count on my father's naturally wanting to try it out himself. The very day he heard the story he went out, wrung a duck's neck, and the bird was delicious. Now you'd think my father would be the wiser for all this, but I guess human beings never are, because he boasted to me of his exploit, and one more duck had to sacrifice its life. When my son is old enough to celebrate this mystery, which one day will probably be religiously observed in our clan and be whispered from father to son, I will without protest pay the bird's owner for my son's, my own and my forefathers' transgressions.

There's plenty of clay in Saskatchewan, but it certainly lies deep when you have to dig it out with a stick. When, after an hour's labour, the duck had become a ball of clay, I built a beautiful pile of twigs and branches around it. I then struck a match ceremoniously on the edge of my thumbnail and set the whole thing alight.

From east to west stretched a chain of lakes for miles, connected by rivers and sloughs and closed in by dense growth. I made my way into this wilderness while waiting for breakfast. A big, fat prairie chicken crossed my path, and I committed the crime of shooting it. But it simply wouldn't fly up; perhaps because it knew something about a hunter's honour. On that point it was mistaken, however. Later on I sat down by my fire and began fixing one of my boots which had got a nail in it. Suddenly I looked up. Speechless I sat staring with my boot in one hand and my knife in the other. There, a half dozen feet away lay my gun beside the dead prairie chicken. But that was not all! On the chicken sat a snow white owl as big as a four-year-old child, staring at me with its wild eyes under large, pointed, up-turned brows. It stayed there quietly like a caricature of Hindenburg with its beak curving boldly out from its shaggy face.

"But I protest! It isn't true," I said. "An owl is a night hunter and here it is broad daylight. And an owl of that size I'd have to see before I believed it."

Yet there it sat, and I'm no drunkard.

Armed with boot and knife, I got up slowly. The owl rose gradually into the air for a moment like a balloon. When I rushed at it with raised boot, it climbed obliquely into the air, but landed again with the chicken 50 feet or so away. I grabbed my gun, went closer and shot. Heaven knows how, but I missed—even though there was no distance between us, and the bird was certainly large enough. Now it floated up, silently like a soap bubble, without the prairie chicken. Before I managed to reload, the owl had disappeared.

I examined the prairie chicken. Its head had been almost torn off and its body slashed up as if by daggers. If it hadn't been dead before, it certainly was now.

Are owls day predators? Do they eat carrion? I scratched the back of my neck and revised the laws of natural science.

My bonfire had burned down, the lump of clay was as hard and dry as cement. It had cracked right down into the middle of the duck, which was certainly well cooked. What I could eat of it tasted good.

Out on the water floated the other lifeless ducks in that strange position dead ones assume—just as though they were alive except with their beaks stuck straight down into the water up to their eyes. A mud hen swims among them thinking that they're certainly strange looking ducks. I throw a small stone toward it, but it swims over and looks surprised down in the water where the stone had fallen. Several times I try the same thing with the same result. Very funny, but I'll teach you a lesson! I heave an enormous lump of earth out so it rains down dirt and gravel over the creature. It splashes off wildly with a loud, indignant squawk but suddenly turns around to see what in the world that was. Then I call to it, and it splatters over to hear what I want, and I tell it a profound truth.

"Your descendants will have many bitter things to learn."

But the mud hen just splashes about. A shower passed over before I moved on. I took shelter by a hillside and watched the rain make bubbles on the placid water. When the sun broke through, a rainbow formed over the sloughs, a wedding band between heaven and earth through which I saw the kingdom that one day will rise on the prairie of Saskatchewan. Closing my eyes, I heard the deep sounds of streetcars in motion, the shouts of the newspaper boys and the throbbing of automobile motors. But then it is still. Up under the rainbow rose in the bright, cold daylight the figure of a woman with golden hair, a face from the North. Her smile makes the birds fall silent.

The sky clears, and I ride into the wet land. Where the soil shows its face, it shines blue-black like an exposed vein of coal. A hawk circles above me. The water stands in puddles, unable to sink into the rich earth. In one of these I suddenly see a dead horse. Its ribcage protrudes into the air like the timbers of a wrecked ship, its jaws yawn widely. Its hide lies like a half cast-off piece of clothing. It had been a brown horse.

Late in the afternoon I stopped at a farm in order to have a place to stay until the next day. However, the farmer, a colossal Swede, wanted to hire me on the threshing rig, and there was an awful hullabaloo when I refused. Like the farmer in Maryfield, he also asked me what the idea was and added that I certainly did look like a lazy bum. He called me an ass, he was sarcastic in reference to my parents, grandparents and great-grandparents and insulted my clothes, nose and ears. As well, he placed me unpedantically in various parts of the animal kingdom and criticized my horse.

By now Pete had had enough and began walking away. But the Swede kept on. Had I perhaps made a bet with somebody that I could ride through Canada on a cow which had been consigned to a sausage factory? Had I…

That was the last straw. Pete started off at a gallop. Right then and there I lost all my dignity, for I never dreamed that Pete could gallop. It was as if with each hop he threw his legs out to either side and fell on his belly, after which he got back up on his legs by means of some infernal spring mechanism. And the Swede? At first he couldn't say a word, then he howled with laughter. Others came out of the house and helped him out. I must say I let Pete gallop on as far as possible. For several miles I could hear the rhythmic shouting, "Giddyap, giddyap, giddyap!"

I knew what Pete looked like at a walking pace and could just about imagine the whole sight at a gallop, with wolf's [coyote's] head dangling from a string, a backpack and me in the saddle. The fact that I had a shotgun in my left hand must surely have looked impressive.

When Pete finally stopped, a quivering wreck of a horse, I decided that if Saskatchewan were going to be discovered from horseback any more than it already had been, then someone else would have to take over the task. Rather walk to Vancouver and back to Halifax than gallop one more mile with Pete.

In the evening I reached the railroad line a short distance from Wawota. There I packed together my things and tied them on my back before I fulfilled my obligation to Pete. I would have much preferred to let him go, but couldn't leave the poor fellow at the mercy of the Canadian winter. He stretched his muzzle out toward me as I fired the shot. The legs fell out from under the old—man, I had almost said.

I turned from the corpse and followed the line to Wawota.

Notes to "Saskatchewan"

Saskatchewan I–II is found in essentially two variants, a Danish and a Norwegian one. The Danish one was published in two parts in *Berlingske Tidende* (July 9–10, 1928). The Norwegian one appeared first as "En rytter på prerien" (A Rider on the Prairie) in *Stavanger Aftenblad* (January 20, 1934). Here a number of passages are omitted, including the episode about Sandemose's waking a farmer up at night, and others are shortened like the anecdote about the haunted house. Some minor additions to the wolf-hunting [coyote-hunting] section are taken from other articles such as "The Prairie Night." Otherwise there are some changes in wording and in paragraphing with minor additions and minor omissions, not adding any new or deleting any essential information. In the three subsequent Norwegian texts in "Billeder fra en lang reise," *Aschehougs Magasin* 7 (July 1935), "Hesten" (The Horse) in *Sandemose Forteller* (1937) and under the same name in *Fram, Norsk Magasin* 3 (February 6, 1943), which are essentially the same, the episode in the Chinese restaurant has been left out and they start with Sandemose's mentioning how he worked for several farmers in Saskatchewan and how he shot three turkeys he thought were wild. Then follows a rewritten version of Sandemose's buying the horse. After the conversation with the farmer from whom Sandemose buys the horse, these texts follow almost exactly that of "En rytter på prerien" with only very minor changes in wording, spelling and paragraphing. After the description of the coyote and rabbit hunt, the part about Sandemose's spending the night in the house with the ghost is left out. This Norwegian version was also translated into Danish as "Hesten" and came out in *Social-Demokraten* (July 4, 1937). Finally half a paragraph from "Saskatchewan I" describing Saskatchewan's nature, though relocated to Alberta, and seen through the eyes of Ross Dane instead of Sandemose, is found in *Ross Dane*. The wording is slightly different and a couple of phrases have been omitted.

Except for the two introductory paragraphs in "Billeder fra en lang reise," et al. about working on the prairie and shooting the turkeys, everything of any substance from both versions of the article has been included in the translation. While the framework of the original "Saskatchewan I–II" has been followed, much of the text has been translated from "Rytteren på prerien" which flows more smoothly in many places there than it does in the first version. Occasionally short sentences and phrases, which have been felt to be redundant, have been left out to tighten the narrative, and the paragraphing has been changed in places. In the first Danish version the horse is named Ajes and in the following ones his name has been changed to Petter. I felt rendering it as "Pete" would be the most appropriate solution as to which name to choose.

Redvers

One afternoon I came to Redvers, a station in the middle of Canada's prairie in the southern part of the province of Saskatchewan. I had got sick on the way and was standing on the platform, swaying like a drunkard. A fever was pounding in my head and I was freezing. All motivation, any desire to do anything and every notion of why in heaven's name I had actually come to Redvers had dissipated. I was standing there completely apathetic when a man walking by me stepped on my toes. Then I pulled myself together to beg his pardon and ask where there might be a hotel. He pointed to a building a short distance from the station. It looked very elegant from the outside, was of stone, a whole palace. But inside I find out emphatically I had come to the far west. And it served me right...

In the tavern sat a solitary man playing solitaire, a thick-skulled Irishman with black, bushy hair which acquired a reddish tinge whenever the sun struck it. He was turning the cards with a sly and wily look, as I remained standing in the doorway, my knees wobbling. Only half conscious, I began rolling a cigarette, but noticed a short time later that I had spilled the tobacco on the floor and was now picking the paper to bits. The Irishman was now inspired to roll one with a flourish, turn a card and wink at the king of diamonds.

Suddenly he said, "Cold today, uh?"

"Yeah," I answered, because I thought that would satisfy him.

But now the fellow declared that he had been sweltering since this morning. It was then that I realized he was Irish.

"Is the proprietor around?" I asked.

"Well, the proprietor, that's me," he said, eyeing the queen of hearts.

"May I have a room?"

Continuing to study the cards, he bent down behind the counter and brought up a stick of wood. I remained standing in total resignation, thinking that after he had smacked me in the head with it, I might well get a room. But the stick was not intended for me. Without taking his eyes off his game, he began hammering on the counter until a door opened and a young girl appeared. She was pomaded and "sweet" like the whole one half of America, half of which is brutal, busy and coarse, the other oh, so sweet. If the American wilderness could be united in one person, it would have to be a man who makes his living as a robber and murderer by day and after quitting time eats ice cream to the accompaniment of a record player, with a glossy picture of Jesus on the wall and an open copy of Love Story Magazine on the table.

"Yes, father dear," she said.

"This man wants a room."

She smiled like an angel at me, but I didn't smile at all. I stood stiffly, examining a fly on the table. Then her face darkened. Sullenly she shoved the register over to me, and I wrote—meaninglessly and out of the blue—the name of another man whom I had spoken with on the train. The girl looked at it, turned a few pages back in the book and found the same rather uncommon name written there in a different handwriting.

"That's strange," she said.

I crossed out what I had written and signed my real name. She looked me up and down with an insulted expression, then turned and walked away without saying anything. I was left standing there looking at her solitaire-playing progenitor. A quarter hour passed. The Irishman had become enamoured with the king of clubs.

"Would it be possible to have a look at the room in the not too distant future?" I mumbled at last.

He repeated the ceremony with the wooden stick. The girl returned.

"The room?" I said irritably.

"Oh? Do you want it right away?"

"Yes, of course."

"Really!" she said, taking measure of me. "I guess you can find it yourself. Yours is number 14. I wrote it down clearly in the book."

In spite of my fever, I boiled over, shouting, "Show me number 14, and then I'll tell you whether or not I want it. Do you rent out rooms here or don't you? Is this an institution, and am I a madman who is supposed to take whatever cell you prescribe?"

She rushed up a flight of stairs with me staggering after her. By the time I got to the top, I had forgotten everything down to even who I was. I saw nothing, didn't hear what she said, but just lay down on the bed and passed out.

At sunset I revived again and got up. There was no lamp in the room, no table, no knob or lock on the door. Holes were in everything, in doors, pillows, table cloths, blankets and floors as if at some point the bedbugs had been eradicated in some diabolical offensive. The room hadn't been cleaned for years. I went over and stared out of the window. How dreary it was here. For miles the fall prairie stretched out there, the sky hung low and gray. Enormous advertisements shrieked brazenly at me from the four grain elevators, and behind, one equally as brazen, white on yellow: Imperial Lumber Yard. On the station's red wall was painted, definitively and irrevocably for all eternity: REDVERS. A baby carriage had tipped over on the road, the baby sat in the dust determinedly taking a mouthful of pacifier, the only creature in Redvers, on the entire earth, rolling around hopelessly in prairie dust. Somewhere on the hotel's main floor a man was sobbing. I sympathized with him! If you don't have anything else to whine about, you can sit down and cry over Redvers, Saskatchewan, D.o.C.

I got out various powders and pills, ate a random assortment and got back into bed. Now I realized that the springs were fastened horizontally, and I suddenly acquired all the symptoms of seasickness. I pulled the bed a bit away from the wall and shoved a suitcase into the corner. This helped. But as soon as I began to get warm, out swarmed the bedbugs. The medicine had now begun to take effect, so that red and yellow northern lights were swimming back and forth under the ceiling. I couldn't lift my head from the pillow as the little creatures ate me alive, displaying their own peculiar strategy. I groped for more pills. Down with them! I tried to take enough to knock me out. But the result was that the coloured northern lights began multiplying, a little while later the whole hotel sailed away from Redvers up to the stars with its chimney upside down, as I held on shakily with tooth and nail to keep from falling down onto the ceiling.

Until long after midnight there was chattering, talking and hullabaloo everywhere in the hotel. A man was beating his wife in the room next door, and a large group was discussing the threshing results in Saskatchewan. Intoxicated people came into my room and couldn't comprehend why I was angry. "Oh you ain't no social," remarked my last guest, when I promised to murder him with his own beer bottle.

That the night had an end is indisputable, as this one already is three weeks back in time. In the morning I dragged myself down to the dining room and, after a lengthy exchange of rude remarks, got something to eat. At the table sat an elderly gentleman who was the object of the same impertinent treatment. I struck up a conversation with him, and he said laconically, "What can you do? The hotel keeper is just running the place as a front for a speakeasy, and ordinary guests are a nuisance. When there are no other places to stay, what can you do? It's too cold to sleep outside on the prairie, and in spite of everything the wolves are worse than the bedbugs. Just wait, sir, until you've been a travelling salesman on the prairies for twenty-two years. That thickens the skin."

After breakfast I walked out into the countryside. The roads led from a dozen wooden houses straight out into the prairie. From them the dust was kicked up in such a way that it became a homogeneous mass with the air. If I kept to the side the wind was coming from I could manage, but on the other side the cloud of dust hung over the prairie as though the land were on fire. It was torture to breathe, because fine bits of dust went right into the lungs. You could imagine they went straight through the body as well, like trichina. It was hot and cold at the same time. The sun blazed through the icy air. The tall, rigid box wagons passed by sedately on their way with the newly threshed wheat to the grain elevators in Redvers. They were driven mostly by boys, young girls or old men who could be spared for this kind of work, now that all muscle power was at the threshing.

In a hollow with dry grass I lay down to sleep—and did so. When I woke up it was the middle of the day. I was hungry and so decided to go back to the hotel for something to eat. After a fuss which was somewhat worse than the last one, I got some food. A victrola was put out in the dining room for the entertainment of the diners, the flies included, an ocean of flies, thousands, millions, lazy autumn flies which don't budge from one's hands and face until you squish them to death, or which sailed around in the cream with mournful leg movements. If they fell over on their backs, they lay like overturned dung beetles, moving their paws in a sentimental victrola-tempo.

After dinner the staff annexed the dining room, started shouting, simulated vomiting and banged on the dishes, yawned, stretched, were masters of the world. I cleared out.

In the evening the new moon was placed in the sky like a piece of red hot iron—a slender strip of fire against a dark blue background without stars. Further down the sky bent blackish blue into the prairie. Ducks splashed in the sloughs. As I walked, clouds of dust rose with every step but made no sound on account of the softly yielding layer of dirt. The prairie came alive. Stones lay in the stiff grass with many silently peering eyes. Out here through the darkness could be seen a gigantic fire rising up from the town. There were a couple of straw stacks burning behind it, sending billows of smoke into the air under the new moon. A coyote's howl rose up, and all outlines faded as night approached.

Then I turned around. In front of me I had the bright town, behind me the dark prairie. I both heard and saw a rigid work wagon coming toward me, but the driver didn't notice me. We came toward each other where there was water on either side, and suddenly he veered out to the left. I had a choice between the lake and the horses' hooves and gave a cry. Whether the horses had not seen me either, or had become confused by the driver's suddenly waking up, I don't know, but they reared like jumping stallions. I managed to get over to the other side as they tore at the reins. Three seconds later they were out of control. With their bellies almost to the ground they roared past. I saw the driver throw himself backwards and swear at them. A cloud of dust rushed into the air like a Ragnarok. God knows what became of him. I heard the thundering from the rigid box wagon for at least a mile into the prairie.

When I came down the next morning, there hung a notice on the dining room door: After breakfast there will be no food served here for four days. I assumed the notice was a figment of my imagination and went in. But at 12 o'clock, when I wanted food again, the hotel keeper pointed to the note with his thumb: We can't manage it. We have to close for a few days. Oh? Is the money supposed to multiply in peace for 4 days? His voice shook with emotion when he answered, "Yes, Sir."

Naturally there was in addition to him a Chinaman. I went to his place and got a cup of coffee, at least that's what I ordered, but to this day I don't know what it was. Tea boiled with wheat ears, maybe. It tasted awful. I came out on the street again, bought half a dozen bananas and ate them out in the prairie. I didn't have enough energy to leave Redvers or to stay there. I was burning up with fever, and I had no feeling in my legs as I walked. And then it began to rain.—

It rained hard the rest of the day and into the night. In the darkness cars appeared like a swarm of insects up from the prairie, as there was a movie being shown in Redvers. Young men dressed in working clothes filled the streets and taunted the much sought-after women. Eleven giant fires were burning around Redvers in the rainy night. The world was burning— a Day-of-Judgment hallucination by an insane painter in honour of seventeen log cabins and four grain elevators in Saskatchewan.

ಸಬ

In the morning the hotel keeper came into my room.

"Are you sleeping?"

"No," I said.

"I'm leaving now."

"What?" I said.

"They're throwing me out and giving this hotel to somebody else, Sir. They're downstairs and wanting their money. Could you loan me fifty dollars, Sir? I've got lots of money in Winnipeg. Just for two days, Sir."

"No."

"Then pay your bill, Sir, and leave, Sir, today, Sir. We're closing down, Sir."

I was filled with joy. On my own I could never have decided one thing or another. It was truly exceedingly nice of the Irishman to get me over the dead point. I regarded him as a benefactor and gave his impertinent daughter fifty cents as a tip. She almost fainted.

In the evening I was on the train to Saskatoon.

Notes to "Redvers"

After the first Danish version called "Redvers" appeared in *Berlingske Tidende*, Aftenudgaven (August 20, 1928), a second Norwegian one was published as "En vandrer får influensa" (A Wanderer Catches Influenza) in *Helgelands Arbeiderblad* (Christmas 1933). It starts with comments about its being a scandal that science has not found a cure for the cold. The content is essentially the same as the previous version, but it is frequently rephrased with small additions and subtractions that don't really add to or detract from the story. It was also printed with a few minor differences in grammar, orthography and wording in *Tidens Tegn*, Lørdagsavisen (February 1, 1936). A second Danish version in *Social-Demokraten*, Hjemmets Søndag (June 7, 1936) is a translation of the Norwegian one with a few insignificant changes in the text. The version in *Sandemose Forteller* (1937) is slightly shortened and slightly rephrased, but nothing of significance has been omitted. Essentially the same article, without the statement about science not being able to find a cure for the cold, was also included in the collections *Årstidene* 9–10 (1954) and *Dans, dans, Roselill* (1965) as "Forkjølt reisende" (Traveler with a Cold). A Swedish adaptation "Rum nr 14" (Room Nr. 14), *Folket i bild* 1 (January 3, 1943), starts with two paragraphs on how shameful it is that science has not found a cure for the common cold, but this is different from the Norwegian text. It follows fairly closely, with a few minor changes, the version in *Sandemose Forteller* but omits several small sections such as the writer's attempt at rolling a cigarette, his being attacked by bedbugs and the hotel staff's trying to get him out of the dinning room. There are some additions as well. The conversation with the travelling salesman in the hotel is expanded and a description of just how sick Sandemose was after buying bananas and going out into the prairie is inserted. Also after the short description of the evening in Redvers, Sandemose tells how he went into a Chinese restaurant and got some mysterious mixture for his cold which he took before going to bed. At the end is a short account of what he did in Saskatoon after leaving Redvers.

Extensive passages in his diary were used by Sandemose to write "Redvers." The translation is based on the first Danish version with some passages taken from "En vandrer får influensa" when it was felt they flowed better in English than the ones in the original. Several sections were also omitted from "Redvers" which were also left out of "En vandrer får influensa" since they did not really add anything to the text. In a number of places I based the translation on the diary entries, especially the descriptions of the hotel, as I felt they were more immediate and lively than their equivalents in the printed texts.

Moving Day

Next to the Rocky Mountains the snow had already come a couple of months before, but further east the prairie still lay with brown stubble fields and black roads. Whenever we were puttering around out on the fields, I often stood quietly for a moment looking toward the distant snow-covered mountains in the west. I wished to be in them right then, but had to stay down on the lowland working, because I had no money. And in the mountains you are soon finished if you appear as a vagabond.

Over the prairie the sky was without clouds. The land lay in a cold and raw light. That the prairie is supposed to be beautiful, I have never understood. It appears to me extremely unpleasant, but of course one always finds a little something to make oneself happy. In the dirty stubble fields the prairie rose was having its second blooming, and there were swarms of large, yellow gophers, which now only rarely gave themselves time to stop on their mounds to twitch their whiskers up in the air. They were busy, as food had to be gathered for the winter.

I had work on a farm during the harvest and was supposed to have left when the season was over, but was asked first to help with the moving of a house. It had been sold to a bachelor who couldn't move it the six miles in question alone.

The whole morning was spent breaking the little building loose from the ground. It was built on a sort of sled which in the course of time had sunk deeply. It was hopeless to try to have the horses pull it loose. In the meantime we hitched up the twelve horses to it to test in advance whether the tension was equally divided among all the animals. Then the driver went into the door and standing in it began to yell at the horses which immediately reared a bit, but then slowly attempted to pull. The house didn't budge. We stood alongside and helped the driver yell, and finally it began sliding very gradually along the muddy earth.

The man in the door probably didn't hear anything in all the commotion, but the farmer beside me and I looked questioningly at each other, for suddenly there was a strange, pitiful cry. What was that? We were informed much more quickly than we would have wished or dreamed. Behind the house something alive appeared. The farmer let out a warning shout.

Under the house had been living two old and six young skunks which now in fright and anger—all eight simultaneously—threw their tails in the air and shot a devilish salvo of musk at us. We were both struck over our whole bodies by the greasy paste and shouted desperately for help. The driver came rushing just in time to be sprayed as well.

It's not too much to say that we wished we were dead.

You blend together a mixture of tar, pepper, lye, glue, shoe polish and sulphur. Mix well with excrement. Then call on your fantasy and season to taste. The person wanting to know what it is like to be sprayed by a skunk is now placed with a cord around his neck at a height that his toes just touch the ground, after which a knowledgeable person rubs his face thoroughly with the mixture. It would be advantageous also to prick the person in question with a needle so that he screams and thus gets as much of the stuff as possible down his throat. Then you will have a faint picture of what we suffered.

We stormed away from the place, threw ourselves in a mud hole and rubbed our faces with earth. It took an hour before we could think of anything but torture. Then we undressed completely and stood naked in the cold—far away from our detestable, stinking clothes—facing the complicated problem of sending word to the farm. There wasn't a person in sight. We had to go ourselves. Hidden behind a bush, we screamed ourselves hoarse until one of the farm girls heard our pitiable cries and carried out all the farm's old clothes to the bush. The house resounded with laughter. Human beings are no different.

But that wasn't all. The smell clings for days to a person sprayed by a skunk. Both wolves and mountain lions stay far away from such an individual. For four days and nights we took up lodgings in a woodshed and had our food brought to us outside the door. We quite understood what it is to be a leper. The farmers in the area teased us many times a day until we hit upon chasing them. I must say they know how to use their legs.

I have never met a tiger and have no desire to, but I think I would prefer to deal with a tiger rather than a skunk.

In those regions where there are many skunks it's a favourite sport to indoctrinate young emigrants with a mistaken idea concerning a skunk's zoology. One impresses upon the young man that when he sees a skunk he should try to get behind it. We explain that the skunk first sprays its foul liquid out on its bushy tail, which is then thrown *forward*, flinging it further. It's true that the skunk makes this movement with its tail, but it does this only in order not to dirty its tail. The stream shoots right out from behind as from a fire hose, and the victim knows better the next time.

The interruption in the moving did, though, result in some good. When we set to again, the first snow of the year had fallen.

To be on the safe side the farmer sent several loads of buckshot in under the house before we began, but the smelly family had long since taken up other quarters.

We hitched up the horses, tied down the furniture and let the house move over the prairie. After we had been under way for a while and were far from habitation, the farmer loaded his rifle and crept up onto the roof. He thought it was possible to get a coyote. Improbable? Only apparently. On observation it would seem that a house hitched up to twelve horses would make so much noise that a shy and cautious coyote would not allow itself to be seen. But a number of circumstances make things stand a little differently. Coyotes are curious. We only stimulated this trait. Secondly coyotes like to keep close to horses. They conceal them in the open countryside, and the strong scent of horse drowns out that of coyote—to the detriment of rabbits and hares.

Suddenly the rifle went off above our heads, but we heard from the man's outburst that he had missed. I stuck my head out the door. There was a lone coyote, standing four or five hundred yards away without making any attempt to flee. The animal's long triangular ears stood out sharply against the white landscape, and I saw the look in the eyes of the hare murderer. Another shot resounded. The coyote made a strange jump straight into the air and stood as before. A third shot. Exactly the same thing happened. The fourth shot, though, didn't make the coyote jump. It lay down quietly as though wanting to rest a bit, but it was a rest from which it would never again get up.

When the dead plunderer was lying in with us on the floor, I felt sorry for it and took all the joy from the hunter by remarking that I would rather see a dead skunk.

After we had driven about half way, there was a sound like a mixture of thunder and avalanche under us, and during the next few seconds all the planks on the floor were ripped up. There was a large boulder in the way, and we were in great confusion as we lay there rolling around with the overturned stove which filled the whole house with soot. We had to stop for several hours and attempt to fix the damage somewhat by driving long nails in here and there to hold the pieces together. Finally we continued on, keeping a sharp eye out for stones.

I stood beside one of the small windows, looking out at the glittering white land which had become so strangely alive after the snow had fallen. The earth had become a living creature which lay breathing under the winter sky. Now and then we startled a hare which darted across the snowfields like a bullet with a tail of blowing snow. The barren and endless whiteness felt like something beyond life and death.

The man had in advance selected a place on the edge of the coulee where he thought it would be possible to sled the house down. We stopped there and looked over the surroundings. The enormous valley stretched from south to north, and in the coulee itself were other hills and valleys, one landscape enclosed in the other. Meanwhile the owner of the house suggested we begin the descent, and the two of them went into the house. The trip down would be a dubious one which could end in who knows what, and I preferred to stay up on the top and watch the result from a safe place. The thing was that not more than a month ago I had been sleeping in a shed which in the middle of the night quite unexpectedly rolled down over a hillside with me in it. I still carried scars after that incident, but that house had at any rate been empty, except for a bed and myself. In this one there were both a stove and a chest of drawers, not to mention a large tool chest full of chisels, hammers, planes and nails. But when it came down to it, I didn't have the moral courage to say no. So we started off.

Even though my worst fears didn't materialize, it still went badly enough. On the middle of the slope we picked up an enormous speed. The stove began an insane waltz, and when I tried to hold onto it, I got into a tight squeeze between it and the wall. I screamed. So did everyone else. The horses, which had the house behind them, threw themselves to the side, and the house continued on, dragging the horses now behind it. This new position caused the stove to turn, and I started dancing a deranged Charleston with it across the floor. The trip continued in reverse with all the horses sliding on their tails behind us.

Finally the journey stopped suddenly. We wisely kept ourselves inside until the horses had calmed down. By some miracle all twelve were unscathed and only the harnesses were broken. The house stood nicely on a little platform. A better place could not have been found.

And there we left the farmer to himself. On a rise a short distance from the coulee we turned around and looked down toward the pioneer. Already a white spiral of smoke was twisting up from his chimney.

Notes to "Moving Day"

Like a number of other of Sandemose's Canada articles, "Moving Day" exists in two distinct variants. It originally appeared in Danish as "Flytning paa Prærien" (Moving on the Prairie) in *Dagens Nyheder* (August 22, 1928). This was followed by a Norwegian variant "En farmer holder flyttedag" (A Farmer has a Moving Day), *Arbeider-Ungdommen* (Christmas edition 1933). The introduction in each is quite different, primarily in the fact that the earlier variant takes place in Saskatchewan and the latter in Alberta near the Rocky Mountains. Otherwise the content of both is essentially the same, except that in the Norwegian one there is a considerable difference in wording and in some of the details from the Danish one, along with a few additions. The third time the article was published was in "Billeder fra en lang reise," *Aschehougs Magasin* 7 (July 1935). This is basically the same as the previous with very minor changes in orthography, grammar and wording. The title was changed to "Flyttedag" (Moving Day) in *Sandemose Forteller* (1937) and in a Danish translation from the Norwegian in *Social-Demokraten, Hjemmets Søndag* (August 8, 1937), as "Alberta" in *Årstidene* 9–10 (1954) and *Magasinet* 25 (June 22, 1957), and again as "Flyttedag" in *Dans, dans, Roselill* (1965). All these are basically the same as the one in "Billeder fra en lang reise" except for a few minor differences in grammar, orthography and wording.

Essentially the translation is based on the Norwegian variant with some sentences taken from the Danish one, though several of the additions Sandemose made to the former are not included. The title is taken from "Flyttedag" and the setting is Alberta, since this is where the actual incident the article is based on took place.

East Coulee

In Alberta, seventy to eighty miles from the Rocky Mountains, the prairie changes its face. Lakes and woods give way to the enormous coulees—deep and trackless gulleys which the spring floods have cut into the prairie through the millennia. Flat land, forests and high domed hills alternate down to the bottom of the coulee where a brook cuts its narrow course. This rugged landscape is situated on a high plain and is a forerunner to the mountains which from the high areas you can see outlined to the west. It is a spectacular sight—clouds and mountains blending into new cliffs and valleys until everything loses its substance, cradled airily under the horizon.

A man by the name of John had bought "East Coulee" and the surrounding prairie land. Now he wanted me to move out there for a while. First he was going to get his house ready, which was no big thing—it was a *shack*, a large house of boards with simple walls and one room. The house stood on sled runners, and after it was fully supplied with a bed, furniture and a roaring fire in the stove, eight horses were hitched up to it, and we drove the seven miles to East Coulee.

The region was wild and desolate. A Canadian had farmed there once, but he was long dead, and several rotten fence posts were the only traces of his work. He had been a bit of a character, and it was said that he would walk up through the valley quite often during the winter nights after his death.

At the bottom of the coulee was a broken up iron safe. It must have weighed a ton or two and probably had its own story. The dead farmer would come and sit down on it at night. When I went down to examine the safe, there was no farmer, just a little owl sitting on it. It hissed at me in comical indignation before it floated off and sat down in a tree. The farmer's soul maybe? If that were the case, it had suddenly begun thinking about changing domiciles, because as I stood looking over at the owl, it fell down dead in the snow. Rather shocked, I gathered it up. It was dead. But then I began thinking that an owl has to die at some time or other, so this occurrence isn't really so strange. But I had never seen the birds of the sky fall down without there being some concrete reason for it. And as I stood in the silent, white valley beneath the huge hill slopes looking at the dead bird, I felt as though something were wrong. It was an oppressive feeling, and it stayed with me.

It was nearly evening when we came to the valley, and at sunset the temperature fell way down. It was as if the air froze, so that we had difficulty walking through it. When the door was opened out to the cold, the opening was filled with mist. We sat up to the glowing stove as flowers of ice grew up out of the floor and formed a wedge over from the door. That night the mercury fell to 53 degrees below zero Fahrenheit. I breathed the frost away on a part of the window and stared out into the bleak Land. There came over me an overwhelming feeling of time, of days long past, and suddenly I got a painful desire to be somewhere else—a thousand miles away from eternity in Alberta. The hills on the opposite side of the coulee came alive and airy, as though they were not hills but an irregularly shaped piece that had been cut out of the firmament, forming bottomless corridors out into the universe. Out there was a living fairy land full of those creatures whose bones or petrified skeletons lay spread around in the valleys—man, dinosaur, sabre-toothed tiger, buffalo, coyote.

Usually when time and eternity are discussed, expressions mostly like tough mathematical formulae are used. But there are times when one visually approaches eternity and encompasses the millions of years with his mind. Perhaps it is not thought but a self-effacement. The self is driven to its knees under an impression of the vastness of life, and under this stupefying effect one relinquishes one's position as an individual and self-willed creature and for a short time goes back to whence one came—to eternity.

The coyotes passed through the valley during the nights. In the stillness we heard them go by out in the shrieking snow. They always stood still a couple of times near the cabin and came to terms with the fact that human beings had come to East Coulee.

The weather changed constantly from dead calm to snow storm. Whenever there was a storm, it sent no breeze ahead, but came roaring suddenly through the coulee, jumped from slope to slope, flailing their hoods of snow. But you didn't just observe how far it went, it used chasms and cliffs like strings on an enormous instrument. To the north a sharp ledge jutted out which shrieked like horses drowning. Then the wind howled over to the next slope, gave a screech and travelled on. We always knew, even during dark nights, where it came from and how far it had gone, until with a whistle it captured the cabin in its embrace.

From hour to hour the coulee changes its mood, eternally the same yet never the same. And if you walk on the hills along it, it opens up visions which remind you of everything you have dreamed, from Denmark to Mount Everest and the moon's dead craters. But you cannot stay outside very long at a time. The cold tears at you, and the little wisp of smoke from the cabin is enticing. So we go home and quarrel.

John and I do not agree on anything at all, and therefore time passes quickly. Through the winters he sits in remote places like this, studying literature and economy. His brain is a storehouse of knowledge, and his opinions are profound and unimpregnable as battleships. John doesn't smoke or drink, and he eats only bread. For twenty years he has shared his time between hard work and the acquiring of knowledge. Now he is forty and will probably never change his lifestyle. And why should he? He is to be envied. "I came to America at the age of twenty," he says, "and from the first day, I have loved this country."

Happy, happy man!

He reads one of my manuscripts. "I will tell you," he says, "that a manuscript I have read gets good luck." And he tells about a young Irishman whom he met once in New York. John read the manuscript of a novel which the Irishman—whose name I have forgotten—had written, but the work didn't particularly impress him. Later the book came out, was a roaring success and raked in for the Irishman a lot of money—and a wife. After a while it was expected that the family would increase in size, and the couple made plans for the boy—you see, it was going to be a boy—long before he was born. They decided to go to Ajaccio so he could be born in the same place as Napoleon. But after three days there, the wife had had enough of the Corsicans, and the boy, who turned out to be a girl, saw the light of day first in St. Paul, Minnesota, U.S.A.

It's almost Christmas, but there is no peace on Earth. Hunters set out to relieve the coyote of his life and pelt.

One day toward evening I went up onto the prairie to catch a rabbit or prairie chicken, since the hermit's bread and tea were beginning to be a bit meagre for my taste. From far off the sound of sled runners screeching in the snow caught my ear. Two coyotes came in my direction, hindered by the deep snow. Far behind them came a sled pulled by two horses, the steam puffing out from the nostrils of the already exhausted animals. Then the hunter opened a box and out sprang four greyhounds which, fresh and invigorated, took over the job of the horses. They circled the coyotes in the middle of the flat prairie. Slowly the man sledded over and waited until he could shoot both animals with one shot. The dogs immediately lost interest and began eating snow. A little later the sled slipped past me. I caught a glimpse of the man's face, red and swollen in the cold, as he shouted in lilting Danish dialect, "I saw a half dozen prairie chickens to the south."

I have seen similar things many times, but the image of this meeting remained in my mind—the Danish coyote hunter swinging his leather whip over his head in a whirring circle, as the rime-covered horses flew over the wild prairie in the twilight.

That night it was again insanely cold. Out in the coulee the coyotes were howling shamelessly. It got colder and colder. We lay tightly wrapped up in the bottom of a box with straw and furs. We kept warm, but the house groaned in the cold. When in the morning we looked at the little column of mercury in the thermometer, it read 61 degrees below zero. When I placed my foot out onto the snow, it screeched like a dozen wounded felines. "It's cold!" I said. John looked up from his incessant book. "Well, the mosquitoes aren't bad here during the winter. That's another advantage of Canada."

That day was a Sunday, and it brought a more frightful storm than a human being can imagine in his wildest dreams. As usual it came without warning, shrieking up through the coulee with an ocean of snow and hail in its lap. Hail? It was sharply honed lumps of ice of all conceivable shapes. They struck the small branches off the trees and clattered on to the roof as if the sky were falling down in shreds. There were rounded lumps like chicken eggs, but otherwise all sorts of grotesque shapes. Some of them weighed nearly a half-pound and had edges like Gillette razor blades. Others resembled candlesticks, ink wells, cream pitchers and matchboxes.

When the storm reached one of the high slopes to the south, it was as though it were being torn up by its roots. Branches, earth and snow whirled from it. A minute later the hail stopped, but the whole world was drowning in a cloud of snow. Nothing, absolutely nothing could be seen three feet away. The storm lasted twenty-four hours. Afterward I understood the accident that occurred near Wayne during the winter of 1926–7. A mother and her child lost their way one night in the snowy rises between the farmhouse and the barn. Both were found the next morning frozen to death. We who live in a country where water and land alternate so the winter is mild and the summer no warmer than is good, have difficulty comprehending this inland climate where the weather throughout the year covers the entire range.

The night that followed was again deathly still. Nevertheless the coulee was filled with evil sounds. Strange creatures fared among the trees at its bottom, while the slopes came alive and stared in over the prairie where the wolf stood sniffing at the badger's lair. Each tree had seeing eyes. The snowdrifts lay out there, their sharp backs breathing in the white night.

Again day came. It tears at a person. The moment you are outside, you want to be free of the coulee, want to get up on top where there are only plains of white snow on all sides. And I know that if I were to *live* here permanently, it would in a short time leave a deeper mark on me than I should care for. Even in the middle of the day *it* comes over me, as soon as I'm alone. It's certainly not completely untrue that East Coulee is haunted. I had there an experience so strange and so contrary to human experience that, now at any rate, it eludes words. There was something that required human beings to set forth, but I dare say it will become silent, if a light-harried city ever should lie in the valley.

Strange things are revealed and personified in the shadow of eternity.

Well, the days passed. We read and argued and went hunting, as our beards grew and the tobacco ran out. Beyond the cabin was the rounded incline of the coulee like a warrior's brow. Owls and coyotes jeered at each other during the nights, and there was a heavy sigh whenever the snow slid on the hillsides.

Snow, snow, mountains of snow which from day to day give the landscape new faces. It's as though one gets snow on the brain at last. Snow, snow, ever more snow as the cold sinks its teeth more deeply. Snow, snow, until you feel certain that the world will burst apart tonight of cold. Something is tightened more and more, and it must end with an explosion! You get used to the cold one day, because after all it is there. But the next day it becomes even more unmerciful. You get used to it too, but you begin to acquire certain confused ideas that the cold will soon have to set fire to the snowdrifts, so the whole world goes up in smoke. Let it be cold! East Coulee is beautiful—a God forsaken model of man's earth.

Still, on the last day, when I was standing up on a hill saying goodbye, it was not East Coulee I saw, but a December in Denmark with the clouds being ripped along the gray and low-hanging sky. I heard the water rippling in channels, and out in the night were lights from many windows. Emigrate, very well. But my right to walk under Denmark's sky I would not sell for the whole province of Alberta.

Notes to "East Coulee"

There is only one version of "East Coulee," found in the Danish newspaper *Berlingske Tidende*, Aftenudgaven (September 29, 1928), and the translation is of this.

The man named "John" in the article is John Andersen, a resident of Dalum, Alberta in the 1920s whom Sandemose helped move a house down into North Coulee (See Introduction). This move is described, if somewhat fancifully, in "Moving Day."

Simon Hjortnæs, King of the Danes in Canada

Travelling around in Canada I was constantly running into the name Simon Hjortnæs, often called *King Simon* or *The King of the Danes*. Mention of him gave me no reason to suppose that he was a beloved man, but on the other hand I quickly found myself in a position to establish the fact that the stories about his severity and brutality are wildly exaggerated. Most of them were from the start judged to be childish tall tales, because if true, the inevitable conclusion would have to be reached that *Simon Peder* or *Simon P.*, as he is also often called, would be sitting, not like a king on his farm, but rather in jail.

Canada, you see, is not a lawless country where you can go around picking off people unpunished when you are in a bad mood. That kind of Canada-romanticism belongs in deranged heads. They were fantastic accounts which were circulating about Simon Hjortnæs, and you scarcely know what you are to believe when you periodically see some of the most hair-raising ones appear in Danish letters-to-the-editor columns where they naively pass for truth and dead seriousness.

Though several times while passing through I was very close to Alida, I put off visiting Simon Hjortnæs, preferring to wander around without any real goal and making only occasional acquaintances. I was taking a whole pile of unopened letters of recommendation back home, when my instincts and perhaps an inborn suspicion drove me first and foremost to hunt up those nameless, struggling emigrants. That an older generation was well provided for didn't necessarily mean in itself that there were also now good starting conditions for young people.

But at last I felt mature enough to visit Simon without being disturbed. And it turned out that I could have been quite at ease. He exhibited little need to force his opinions on anyone. The reason for his unpopularity, which was and is indisputable, was rooted in his tremendous energy and joy of work that formed the background for an intense hate of everyone who had no desire to work. To them he showed no pity, but it should be immediately said that he well understood how to differentiate between those who *could* not and those who did not *want* to. And of course the man must be understood against his own background which it is to be hoped will be evident from the following.

In the 1890s when Simon was eleven years old, he came with his parents who were poor tenant farmers from Vrensted in Vendsyssel to North Dakota, U.S.A. Nothing much is reported about his early youth.

At an early age he began working on his own. When he was eighteen he tried his hand at dealing in horses but had no luck, as one fine day his whole flock of horses disappeared. However, he found them again after a long search, because a clairvoyant Norwegian informed him that they were at a certain place up in Canada. Sure enough he found them there, and he also took such a liking to the land that he took out a homestead.

After having broken up the legal minimum amount of land, he did roadwork and other similar jobs in Dakota and Montana in order to get a little money. Then he fell in with a couple of Germans who wanted to start a ranch. It was soon agreed that Simon would be their partner, and together they bought thirty wild horses. Of these thirty horses, four were broken in so that they could be hitched to a wagon, made out of the remnants of an old mowing machine they found on the prairie. Then they went north, and after a month they had covered 400 miles up to Milk River Canyon. At night they kept watch over the horses. It was impossible for them to get proper shelter, and the weather was extremely changeable. Day after day broke with brilliant sunshine, but on the other hand there was thunder, lightning and hail night after night.

One night when they had camped by a railroad line near the Missouri River, the horses were frightened by the train. For a whole day and night they struggled to gather the animals together. Finally everything was ready to make a fresh start, but two minutes later the mowing machine's cast iron wheel broke on the train tracks. Now they were in a mess. After some deliberation they tied a couple of thin logs under the vehicle and slid on, leaving a furrow behind them. Simon grinned at the recollection of it. "It darned well looked as though we were trying to cut North America in two lengthwise."

In the meantime they reached the Germans' homestead where the ranch was supposed to be situated. There had been poverty here while the men had been away. The seed potatoes had been eaten, and the peels had been planted—incidentally with favourable results.

Simon's life as a ranch owner was a short one. He had a falling out with one of the Germans and rode off taking his horses with him. On the way to his homestead he met an elderly Dane who was looking for some property, and they lived together for a while in a dugout on Simon's land. But that friendship didn't last long either. They procured a flock of chickens, but one of the hens didn't find favour with the rooster which pecked and maltreated it. One day Simon became so angry that he grabbed a stick to chastise the rooster which in the meantime would not stand still. Incensed, Simon chased after the rooster, caught up with it and killed it. Triumphantly he returned, but the old man made such a fuss over the incident that Simon gave him five minutes to clear out.

A while later a Swedish vagabond came by, and Simon made a new friend. He was just in the process of building a house and had for that purpose acquired some boards, a hammer and a box of nails. When the house was finished, the hammer disappeared. Since there were no people around for miles except Simon and the Swede, it was not too hard to figure out who had taken it. While Simon looked for it, he mumbled spitefully about what kind of *son of a bitch* had run off with the hammer. The Swede said nothing, but he became gloomy and said scarcely a word for two weeks. Then Simon went out shopping and came back with a bottle of liquor. That uplifted their spirits, and jovially Simon patted his companion on the back and asked, "Why are you so sulky?"

"You have offended my honour," said the Swede gloomily.

Simon was a bit surprised at the remark, which did not correspond to the usual tone they used between themselves.

"What!" he said. "Have I offended your honour?"

"Yes," said the Swede, "you asked what *son of a bitch* had run off with your hammer, and that was a shameless thing to say, when you well knew it was me."

Without a sense for the comedy in the situation—until later—Simon grabbed him by the back of his neck and screamed, "Oh, so it *was* you!"

The Swede was immediately banished from Simon Peder's domain.

The Simon Hjortnæs living today should be seen in the light of the incomprehensibly difficult circumstances under which he worked himself up to prosperity. It's not advisable for the one who wants to shirk away from everything to get close to the man who has begun with a couple of bare hands on the naked land in a half wild country. Simon toiled like a beast of burden, but he always kept his head fresh and receptive. From his mouth could come words so wise that they might have been uttered by an Anatole France. He read a great deal, had learned German in addition to English and speaks the purest Danish. Usually the emigrant mixes two languages together in a hideous gruel, but when Simon spoke Danish, it was *Danish*.

Not strange that he is misunderstood; he towers so high over the average emigrant that most of them don't understand him at all. He's not completely without blame. People have played practical jokes on him so often that he does the same back, and strangers don't always understand his rough humour which chases the weak person into a mouse hole. One particular event can illustrate this:

A young man came to Simon and asked him for work. Simon inquired whether he knew anything about farming, and the man answered yes. Simon got him a job, but two days later he returned out of work. Well, that sort of thing happens, and Simon got him another job. But when he came back shortly afterward, Simon had discovered that the man was not a farmer, but a half apprenticed saddler, and had absolutely not a clue about farming. The fact is he had committed the most foolish of all blunders—he had looked for work under false pretences. What did Simon Hjortnæs do now? He took the man over to a place where they could be alone, looked him straight in the eye and said, "I get people work once. I get them work twice. But when they come the third time and I find out they've lied to me, then I dig a hole behind the barn and put a bullet in my rifle. *There are a couple of them lying over there before you!*"

The saddler took to his heels. He had no doubt that Simon was serious. Have anyone's eyes ever flashed, they have been his! Whenever King Simon became angry, and he often was, it was like witnessing an erupting volcano. He swept aside the object of his wrath as if it were a feather and spat out a remark that struck to the core of a person's soul. The least dangerous side of this sturdy farmer was not that to a surprising degree he was a master of the language. A word from him could be like the crack of a whip.

But it's a fact that his people were fond of him and did not at all feel themselves oppressed. The conversation at the long table where they ate was unconstrained as Simon presided at the one end and his old mother at the other. He looked down at her thoughtfully one evening and said, "Mother says she was lucky to have me. But I was luckier, because I got her."

That was his natural form of expression, but I felt the emotion behind the words.

Already in the early years when Simon was poor, he had married a girl from the island of Fyn. Karen Hjortnæs became the warrior's better half; the moment she spoke, Simon's eyes grew soft. Once when we were sitting out by a slough lying in wait for ducks, Simon said for no apparent reason, "Karen is the wisest woman in Saskatchewan!" Though I thought this an exaggeration—with all due respect for Mrs. Hjortnæs—but didn't want to intimate any such thing, as that would quite likely have got me a swim in the slough, I chose to remain silent. Since Simon heard no objection, he took a step forward and said, "She's the best woman who has ever left Fyn!"

I said nothing, and a minute later Simon remarked emotionally, "You can bet that a finer girl has never crossed the Atlantic! And a good woman is the best thing a man can win in this world."

It was Simon's greatest sorrow that they didn't have children. "Otherwise the Lord has given me all that I could wish for," he declared, "if only I would take the trouble to acquire it. My brother, he's a real Hjortnæs too… he has thirteen children…" Simon gave a sigh.—

When emigration to Canada gained momentum and the colony of *Dannevirke* grew up where before Simon had lived alone, he became very preoccupied with what could be done for the emigrants—in other words, the women. He saw that many of them suffered by being transplanted, especially because they couldn't stand loneliness.

One should never bother about a man, according to his view, for a man should look after himself and lie in the bed he himself makes. "A man," said Simon, "he can get into trouble, and so what? He's a man. He can lie down to die of hunger, but at the last moment, he thinks better of it and gets up again. But women. We have to watch out for them, because after all they're not men."

In his work for emigrants Simon suffered great disappointments. Not least did he feel indignant at the stream of letters begging for things. Some desired not only help with the trip over, but land, shelter and ready cash which they wanted to "work off". Young people who were not received as princes at King Simon's smeared him in the press, and since he was least of all a parliamentarian, he was soon quarrelling with most of those who worked with emigration.

Like a bull he's not afraid of a locomotive. He castigated the railway companies, the ministers, the government and the emigrants. Several hundred miles from Alida I met a minister who turned pale when he showed me a letter from the King in which the latter wrote, "I'm going to come soon and pound some sense into your stupid head."

Irritated, Simon finally broke off all cooperation and on his own did what he could. But it certainly became apparent that Simon Hjortnæs is lucky only where his will is law.—

I hear that Simon Hjortnæs has now sold his farm to begin all over again starting up a new one. It's not the first time this has happened. He is the eternal pioneer, becoming uneasy when the goal is reached. Start over again!—But I will always picture him on the old place under an autumn sky with the straw fires blazing. How far away that is! A little memory tells me *how* far away it is. Early one morning Simon was standing and giving people orders. I stood looking out into the wet falling snow. A coyote appeared up on the road. It turned its head many times and shuffled uneasily until it continued its walk, disappearing in the darkness. A coyote walking past the farm gate—indeed, that is far away from here.

The same day I was in the field with Simon. He wanted to see me plow, and he thought I "would turn out to be pretty good at it." I then stood, following him with my eyes as he drove the five horses down over his field where large stones could fling the plow several feet into the air, so it was remarkable that Simon plumped back down onto the seat again. Behind him the prairie turned its black face toward the sun, but here, far from the sea, no screeching seagulls followed the plow.

When Simon caught up to me again he said with a little smile, "There's nothing in this world as good as turning the earth with a plow and seeing that the furrow is straight. No place can you be better off than on a plow. There while the plow is going you can think so well about the whole world and your wife. You bet, you who are a poet. You can send greetings and say at home that it was a good thing Adam and Eve were thrown out of Paradise."

King of the Danes—the name was tacked on to him sarcastically once. *But it was a name that fit*, and those who wanted to make fun of him with it are those who now see red when they hear it! Simon Peder Hjortnæs is a prince in the tradition of the farmer and chieftain of Denmark's oldest history.

Notes to "Simon Hjortnæs, King of the Danes in Canada"

"Simon Hjortnæs, Danskernes Konge i Canada" (Simon Hjortnæs, King of the Danes in Canada) was published in Danish in *Hjemmet* 1 (Copenhagen) (December 24, 1929).

The only real difference between the translation and the original article is that some changes in paragraphing have been made.

For more information about Simon Hjortnæs see the Introduction to this publication.

The Last Duck Hunt

In Winnipeg it began to get cold during the nights even in September. I woke up one night with my teeth chattering in a bed with too few blankets and had to get up to put on more clothes. The northern lights were moving quietly in the sky and warned of increased cold. The suburb in which I was living lay still and deserted during the day. Frost had stripped the leaves off the trees. One day was like the other, sad and quiet. I had soon become tired of the sights of the city. As is the case with most western cities, Winnipeg has a highly advanced civilization which has appropriated all technical innovations into its service. Civilization marches triumphantly over the great continent, but the culture of the arts has still not reached farther than to Montreal.

One day I was wandering aimlessly in the city. It was warmish where the sun was shining, and the flag was waving over the *Manitoba Free Press* building because it was Christian X's birthday. I came down to the Red River, the lazily flowing stream which goes through Winnipeg and by the banks of which houses, refuse dumps and bushes supersede one another. As I stood on one of the half-rotten landing docks, an elderly gentleman came down onto one of the dumps, emptied his pockets of papers and made a bonfire out of them. Next he rolled a cigarette and lit it with a burning envelope. Afterward he stood absent-mindedly looking at the fire as it quickly spread over the dock. Then he pensively walked away.

I disappeared as well, as I had a clear idea of what that fire there among the wooden sheds could develop into, and I was the only person around. If you have to suffer punishment for arson, whether or not your conscience is clear seems to me a trifle.

When I came up onto one of the streets, I met a young Dane from Vendsyssel—Canada is crawling with people from Vendsyssel—who had got himself a gun, and who now proposed I come with him on a trip to Lake Manitoba after ducks. I welcomed the invitation, and the next morning we started off in a Ford, a 1907 model or thereabouts.

You cannot grab a bicycle and head out into the prairie. The roads are impossible for that kind of thing, and it's too far between people. I remember a bicycle trip I took once in Denmark. Everywhere there were farms and houses behind the hills. Each minute a new view opened up with a constantly changing sky over the constantly changing landscape. Such an equally long trip almost anywhere in Canada would only be a depressing and boring chore. Perhaps you wouldn't see a living human being on the way, and your place of destination would look the same as the one you came from.

It's seventy miles from Winnipeg to Lake Manitoba, which we reached in the middle of the afternoon, after a couple of flats and with four jackrabbits on the floor of the car. The lake was a disappointment. We had come to shoot ducks, and indeed there were a lot of them. You could hear their quacking everywhere in the enormous swamps that stretch for miles behind the sand dunes surrounding the lake. But the reeds were two or three yards high in the marshes. You couldn't see anything as soon as you ventured into them. It wasn't exactly safe, either; several times we were up to our waists in quagmire. When we finally heard hundreds of ducks quite close by, we would have needed a boat to get any nearer to them. That hunt was hopeless without a boat and a dog. Where there finally was a tiny possibility of getting through, signs were hanging: No trespassing, no hunting. Only one single duck came within shooting distance, but it was a strange bird, impervious to buckshot.

The hills by the lakeshore were covered with forest. Here were the summerhouses of the citizens of Winnipeg, standing empty, and below them the surf surged in from Lake Manitoba. You never really overcome your amazement that you can go down *and drink* this water, for it's an ocean roaring against the coast.

My companion sat down on a slope and looked out at the surging spray. Then this big, robust man burst out, "You can't imagine how I longed for the sea those first years on the prairie. It was like being locked up. I lay awake at night and thought I was thirsty. But it was just because there was no ocean, only all this land…"

I made my voice as expressionless as possible, so as not to frighten him. "Well, I guess we're all like that."

He looked at me out of the corner of his eye. A little later he continued, "I was almost sick because of it. Then I maintained that conditions were far better in Denmark—because I naturally wanted to keep a backdoor open for myself, you see. It just wouldn't do to say that I couldn't stand being here because there was no water. People don't like being laughed at, either."

Then after a pause he said a most surprising thing which I never would have expected from that man's mouth, "Then I discovered that the prairie too is really a kind of ocean."

I tried to draw him out again, but now I didn't get any more out of the tough, long-legged fellow than a touching dream about a girl on a Danish estate. "But it's not easy to write to a woman, you see," he concluded, "when you can't even write. It's like swimming where there's an undertow. If you send a piece of writing like that off, she'll laugh at you and show it to the other girls. Then you're left standing there like a damned fool!"

Ah well, let us keep our dignity and nobility on the wide-stretched field of vanity.

ಸಿಂ

When we drove home there was a mist over the landscape—strange formations which turned the deserted region into an unsuspected fantasy. At one place where we had to stop, a rabbit kept on running round and round in the beams from the headlights, unable to find its way out. It was a meagre prize, much too meagre. We chased it ourselves into the darkness. Round about the countryside shone the red straw fires. It was far between human habitations.

A little before you come to the railway junction at Portage la Prairie is the town of Poplar Point. It was getting very dark when we got there, and we stopped to buy gas. But there was nobody in the house where the pump was, and we decided to continue on to the next town. As my companion was about to start the car, we both happened to look into the garden by the house—and stared in astonishment. A big old tree there started slowly rocking from side to side. A little later it lifted itself up out of the ground with its roots and a large clump of dirt.

I looked at my companion, and he looked at me. "Do you see anything?" I asked.

"Do you see anything?" he answered.

"Yes," I said, "I see a tree pulling itself up by its roots."

My companion rubbed his eyes, "I see it too, but I suspect it's imagination."

As he said that, the tree lifted itself up a bit higher and floated down into the back of the garden, where it disappeared. We leapt out of the car and down into the garden. There was a fresh hole in the ground where the tree had stood. The garden ended in a woods, but there the trees stood quite properly.

"Now I think we'd better drive home," said my companion.

I agreed with him, and we drove in silence from Poplar Point. Some distance from the city we came to a crossroads where we did not know which way to turn. But in the field stood a sign which we presumed was a signpost. We got the car turned so the headlights shone on the sign, but it was no signpost. On it was painted in large black letters on a white background: *Keep smiling.*

For a moment we stared at this request, then my companion said with a solemn voice, "It's a sign from above. If we really size up the situation, we might just as well laugh at that tree too."

That was what we did and drove on.

After a while we got to Portage la Prairie and late at night reached Winnipeg. We were careless enough to talk about the wandering tree in Poplar Point and were forced to listen to many impertinent remarks about the strong water in Lake Manitoba. That wasn't fair, for either you're a teetotaler or you're not. And the tree's walking, or more correctly swimming or floating, is a fact. But the entire way from Poplar Point to Winnipeg I had a feeling that someone or other had tried to make me look foolish. The trees stood along the side of the road roaring with laughter as we swept by.

ಶಿ∝

Toward evening the following day there were a few degrees of frost, and at nighttime it was snowing. Outside my window were a couple of high lamp-posts. They reached up to the fifth floor where I lived, and each had a bulb that lit up the snow so that it was dancing in the shaft of light around. They threw the light down onto a railway yard and a wooden shed which was the only thing clearly visible of Winnipeg. A freight train went by. The bell on the engine was reminiscent of morning services in the church at home. The sound gradually died out far away, while the cars still were gliding by. I counted over a hundred cars and lost count. The train continued by. At last it was as though it had driven through the shaft of light for an eternity. Finally the last car passed with a blue light on the top of its roof. When it too was gone, it was as though there was something missing down there in the blowing snow.

ಶಿ∝

There was no more duck hunting that year. When I left the city I saw only one duck, sitting in the middle of a frozen lake, half on its tail, glancing at the train.

Notes to "The Last Duck Hunt"

"Den sidste Andejagt" (The Last Duck Hunt) was published in Danish in *Aarhuus Stiftstidende* (May 17, 1930). The story of the tree uprooting itself in Poplar Point on Sandemose's way back to Winnipeg from Lake Manitoba is found in the chapter "Centralblikket" ("Central Vision") in the Norwegian novel *En flyktning krysser sitt spor* (A Fugitive Crosses His Tracks) (1933). Here the wording is quite different in many places, but the content is essentially the same, except the man from Jutland has became a farmer from the Norwegian district of Jæren. In the reworked version of the novel from 1955 the same version of the story appears under the chapter title "Ut i mørket" (Out into the Dark).

Except for a few changes in paragraphing and the elimination of a couple of passages that only a person having an intimate knowledge of Denmark in the 1920s would understand, the translation follows the original article.

The Whisper of the Blood

I'd had it with this perpetual racial talk! I took my gun and left. Out on the prairie I calmed down enough so that I could begin to think things over. Even the least prejudiced farmers had objected to the fact that the Galicians built their houses differently. Why did the Galicians do *that*? And why could they never learn proper English?

The farmers didn't know that the Galicians asked the very same questions. Why can't these *Swedes* build their houses like ordinary people? Why can't they learn proper English?

Neither group could speak English. Each individual thought he spoke "fluent English," but to Canadians it was some strange language. The Scandinavians spoke a tongue with a Nordic wash of waves—the Galicians one with a Slavic undertone.

The immigrants' linguistic tragedy was rampant in both camps. People spoke fluently, yes indeed, as long as they were on their farm. But they spoke the colony's local language, regardless of whether the colony was Polish or Swedish, a language which only had expressions for the necessities.

"What do those people mean calling us Swedes?" asked the Danes indignantly. And the Hungarians and Ukrainians wrinkled their eyebrows when they heard the word "Galician." "Why do the Swedes call us that?"

I often left when the discussion among the Scandinavians got too heated. A cloud of nonsense formed every time the subject of race was brought up, and that happened quite frequently. All these fine people went crazy on this point, and it gradually occurred to me that it was the desire for self-assertion that played the most serious tricks on both the Nordic and the Slavic peoples. Immigrants in America discover very quickly that they are not regarded as people of the highest degree. But they are powerless when faced with the natives' enormous majority and established security. Therefore they create their own pecking order.

There is no limit to how high a Swede, Dane or Norwegian after three months' stay in Canada or the U.S. can feel himself raised above the Poles. It's a self-importance of such monstrous dimensions that there's nothing to do except look for the explanation in the man's own mind.

The fact is, no valid grounds exist. It's the same old thing: we are held down, so we also want to keep someone down.

The aversion to everything that's *different*—isn't it the same everywhere? The fear that somebody might *believe* that he is equal to you? If that's the case, racial hatred is identical to the insult the wife of carpenter Hansen feels is directed to her when the wife of shoemaker Sorensen parades about in a gaudy new hat.

We all know that such reactions are the basic motive behind the racial talk coming from Germany. It's the great ones who leave it to the small ones to keep themselves down. The ruling group which has something to hide entices the ones deceived to fly at each others' throats. My God, if it weren't so tragic, there could be good grounds for laughter. What does the average SA man know about the Jews? What does he know about race? What did Hitler, Feder, Goebbels and Streicher know about these things? They knew absolutely nothing. Not a blessed thing.

But back when I regularly escaped out into the prairie once a day to avoid the problem, there was no Hitler sitting at the helm in Germany, and I hadn't exactly anticipated his coming. I thought, like most more or less reasonable human beings, that the easiest thing to do was disappear when people were talking too much nonsense. I imagined that would be sufficient...

I walked around on the fields with the dog Jim at my heels and played "exceptional person." I had been best friends with a Negro and fallen quite in love with an Indian girl who, however, didn't share my desire for racial treason. She had that strange green glint in her eyes you only see in half-Indians and which you go around thinking about for many years, especially when the owner has preferred an Indian hunter living some place up in the Northwest Territories...

To my great sorrow the girl has nothing to do with the story except that I think more about her than about racial theories. But then suddenly one day fate caught up with me.

Whenever I now, eight years later, look back at the racial struggle that broke out between Jim and me, and in which I represented the inferior race, I have a need to feel a little proud of myself and maintain that in reality it was I who had the finest blood.

The difference between Jim and me, from an Aryan point of view, must have been in my favour. Jim was black, walked on four legs and wore, so to speak, his scandalous family tree. His forefathers had disgraced themselves shamefully with anything that even resembled a dog.

I was the direct opposite of Jim. In the first place I walked on only two legs, and in the second place I was fair skinned, a Nordic nobleman of Class A, Category I. There wasn't a trace of any sort of inferiority in me. My family tree could for that matter be traced all the way back to Odin without any kind of embarrassing spots.

As Nordic nobleman I ought to have spent my time regarding Jim with the deepest disdain, but that was something I hadn't learned yet. Besides, he hadn't given me any reason to do so—which naturally means little and shouldn't have prevented me from my Nordic duty. But Jim went hunting with me and on the whole kept me company. It was in Alberta, Canada, and Jim was a good friend to have in a new and half-wild country. He had eyeteeth like a walrus and a chest like a bear. Whenever Jim jumped up on me to ascertain that I was the best human being in the world, it most often ended with my tumbling onto the ground.

But then it happened that fate caught up with me. I was walking to the farm from the town with that pleasant feeling of human worth being equipped with new boots gives one. They were good boots with thick soles, and also I had got them for a good price after the necessary bargaining. And there came Jim flying across the fields to greet me. He rushed up straight as an arrow...

It wasn't easy for me to realize that Jim had come to take my life. I had, as already mentioned, had little interest in the question of race.

It was an ugly battle. An attack from a good friend is dangerous and disgusting. You think it's a joke for much too long a time. When it finally dawns on you that it's serious, you don't resist with all your might. You haven't had a declaration of war and you haven't had time to adapt yourself. Maybe...? Maybe this is after all some kind of joke. I will certainly tell him afterward that I did not like it.

But then it goes too far. You fall, start bleeding, and receive another blow. And then that rage which breaks down all barriers surges up. The former friend comes to realize that he has unleashed something he had not imagined. He's pursued for twenty years afterward, until he believes it was *he* who was attacked and pursued for eternity for no reason. And he's right. There's no connection between the attack and the retribution. But he forgets there's something else and greater than the attack to be avenged.

The snow lay trampled and bloody where Jim and I concluded our friendship. I still have white scars on my hands and arms after the battle. Jim actually got off lightest. I didn't have four long eyeteeth nor a knife, either, which could have substituted for teeth. But I got hold of my crazed friend's throat and squeezed hard, all the while on the point of tears at the sight of Jim's eyes being pressed almost out of their sockets. Finally the farmer came and got a rope around the dog's hind legs.

Foregoing stronger expressions I can only say that I really didn't understand what Jim meant by such conduct. I stood there looking down at the animal which had got an attack of a deeply guilty conscience—an attack which moreover lasted for a while—and I feared that precisely this guilty conscience would make Jim run amok once more. That didn't happen, but I always was on the watch for it afterward, and our friendship was definitely over. He never greeted me again. He just looked furtively at me from a distance like a tamed coyote.

In the kitchen I had my wounds cleaned with iodine and bandaged. There was no infection, and the day after I was already doing my chores as before.

But there in the kitchen came the explanation. For after I was bandaged and was sitting over a cup of coffee following my fright, I showed off the new boots I had bought in town. Jim had unfortunately sunk his teeth into them too, and faint traces of them could be seen on my feet.

Then the farmer understood everything, "You bought those boots at the Galician's!"

Yes, indeed I had. But the Scandinavians in the colony didn't usually shop there, and they often let the man feel their contempt.

"What a smart dog Jim was! A hell of a dog! He caught the scent of a Galician when you came in those boots! Good dog!"

I was a bit confused on account of the turn the matter had taken. People were bragging about Jim to high heaven. There you can definitely see proof that there is something wrong with those Galicians! Even dumb animals understand that...

At the time I was for my part aware that Jim understood nothing. It has been for him a source of eternal wonderment why he got a whipping and was not supposed to kill me. Poor common SA man that he was.

With brilliant logic the people placed the damned critter on a level with themselves and far over the Galicians, because they had succeeded in bring him up with their prejudices, and on account of the nature of the case he could never come higher up the ladder than to the dirty job of the executioner. But now they talked about *instinct*, about *the whisper of the blood* and about *the nobility of the soul* so that I as noble human being stood quite humiliated. The whisper of the blood! Have you heard such a thing!

Notes to "The Whisper of the Blood"

"Whisper of the Blood" exists in five distinct variants. It first appeared in Norwegian as "Blod og ære" (Blood and Honour) in *Maidagen* (1935), and then in a second variant as "30 juni" (June 30), again in Norwegian, but in the Swedish newspaper *Göteborgs Handels-och Sjöfarts-Tidning* (May 24, 1935). A Danish translation of "30 juni" with a few additions and alterations was published as "Racekamp" (Racial Struggle) in *Politiken* (June 12, 1935). The third variant reverts to the original title "Blod og ære," is found in the short story collection *Sandemose Forteller* (1937), and is quite similar to "30 juni" except it has a new introductory paragraph and some minor alterations, additions and omissions. A considerably reworked Norwegian variant came out during World War II as "Dumhetens opprør" (The Revolt of Stupidity) in Sweden in *Utenfor norskegrensen* (Outside the Norwegian Border) (Stockholm: Bonniers, 1943), and this appeared again under the same title and with extremely minor alterations in *Magasinet* 33-34 (Oslo) (August 14, 1948). The final variant, considerably rewritten from the previous ones and retitled "Herrefolk" (Master Race), was published in *Årstidene* (October 9, 1954). All of these articles have the same story of Sandemose's experiences with the dog Jim and his boots. This incident is also mentioned in

"Danskeren i Canada," *Danmarksposten* (June 1928). The differences in these variants mainly lie in the introductions and conclusions which in various forms discuss racial hatred, Nazism and what Sandemose considers the reign of stupidity.

The translation follows closely "30 juni," except I have omitted the final paragraph as being basically superfluous. Since the significance of the title of this version would perhaps not be readily apparent to the modern reader, and since using one of the other titles would strictly speaking not be correct, I chose to call it "Whisper of the Blood," a phrase Sandemose uses in the article.

It was on June 30, 1934, the "Night of the Long Knives," that Hitler carried out his bloody purge of the SA.

The story about Sandemose, Jim and the new boots has some basis in fact. In the early 1980s, when interviewing the sons of Peter Sorensen, the farmer Sandemose stayed with near Holden, Alberta, I asked each one separately whether they remembered the author. Though boys at the time, both immediately stated, "Oh, yes, he was the one our dog attacked when he came home with new boots he had bought at the Galician's store."

Go Back

During the winter of 1926–27 I lived on a little farm in the province of Alberta, close beside the Rocky Mountains.

It was very lonely there, and in the severe winter with the heavy snowfall, it happened that in the morning we could follow the coyote tracks in the snow over the roof of the house we lived in.

I was very depressed in those days, and in addition to everything else the deserted stretches of snow got on my nerves. I had had sad news from home, and there was no work that could occupy my thoughts. On the farm there was just one single room. Virtually everyone occupied it most of the day. Writing was impossible, and anything readable had been read many times over.

It happened that every day I wandered around with my gun. It was a countryside with large, sweeping hills of soil, often very high, and with deep valleys which they called *coulees*. I haven't seen a similar landscape anywhere.

To get up and down the hills in the deep snow was exhausting, and I don't use skis. There wasn't much game. The coyotes seldom came within rifle range—I shot two that winter, and strangely enough it was on the same day. Otherwise there were prairie chickens, hare and rabbits. The last mentioned were a plague.

One day toward evening I was working my way up over a steep hillside. It was an awful chore, but I was deep in thought as I struggled upward and wasn't thinking much about my surroundings. Finally it was a bit less steep, and I could walk more quickly.

Then it happened: A hand was placed on my right shoulder, and a voice said half-aloud, "Go back."

I whirled around, deeply dismayed—for no one was there. I stared at the snow where only my tracks were to be seen. I let my eyes wander over endless fields of snow. There wasn't a person anywhere.

I felt a streak of cold down my spine. And indeed it's true that the hairs can stand up on your head.

It was a good while before I continued upward, and now absolutely not lost in thought. My nerves were strung out, and I listened intently.

And it repeated itself. The hand was placed on my right shoulder, and the strange voice, this time louder and more urgently than before, said, "Go back."

I have never really liked telling what I experienced there in *East Coulee*. I don't want to be cited in support of all kinds of confused superstition. But what I'm relating did happen.

The second time I didn't turn around but remained standing, stiff as a statue and staring at the gun I was holding in my hands. "The hand" was removed from my shoulder, and the voice repeated—in a tone that sounded friendly—"Go back."

Then I slowly turned around. There was nothing to be seen, absolutely nothing, no other tracks in the snow but my own. Then suddenly I became angry. What was this? Had I gone crazy? Was I now beginning to hear harps in the air?

I certainly didn't want to go back. I went upward.

But there was a difference. I walked very slowly now, and was on the point of stopping at every step.

Naturally I was extremely excited and afraid, but also indignant. The encounter with a spirit had gradually made me furious.

For a moment I stood still and listened and looked behind me. Nothing. Then I carefully wanted to take one more step upward—but pulled my foot back and didn't budge an inch.

※

It happens now and then, especially during the spring flooding, that there's a landslide in these enormous hills. That had happened here. If I had continued as before, lost in my thoughts, I would have plunged fifty yards down and been killed on the spot.

※

There I stood staring down at three coyotes, stripping the carcass of a dead horse. The horse had not had anyone to warn it.

The coyotes looked up. They stood like myself without moving for a while, staring at me with their body-snatcher eyes. Then they disappeared with lightning speed through the narrow passage. I looked after them without shooting.

※

Once I told a man about *visions* I had had which had not managed to shake my conceptions about life and death. I told about a close relative who had shown himself to me several years after his death. When I was through with this, I began to explain how all of this had come about. That this relative had really been in the room, even though I had seen him clearly enough, I did not believe for a moment.

Then the man I had been speaking with jumped up from his chair and was raging mad. (He easily gets this way when he is not so already. He is constitutionally offended.) He struck his fist on the table and fumed, "This is intolerable! *You* see what I believe! I never see it, but I believe! It's unreasonable and incomprehensible that somebody like you should have second sight!"

I could have said a lot to this if I had been allowed to. I both hear and see a fair amount that is ridiculous and impermissible to see now that we live under the conventions of the machine age. But I think it is good when second sight is combined with common sense.

What happened in *East Coulee* seems to me quite simple. I knew it could be dangerous walking around there when the snow was deep and hiding dangerous precipices. So I was walking there and was daydreaming until I was warned by my own slumbering consciousness.

Notes to "Go Back"

First appearing as one of Sandemose's short essays which he wrote under the rubric "fra Kjørkelvik" (from Kjørkelvik [Sandemose's farm in southern Norway]) in *Aktuell* 24 (November 26, 1949), with no title, a virtually identical version was published with the title "Gå tilbake" (Go Back) in *Årstidene* 9–10 (1954). The incident is also mentioned in "Han gad ikke flytte sig" (He Couldn't Manage to Move), *Dagbladet* (May 16, 1935), and it is used in the novel *Ross Dane* in conjunction with one of Theodor's hunting trips.

The translation, except for the omission of one superfluous sentence, follows closely the original.

The Prairie—Long Ago

The western horizon was flaming red after the sunset when I came out onto the veranda, and it reminded me suddenly about something I had forgotten long ago: The red sky which I thought was a fire—once in the province of Saskatchewan in Canada. I was on the way out to see to the horses in the evening, and I have never seen the like of it either before or after. It was the moon rising. I count on my fingers and think, heaven's sake, that was thirty-eight years ago. It's certainly true that time flies. I read some place or other that it makes real headway. And I can add: Gradually it quite quietly does away with us all.

A great deal must have changed. It was twelve miles to the closest neighbour and no roads. You sat up on a horse and said, "Get up." Even though a horse could break its leg in a badger hole, there was no danger, not even a tame Indian. Now they probably have super highways and don't know what a horse looks like. In addition to twelve or fourteen horses there was a herd of pigs, a lot of chickens and two cows. In the evening we went out and threw stones at the pigs. That was our little diversion. We didn't need any scorecard. The pigs kept score themselves.

※

I remember something I experienced which was a mixture of comedy, foolishness and personal danger. The wheat fields were so large and the working day so long that it wasn't always possible to get back to the farm in the evening during the busy harvest season. Then we lived in a "caboose" which most resembled the circus wagon that older people remember from their childhood. We lay there on straw on the floor, and the unwieldy rig would be moved from place to place by a swarm of horses. The threshing machine followed along as well. It was in October and there was frost.

One evening we were sitting playing cards (we had no pigs to throw stones at) when one of the men had to go on an errand. He had just come in the door when he let out an ungodly screech and fell over backward.

I had good cards. I pressed them against my chest so that no one would see them and ran over to find out what was going on. I tell you I got a shock. There stood an enormous, shaggy grizzly bear, sticking its paw out at me. The forest limit was not so far away, but nevertheless no one dreamed of encountering a bear. The explanation is that it was an old male—I was told afterward—which hadn't eaten enough before it was supposed to go into hibernation, and these roam around uneasily and normally die. They are usually killers, because human beings are comparatively easy prey.

Now it happened that I didn't want to lose the good cards I had in my hand, nor did I want to be taken by the bear. Therefore I poked at it with my right fist. In the same moment it had ripped my coat sleeve—without my having received a scratch. Simultaneously a crash shook the caboose—and me. It was a bearded fellow from Copenhagen, originally a baker's apprentice, who had fired his rifle right next to my ear.

The bear sailed over on its side like a haystack and there it lay. In spite of my being almost deaf, I heard someone yell behind me, "You've gone off your goddamn rocker! (it was me and not the bear he was speaking to). Your father must have been standing on his head when he sired you! Idiot!"

I was suddenly very agitated, familiar as I was with the level-headed Copenhagener's mode of expression. He did what a kind mother would do in her great fear—box the child's ears when it just barely avoids being hit by a car. The baker was white with fright on my account, but only he and I understood that.

Later I was made fun of unmercifully for a long time, "There he is! The guy who wanted to kill a bear with his bare hands. No, with just one hand!"

༄༅

It was in Canada I made the final decision about my future, even though it took three more years before it was realized. I had been split nationally since I was a child, and I had at that time ended up with the idea that I could turn my back on both Denmark and Norway—and emigrate. Choose a third. But I saw in Canada the complete denationalizing that would be the consequence of that, and I saw that the one who thinks he has got rid of the national [identity] always gets into a miserable situation. You see, he hasn't got rid of it. He just becomes confused. I have said many times after: He who emigrates chooses the cheapest way to make himself unhappy. You see the clearest trait already before the person changes countries. He leaves with scornful words for the old country, and he disdains it when he's home on a visit—but in the new country he keeps to his own people, and it's a rule that he never learns the new language, however much he thinks he does himself. The lack of a cultural atmosphere on the prairie was total. An idea often occurred to me: If you put one or another animal in a box and let it loose on the other side of the world, and it can get food there, then it will settle in as if nothing had happened. But it encounters so many strange things that it has to accept and regard as normal, and it will never, deep in its dark soul, get rid of a consuming unrest. No animal has ever been at home in a zoo until after several generations, and most of them never become so.

༄༅

Canada taught me a third thing. I had come from a different background and could never move into Canadian culture—perhaps just touch on a corner of it.

Even though I have written three books about farmers in Canada and have been quite well acquainted with the conditions as they were back then in the twenties, the country has become quite distant for me. Names of people and places are hazy, something which certainly is connected with the fact that I left there with such a definite feeling that it could never become my country. Perhaps a year ago I got a letter from a man over there. It was clear we must have known each other quite well, but it was impossible for me to place him in my memory.

What is clearest in my mind are some hunting trips on sleds on the prairie for coyotes, bushes of prairie rose, the distant horizon and perhaps most of all the flocks of working horses in the harsh winter. They were let loose when the harvest was finished and managed remarkably well in the cold and the deep snow. They were sleek and fine all winter. It was my job to go out when evening approached and give them a little salt and a fistful of wheat each. That kept them more or less in the area. Otherwise they were given nothing. When a crust had come on the snow they got bloody hooves from kicking down to the meagre bits of grass.

Most of the prairie life is distant, endlessly distant. The machines, cars, roads, the radio, television and the telephone must have changed everything, and probably only people over fifty remember how it was.

Notes to "The Prairie—Long Ago"

"Prærien—for lenge siden" (The Prairie—Long Ago), *Aktuell* 4 (January 25, 1965), is Sandemose's last Canada article, written almost eight months before he died on June 8, 1965.

The translation follows closely the original except for some changes in paragraphing.

FICTIONAL STORIES

Cover-Up

Vilfred Larsen stopped the self binder, crept down off it and walked over the stubble field toward the men who were tying sheaves together. His look was gruff. The six men glanced out of the corners of their eyes at him. What now?

"Fred and William," said Vilfred coldly. "This evening you can get your pay."

"All right," snarled Fred.

But William took measure of his employer. His small pig-like eyes glowed.

"Don't we work hard enough, Vil?"

"No," snapped Vilfred, "not according to my way of thinking. I'll drive you down to the station, if you want."

Nothing more was said. Vilfred went over to the other self binder and helped the farm-hand fix something that was wrong with it. Then he started driving again with his own.

It was windy and cold. The sky was covered with clouds. Vilfred Larsen was reddish blue in his face. He frequently cast a glance to the north and mumbled to himself the same words: "Late fall and early winter. There's no use for lazy apes here."

He saw that William and Fred were slacking off even more. Fine. This evening they'd be gone. The other four men were OK. They didn't seem to be that busy, but they got the job done. None of them made a superfluous movement. But without stop the sheaves steadily rose up after them. Vilfred nodded approvingly to himself. Those four wouldn't regret it, if they remained with him during the threshing too.

Fred and William didn't want to accept any favours from the stuck-up Dane Vilfred Larsen. In the evening they went to the nearest wheat farm, while Vilfred alone in his old Ford drove to the station to see if there were any people needing work.

The station master said that there were a couple over at the Chinaman's restaurant. One of them was a large man and the other a boy. Both of them Danes, as far as he could tell. Vilfred went over to the Chinaman's and hired the two of them, though he had some reservations about the younger one. They were, quite rightly, Danes but for that matter knew nothing about each other. It was a casual acquaintance from the train. The "boy" was probably twenty and called himself Hartvig. He was slender, and his hands weren't used to work. A runaway clerk out for adventure in the wild west, thought Vilfred derisively and tried to catch his glance. But half of Hartvig's face remained hidden under a ragged straw hat. He was probably embarrassed, because his face was disfigured by what may have been a birthmark.

Well, anyway, Vilfred would give him a chance. Often there was energy in such frail fellows after all.

Vilfred Larsen was a self-absorbed man. He didn't pay much attention to his hired help, only to what they accomplished. And when it came to Hartvig, Vilfred was moved by a kind of pity. It was so clear that the young man did everything he could to keep up, even though the results were not stellar.

Five years had passed since Vilfred Larsen had given up his position as manager in Denmark to make his way in Canada, and he had been lucky, though what he had going for him was not luck but iron-hard energy. He had always liked working, but he'd never toiled as here on the prairie, where it wasn't only desire that drove him forward, but the need to forget a past. It could still shock him when he remembered the humiliation he'd suffered. At the memory of it his cheeks could get even redder than the prairie weather had made them, and through his brain could pass indistinct ideas of his working and toiling here in this country so that sometime he'd be able to take vengeance.

It concerned a woman, naturally. Her name was Else and she was the daughter of a man who lived off his money. The thought that she belonged too high up in the social ranks for him had never occurred to Vilfred, even though he later saw clearly that she herself had thought this was so. He snorted full of contempt. Such a little thing her brain had been! She was pompous and provincially comical, he told himself—tremendously conceited because a local newspaper had praised her as a pianist, and her father didn't have to work.

This last fact tormented Vilfred the most. Work and the work ethic were for him the only things which in this world could give a man a measure of nobility, and deep down he had in reality despised Else's father who in his best years shoved all work aside because he'd got an inheritance.

Else had toyed with him, yes, and he had allowed himself to be toyed with. When he took her seriously, she'd made fun of him. Some unimportant townspeople had enjoyed his defeat.

Vilfred had written her off, as he himself expressed it. But all the same he couldn't forget her. He was ashamed at his weakness, but that didn't diminish it. And since Vilfred was not one of those who go around being sentimental and displaying a wounded heart, one fine day he went his way.

℘ଔ

The weather became colder, and when the threshing began there was severe frost during the nights. The hillsides to the north were white with rime during the days. The farmers buckled down to it. The smoke and the splintered straw surged out from the threshing machines in drifting clouds. Dismissal without mercy was the consequence for anyone who couldn't keep up the tempo. Long before the sun rose, the wagons began to drive and the threshing machines to hammer. From many places in the province there were reports of snow.

For Vilfred it was prosperity or ruin. He almost didn't sleep any more, and he worked as three. His whole mind was turned toward the one thing—to save the harvest. He laboured mechanically like a machine, overworked and suffering from lack of sleep.

Then he was dealt a blow that was as brutal as it was unexpected. Shortly after the threshing machine had been started one morning, it refused to function. Vilfred worked on it for a while and was half crazed with rage when he found out what was wrong: all the oil cups were full of grinding powder.

As quick as lightening all the names of those who might be his enemies went through his mind. Which one of them had committed such a spiteful outrage? He couldn't comprehend it. He admitted he had enemies. His nature was such that it couldn't be otherwise. But they were all honourable people—he could suspect none of them of dirty tricks. He stood stooping with an oil cup in his hand and stared with his tired, bloodshot eyes at each man. They were diligent, hard-working fellows. The only one who was a bit strange was little Hartvig, who never met his boss' glance and always kept himself at a distance. But no, the fellow must be thankful that he was allowed to stay here. He was so puny—and unsightly. The birthmark on his face was ugly…

A man came up and said softly, "Fred and William are hanging around the neighbourhood. Nobody has wanted to keep them."

Vilfred looked sharply at him. "Well, what's done is done. Now we have to get the machine going again—and keep an eye out."

Twenty-four valuable hours were lost for Vilfred Larsen, and yet he had to be glad the damage was not greater. When the reparation was finished, he walked around on guard with his rifle over his shoulder beside his threshing machine and never left it day or night as he goaded his men through the fifteen-hour workdays. The other farmers grumbled at the high wages he was now paying. They neither would nor could follow suit, but Vilfred chased them away anyhow—here it was he who was in charge!

And his crew was achieving the incredible. However, he could see that Hartvig could not go on. True, his hands no longer bled—their skin had grown thick—but twice Vilfred had seen him pass out over the sheaves. He had acquired a real respect for the little chap who each time got up and staggered on again. What a youngster! Many a big strong fellow should have half Hartvig's fighting spirit!

Then a sturdy worker from the station came out to Vilfred's looking for a job. Vilfred hired him immediately and called to Hartvig.

"You've been all right," he said curtly. "But I'm tired and can't manage to look after the chickens on the farm as well. That's your job now. Go home."

Hartvig didn't look up. "All right," he said faintly and left the threshing machine.

In the cold night Vilfred sat in a straw stack near the threshing machine, nodding. Now and then he straightened his head up and looked at his precious machine. There would be the whine of a rifle bullet if anyone got close to it.

His eyes tried to penetrate the darkness lying over his fields. No, they wouldn't strike him down. If they thought they could, then they didn't know the Dane Vilfred Larsen.

He smiled, tired, and nodded again. It became so remarkably light over the countryside. It was as though the darkness retreated … it was indeed not at all a raw autumn night. The prairie lay bathed in the rays from the rising sun. It was spring, spring. The dew gleamed on the green grain. Soon she would come… there she came, Else. She nodded smiling at him as though they had seen each other only yesterday. Never had anything come between them.

෨෬

With a happy smile on his lips, the exhausted man lay back in the straw stack and slept, while a coyote howled at the moon far away which became visible for a moment as though falling down through the scudding clouds. He slept, slept like a rock, more unconscious than sleeping.

Somebody was shaking him. For a long time he didn't notice. His listless eyes finally opened slowly. He saw someone bending over him.

"Are you hurt? Answer me, Vilfred!"

Suddenly, like an animal, he jumped up. It was light over the prairie. Round about stood his men with horses. "Come on, come on," said a man on the verge of tears, "there's trouble again."

Vilfred ran with him over to the other side of the threshing machine. There lay two lifeless men. One of them was William. His face was full of blood. The other was Hartvig. The blood lay clotted on his one shoulder from a knife wound. Vilfred's thoughts were quickly on the threshing machine. A pile of hay had been burning up next to the machine. God bless Hartvig!

They were both alive. Vilfred asked for water and loosened Hartvig's shirt. Just as he reached his hand out for the water, it sank powerless. Shaking and white as a sheet he jumped up at his men who were standing in a circle, "Go away! Are you deaf? Get out of here!"

They moved, nervous at his vehemence. With a gentle touch he washed the wounded chest which belonged—to a woman. Then he stretched out his hand for an oil can and rubbed the red scar "Hartvig" had on his face. It was a fake.

Vilfred forgot everything around him. He carefully lifted Else up and walked with her to the farm. His features were as calm as stone, but five years of stored-up anger had melted away in an instant.

How much had his Else been worth after all. She had really loved him... When he was gone, and she had only the town dandies left, the months and years that passed had told her whom she was in love with ... but they had told her more: that she had scoffed at a working man and had wounded him in the heart by doing so—and had incurred his contempt. That could not be erased with a word.

Vilfred Larsen laughed quietly, a good happy laughter, his first in many years.

Notes to "Cover-Up"

The original title of "Cover-up" is "En Pige gaar til Canossa" (A Girl Eats Humble Pie) in the Danish journal *Søndags B.T.* 33 (August 18, 1929). There is no other version.

In the translation the paragraphing has been changed somewhat and a few very minor sentences and phrases have been omitted to make the text flow more easily in English. The title was altered to make the ending of the story a bit more unexpected.

Norwegian Amazons

Whether the two Huseby sisters had left Norway because they had been disappointed in love or in something else, they hid it well, perhaps because they didn't know whether they should be disappointed more than most people.

Kaja and Marie Huseby were sisters, but not twins, though they resembled each other almost to a fault. There were reasons for rumours to circulate around the two of them. They were enormous women with arms and legs like posts and unusually large feet. They had a long, horsey look in their faces, strong jawbones and large noses and ears. Their blue eyes were calm and sharp with authority.

Anyway, ugly they were not. Or they were, but only to someone with poorly developed taste.

To see one of them behind the plough was like watching the legendary giantess Gefjon ploughing the Danish island of Zealand out of Sweden. For Kaja and Marie farmed and did so with a perfection which put both Scandinavians and Germans in the neighbourhood to shame.

They had drawn attention to themselves the moment they had left the boat in Quebec, and probably they had also done the same on board and back home in Norway. At the emigration office the authorities were a little confused; to which housewife dared they send one of the giant women, or perhaps even both of them?

They telephoned east and west. Everyone was dismayed at the description and declined with thanks.

"I understand so well," said the immigration inspector and laughed almost hysterically. "First you'd have to install reinforcements in the house those two ladies are going to turn around in! And just look at their hands—I wouldn't want to get into a disagreement with either of them."

In the meantime the sisters sat dominating in the middle of the hall on the enormous pieces of luggage they themselves had carried in on their backs. They waited quietly until most of the others had been attended to. Neither of them said a word, but they observed everything. At last Kaja said, "Well, Marie, I guess we'd better find out how you get to this Sasperastesevan."

They intended to go to the prairies to the province of Saskatchewan.

At last a small, scrawny man stood before them and asked what they actually had in mind. He spoke a language he thought was Norwegian, a belief the sisters did not share and therefore they regarded him rather coolly. Others came and stood a ways behind them. He pointed at the luggage and the sisters and asked, "Where you go?"

"Saspekarasje—eh," said Marie.

"Where?" the man repeated.

Kaja took out the papers. Oh! The man was delighted. These were then two farmers who had money and wanted to buy land in Saskatchewan! One might have thought so right away. But the man was still bewildered.

How much money did they have? Kaja spoke up and declared that she didn't know it was anyone's business. The man inquired how large the cheques were which had been issued to the sisters, but none had been issued! Kaja had cash on her some place…

Then they took the train west. There was a woman who was supposed to look after the female immigrants. She was Norwegian-born and took her position seriously. She glided upright and stiff into the car where Kaja and Marie were and read from a piece of paper without first deigning to give them a glance. "Kaja and Marie Huseby, is that you?"

She lifted her eyes and looked authoritatively at them. But her authority faded away, and her jaw sank when she caught sight of the two. They looked for a moment at her. Then Marie said in a calm and deliberate voice to Kaja, "It's strange how many there are who want to stick their noses into other people's business here in Canada."

"Well...eh..." said the woman, and shrank at least a foot. "I'm here to look after young girls travelling..." Kaja and Marie smiled imperceptively. The lady disappeared without giving any directives.

They attracted considerable attention in the little town in Saskatchewan. The Ukrainian who sold land was overawed for the first time in his life when he sat alone with Kaja and Marie in his office. Marie had sat down by the door, while Kaja stood in the middle of the floor and expressed herself with some curtness as to how the sale should be arranged. The little salesman kept glancing at the door, the windows and the telephone.

"Well...eh..." he said, confused, and looked furtively from one to the other. He got out one of his standard contracts which it later turned out the sisters knew by heart. Kaja cooly struck out a large number of paragraphs in it and suggested a different price.

"Well...," said the man.

"Fine," said Kaja, entered the figure herself and signed below. She gave the Ukrainian the pen. He dipped it nervously several times, but signed with a start when he heard Marie get up and cough. She signed as well, after which Kaja undid several layers of clothes on her broad chest, took out a heavy leather folder with copper mountings and paid with crisp, new dollar notes.

Then they said goodbye, but not thank you, and left. The same day they had the plough in the ground. The Ukrainian was left sitting shamefaced, but concealed his defeat with great care. "Oh yes, not a bad sale," he said to his neighbour, the doctor. "Do you think there are many such ladies in Norway, doctor?"

It wasn't until two years later, after one evening having drunk too much moonshine whisky and lying under the table, that he confided whimpering to a lively party how miserably he had been cheated by those two Norwegian giant women. "They were as enormous as houses," he cried, "I knew they would kill me if I contradicted them, but I was alone—the sheriff was away. Besides, do you think they would have cared about a miserable sheriff? Of course I've cheated all Norwegians as well as I could, but still, I haven't nearly recovered the money."

When the first surprise at the two women had died down, people quickly got used to them. At home they had often seen, for example, widows doing farm work, so this was perhaps not so strange. And Kaja and Marie Huseby did a good job of minding their own business.

Therefore people didn't have anything to talk about except their appearance—which, it's true, gave them the opportunity for many a witticism. But yet it was as though there wasn't any real colour to the joke. In fact they feared each one of the sisters to the same extent as they had feared their childhood teachers. Whenever one of the Husebys appeared, men were at a loss for words and didn't really know what they should do with themselves. A question from one of them was answered by big, strong men in a slightly quavering voice as their eyes wavered.

"They're good enough," said a Danish farmer one Sunday at church. "If it wasn't because I knew they'd say no, I could well imagine getting married to one of them myself."

Well, that Jens Pedersen was always pretty loose-tongued. But the group quieted down as several of them became pensive. The sisters were good, capable girls who to tell the truth also had a sort of beauty…and they had a heart for those who suffered misfortune—anyone taken by a Huseby might be in for a lot of fun!

The colony was primarily Danish with a few Norwegians, Swedes, Germans and Dutch. It was as if the Huseby girls wanted not only to manage by themselves, but also without fellow countrymen in the vicinity. They must have had to put up with taunting all the way from childhood back home in Norway. How could it be otherwise? Those who are peculiar have to suffer through that wherever in the world they may be.

One evening into the fall when the Huseby sisters had been farming for a couple of years, a man came to a farm in the colony inquiring about work. His name was Torvald and he was from the west.

The owner of the farm was repairing the self-binder and didn't have time for talk. It was in the middle of the busiest harvest time, and the radio had just sent out a weather report which wouldn't serve to calm anyone. No, he didn't need help. He glanced quickly at the man and continued with his work.

Torvald didn't awaken any sympathy with him, either. He was a bearded man of average height in his late twenties and with a constantly self-conscious and easily offended look. A moment later the farmer looked around for a tool and discovered Torvald again.

"Well actually," he said, his head disappearing back into the machine, "I heard today that they have use for a man over at Huseby's."

"What kind of people are they, anyway?" asked Torvald curious.

"Are you picky?" snarled the man from inside the binder. "They're the kind of people who pay a man exactly what he's worth. They are the Huseby girls."

"Girls?" said Torvald, a bit bewildered.

The farmer lifted his head and pointed.

"That's the red buildings over there. They are two Norwegian sisters who run the farm alone. They have no help at the present. It's well worth your putting on the charm for them," he concluded derisively and kept on with his work.

Torvald gave him a hostile look, but now had something else to think about. For a long time he gazed over at the Huseby farm, but was gone when the farmer again looked up from the self-binder.

The next morning Jens Pedersen went over to the station to get the mail. On the platform stood the stationmaster taking in the sun. "Hello, John," he said, stretching. "Isn't there any peace around this fine place anymore?"

"Peace?" said Jens. "What are you talking about?"

"One of your countrymen came here and took the train east this morning. He looked as though he had been straight through twelve threshing machines. Yes, sir. He was hanging his head. His hair was gone, and the bits of beard didn't exactly improve his looks. He was limping and holding his stomach."

"Don't know anything about it," said Jens. "Did you ask him?"

"Yes indeed. He said a team of horses had run over him, but I think he was lying. It was the new man who came yesterday."

Jens Pedersen forgot the story; he was very busy. But that evening he was reminded of it by Kaja Huseby, who came to buy baling wire.

"I don't understand what sort of countryman of yours it was who came to visit us late yesterday evening. It wasn't Saturday night, either."

Jens suddenly remembered what he had heard that morning and started questioning Kaja.

"I tell you, Marie and I were lying in bed almost asleep when we heard somebody coming into the house. We wondered who could be rummaging around in there, but we stayed in bed because we were tired. Then somebody turned the doorknob and opened the door. Marie and I raised our heads and asked who it was. He said, 'Shh, you don't have to be frightened.' You see it was a man."

A broad smile appeared on Jens Pedersen's face. It was a comical thought that someone had asked Kaja and Marie not to be frightened.

"We were a bit surprised, you know," continued Kaja, "and Marie says, 'Who is it?'"

"He said, 'Shh, I just want to say hello to you. Don't be frightened. I'm not a people eater.'"

"'No, then you'd be the first one of those I've run into,' I said. Then he laughed and got quite bold."

"He said, 'I thought maybe since nobody knew there was anybody visiting around here…' and he smiled foolishly."

"'Well,' I said, 'but be off with you. We want to sleep.'"

"He laughed at that. On the whole he was quite mirthful," continued Kaja. 'Idiot,' I said and I turned over on my other side. 'Get out.'"

"But I declare if he didn't come over and sit on the edge of the bed beside me."

"'Do I want you sitting there?' I said. He was still just as silly and wanted to hold my hand."

Jens Pedersen was on the point of choking as Kaja blithely continued, "I let him do it too, but it was as if he didn't really want to when it came down to it."

"'Ow, darn it,' he yelled, 'what are you pinching my fingers in…'"

Kaja looked smiling at her large, muscular hand. No, it seemed he didn't like holding Kaja Huseby's hand anyhow. "Since he kept on yelling, I pushed him back into the bed so his legs were kicking in the air. Now he didn't yell any more, but he struggled bravely… I think he was just about to cry, because he didn't know where he was. Maybe he thought he was in a threshing machine…"

Jens Pedersen squirmed with delight and said, "The station master thought he had been through twelve of them!"

"Oh, no, two can do the job," said Kaja calmly. "You see, my sister can get quite riled up and she wanted to get her night's rest. When she caught sight of the man's legs almost up to the ceiling, she went completely crazy! She said, 'Have you ever seen such a vulgar fellow!' and she raised herself up in the bed. Then she took the man by the legs, whirled him around over her head and threw him against the door."

Jens became pale and didn't laugh any more.

"You know our doors don't amount to much. They were just temporarily thrown together. And this door didn't hold. Pieces of wood and the man flew right out into the front room. He lay out there wailing. Marie said, 'Shut up!' and she lay back down. But I stood up to see whether he could get home by himself. Otherwise we would have let him stay in our house in spite of everything, if he had wanted to…"

"Could he walk?"

"I don't know," said Kaja thoughtfully. "But I tell you, he could run."

"He got a real fright!"

"Do you think so?" asked Kaja innocently, as she took the sack of binding wire on her back and prepared to go. "Well, then we're bound to get a good night's sleep, my sister and I."

Notes to "Norwegian Amazons"

"Norske amasoner. Fortelling fra Kanada" (Norwegian Amazons. Story from Canada), *Hjemmet* 12 (Oslo) 12 (March 19, 1932), is the first Canada article or short story that Sandemose wrote originally in Norwegian. Two years later it was translated into Danish and published in *Hjemmet* 19 (Copenhagen) (May 12, 1934) with the title "Norske Amazoner."

The translation follows the original, except a few minor short passages are omitted to make the text flow more smoothly in English, and the paragraphing has been changed somewhat.

Happiness

The city of Calgary is situated at the foot of the Rocky Mountains. I had been there several days waiting for money but was otherwise not suffering any privation. I just didn't have enough cash to travel on east, to Europe. After a difficult time everything had turned out for the best. Now I was going home after two years of roaming around in order to begin exactly where I had started. A newspaper had sent me out for six months, but after they had passed, I'd taken work on a farm, stopped writing for a long time and thought quite a bit about staying in the country for good. Not because I liked it there. I didn't like any place that time. Then it came over me one bitterly cold winter day that I wanted to go home.

It was awful in Calgary. I don't mean that as an insult. It's said that Calgary is a pretty city, that is for a prairie city, and no doubt it is, too. But now I wanted to leave.

I currently don't remember anything from Calgary except a bridge, a river under it and a gorilla that laughed. I was standing on the bridge looking down at the ice where there was a pitch-black channel with rushing water. It was snowing a little and windy. Then someone laughed beside my ear. I quickly turned around, expecting to see one or another of my acquaintances from the prairie, but recoiled at the sight of an abominable face grinning at me. A hairy creature with a broad nose which had fallen in by its roots, hair everywhere and a yellow row of teeth. But its eyes were gentle. I have never seen such kind eyes. Its arms were the most unbelievable graspers any man has ever had. They could crush the rib cage of any human being.

Somebody said, "Come on," and took a friendly hold of the animal. They walked on over the bridge. So that's the way a person could look. Such things are otherwise only seen in dreams. There was no doubt that the poor thing's mental powers had been extinguished. He was led off like a kindly bear.

The strange individual was certainly not insane. His soul was well off in accord with his animal shape. I had seen *the missing link* large as life. A tame half-man which a human being was leading by a rope. Recovery? The creature was not sick. Nothing was wrong with him. He was what he was. I feel the same way now as when I have previously spoken about this encounter. I try to avoid the designation *man*, *person* or *he* regarding the phenomenon. But since it is certainly a scientific fact that the thing was a person, a man and a he, I will use the words anyway, for the sake of convenience, even though I think they sound strange here. It was not a person. Perhaps I can best express it by saying that I consider it natural to call the character a he-person. Then it's as though he is categorized.

That same evening my train left, and I went to bed the moment the bunks were pulled down at nine o'clock, turned on the reading light and cuddled up with a book. It was a blood-curdling story called *Cold Harbour* which described a father who really abused his children. He made them imagine that the farm where they lived was full of ghosts, after which he himself played ghost at night and made tracks of blood after him with beet juice. No punch was spared, and the concluding deaths were entirely satisfactory. The book was furnished with a dedication to Dr. Axel Munthe who, among other things, also sells the books their authors give him.

As the train trundled eastward with the modest speed the blatantly advertised trains manage to work themselves up to on the American continent, I naturally dreamed about ghosts and inhuman fathers. It was an average nightmare that woke me up—a hairy hand on the throat, you know, and a scream for help, except that you're not able to scream. And there stood the ghost, grinning, evil and alive without a thread of clothing on its body.

The curtain of my bunk was drawn to the side, and there stood the hairy person from the bridge in Calgary. Someone came padding on naked feet, "come on, you, come on now. Look here my friend, here's your bed."

He looked frightful. Hairy as a bear with in-turned knees and parallel thighs, a rib cage like a syrup barrel. He nodded at me. His eyes were smiling. Whatever he was, he had the world's most beautiful human eyes!

The other one led him away and came back a while later to give me an apology. He introduced himself, Mr. So-and-So, something about the police. On the way to Bulgaria with that there person—

Bulgaria?

Yeah,—it was like this. The sick fellow had entered the country as an immigrant, no one knew how. Perhaps he had been trained to appear rational for a time, or whatever.

I asked if it wouldn't be cheaper to place the man here in Canada.

Well, maybe, but of course he has quite a constitution and is only twenty years old. He could live for seventy more years. As you see, he's no desirable emigrant. Unfortunate material, if I do say so. And the law, Sir, remember that. The law says we have to send such people home. And the law is not that stupid. We have to teach the Bulgarians that they can spare that sort of thing here. As far as we're concerned they can send their sick people wherever they want to, or build themselves an asylum. There must be some method in the madness, if I do say so.

I clearly got the impression that the policeman had in no way protested a vacation in Bulgaria, half way around the world. Perhaps he himself had sneaked the unfortunate person through immigration in order to get himself a trip to Bulgaria afterward. Or there was a sinister agreement among many functionaries who divided the trip among themselves. A lot of strange things go on.

The next morning I would get another shock. I was standing with my head in the washbasin and rose up to look for a towel. For some reason or other you can never find a towel. Instead I found the gorilla. He was standing behind me, clad in all his hair, but otherwise completely naked. Some people protested, but the Bulgarian just smiled. And when we totalled a dozen grown men and together felt ourselves secure, we also began to smile until the whole group laughed.

Into the room came the keeper, fuming with rage. But then he too began to laugh and pulled a shirt down over the wildman's head. "You have to understand you're not supposed to do that," he said in a fatherly tone.

The man hadn't done anything at all.

It was soon that everyone on the train felt responsibility for the hairy one, not least the ladies. They enjoyed giving him cigarettes which he turned over many times before tentatively eating one, just as an ape would have done. No human experience seemed to have left a trace on him. He didn't understand a word of any language. He merely smiled that inscrutable smile of his.

This human being who was without spirit supplied the passengers on the train with a new spirit. Whenever someone was sitting in conversation with a lady the hairy one could appear, and the tone of the group immediately changed. How can I express it? He was a bridge from one sex to the other. Whenever he sat between a woman and a man the three became one.

Perhaps no one at all discovered anything until afterward, but there was a conjugal-like atmosphere over the sleeping car. We were all on a honeymoon with each other. An elderly Miss from Vancouver fell so in love with men that it was purely remarkable, and her eyes acquired a sparkle they certainly hadn't had for many years.

Then came the scandal: The hairy one disappeared at a little country station. We had to do without him or his keeper for the rest of the trip to Toronto. The atmosphere was quite aboil. We had endless discussions and bought every single newspaper at every station. There wasn't a word in any of them regarding the matter. One would have thought it was the Governor General himself who had disappeared. If one of us others had got off the train for good, even if he had intended to go to Bulgaria, scarcely a single individual would have given it a second thought. But now it was an absolutely unimportant individual who didn't even belong to the human race, and that was something else.

We all became friends and confidants, and when the train eventually reached Toronto, it was as though we couldn't part from each other. We were almost like a swarm of bees when the queen has disappeared. The elderly Miss from Vancouver stood with dull eyes on the platform, thinking of vanished happiness.

Three months later I was sitting one day on the top of a bus in London—and suddenly let out a triumphant roar. Down in the middle of the street stood the hairy one causing a traffic jam. The keeper was the same one as before. He was trying to clear a path out into the street where taxis and busses were honking in a maelstrom around the half-human—who stood smiling with his thick hair down in front of his eyes. Now the keeper got his hands on him. Curses and shouts of surprise rained down. My bus rumbled on. I stood up on the seat and stared through the misty rain. It was as though I had finally and irrevocably lost a brother.

Notes to "Happiness"

The first time "Happiness" was published was in *Lørdagskvelden* 15 (June 8, 1935) where its Norwegian title was "Den glade mann" (The Happy Man). The next time it appeared, in *Sandemose Forteller* (1937) its title was changed to "Lykken" (Happiness). This is slightly shorter than "Den glade mann" with several changes in wording and orthography. The story was translated into Danish ("Lykken"), *Social-Demokraten, Hjemmets Søndag* (February 6, 1938), and Swedish ("Lyckan") *Lørdagsexpressen* (December 23, 1944). Virtually unchanged from the version in *Sandemose Forteller*, except for a few differences in wording and orthography, it came out in Norwegian again as "Lykken" in *Kring jul. Radiogavefondets julehefte* (1951), and as "En lykkelig mann" (A Happy Man) in *Årstidene* 9–10 (1954) and *Dans, dans, Roselill* (1965).

The translation is essentially of the "Den glade mann" but some of the phraseology is taken from the other versions when they seem to flow better in English. Also, a few contemporary references are omitted.

The Wolf Trap

If there's a stupid person in a house, it's stupidity that reigns. The stupid person doesn't let himself be raised up. It is always he who drags others down, because if they are to defend themselves against the stupid person, they have to use *his* weapons and not their own which are ineffective on him. It's not always that you can go your way and leave stupidity to itself. Some of the deepest tragedies in history and in private life are due to people having been handed over to stupidity. We will let historical events speak for themselves here. In private life the one who's best armed can often be completely in the power of the lesser one. It can be children who bind one; or the lesser gifted person can be in possession of traits one has grown fond of, so that it's an even greater misfortune to cut the bond rather than to let it be.

In Canada I once worked on a farm for a childless, middle-aged couple. They sat there on that remote place and had nothing else to stare at but their farmhand. They observed him from early morning to late in the evening with close attention, and nothing escaped them. No place in the world can life unfold so provincially, with such an almost naked stupidity, as in the celebrated free America. Modern authors have at last cut deep down into the dogma that all Americans are happy, wise and rich.

What plagued me most about these two was perhaps the language. They say that the eyes are the mirror of the soul, a phrase which is true nowhere. The mirror of the soul, or if you like, its tone, is naturally language. In their reports policemen ought to mention a person's vocabulary, whether he or she is in command of 100,000, 50,000, 1,000 or three hundred words. The farm couple I had sold myself to had 34 words.

I took the job during the spring and secured myself the right to stay over the winter. It is—or was—very common to make such an arrangement. From spring to autumn there was too little manpower, and the farmers fought over it. During the winter there was no use for people in the extensive farming, and the jobless flocked into the larger cities where they soon suffered bitter privation. Many did as I did—got work from spring to fall with normal pay, but with the right to continue over the winter without cash payment. It was not all who could get work in the forests, and others wanted to have the chance to get paid work. They seldom found any.

It was into October, and I had no desire to leave, though staying was a pain. I had money, but not enough to live on for more than a couple of months, and then only if I were careful. The last half of the winter would be a time of hunger and cold—and then I had to begin from the beginning in the spring without having come any further than the year before.

Both the farmer and his wife were incredibly curious. They asked and dug and ascertained. They were intensely occupied with my parents, how many brothers and sisters I had back in a country they had never heard of, if they were married, had children, how many and how many of each—if I myself had been engaged or married and even why no answer had come from a man they knew I had written to a couple of months before.

In the outbuilding where I lived and which I had to keep tidy myself, the woman had been sniffing around every day when I had been far enough away. I soon began laying small traps for her and knew that never a day went by without everything's being examined. A little piece of a match, which every morning I put on top of my unlocked suitcase, was never there in the evening.

I know, it was petty and mean of me. I could have just let the old lady rummage around.

But that's the way it is being in the claws of stupidity. If you don't get stupid from it yourself, then you don't at any rate get any wiser. Besides, there were letters in that suitcase, sad letters that I didn't want in stupidity's hands, letters about sorrows I couldn't remedy, even though I wanted to.

It happens you hurt people without wanting to and without actually doing so either, but by the mere fact of your existence are guilty of those bad things. I had been a person's misfortune and couldn't help it. Who wants stupidity to have its claws in such things and give its interpretation? Now those letters have been burned long ago, and I could have burned them at the time, but it can be so strange with the outer things. They are an indifferent shell around the inner and actual things. Reason tells us that. But the senses must support themselves by these outer things, and we have to keep them close to us or a dream dies out of them. It happens that the dream never dies out of a child's shoe you have locked in a drawer. Only stupidity derides the one who keeps a splinter of the cross of Christ.

No other letters came to the farm besides those I received. When the first letter arrived, the couple settled themselves in a chair to hear what was in it. It didn't occur to me until a good while later that I had offended them cruelly by putting it unread in my pocket in order to read it in peace later on. Later it was like a magnetic storm every time a letter came for me. The air crackled, the voices of both the farmer and his wife trembled.

What is stupidity? Is it striving toward a collective humanity with a common circulatory system, a circle of people who have grown together at the hips? At any rate it is the first distinguishing characteristic of stupidity that everything is to be mutual, absolutely mutual. You are not to have any thought to yourself. You are not to have any secret with your wife or your child, and stupidity wants to know what's in every nook and cranny of your house. Nothing is to be your own. It's to be thinned out in the blood of the stupid mass of humanity.

Then one evening when I came in the farmer had gone after the mail, and again there was a letter for me. It lay prominently on the table like an accusation, and the couple sat in their chairs, silent, almost without breathing. They did not, as usual, have their covetous eyes on the letter nor on me. And they had been lucky. The letter was in English, and they had understood it, as far as they were able to understand anything.

I went over to the table and took the letter. Yes, it was from her. I turned it over. Yes, it had been opened, clumsily so you could see it a mile away.

What was I supposed to do? I couldn't leave. I had to live with these inferior people, and everything in me hungered for retribution, for revenge. That was probably why I did nothing. I went out into the outbuilding and sat there for a long time without lighting the kerosene lamp. A letter I had longed for for an eternity—here it lay, soiled by stupidity's covetous fingers. It is, as is so often emphasized, not easy to be young.

Meanwhile I read the letter, but still today I feel the pain: These painful words, these timorous caresses, these hidden allusions—it had been in stupidity's hands. All this which had been sent perhaps a hundred miles to come only in front of my eyes, the toads had sat regurgitating before I got to see it.

What does a young man do. Does he take revenge? Does he burn down the house over those who committed sacrilege? Seldom. He still doesn't actually think it's true that somebody does such a thing. He doesn't comprehend it until some time has passed, before revenge is too far away. The hasty reaction and the act of violence is more often found in the older person, the one who has mortgaged the years for what he suddenly sees dirtied and spat on.

The young person has the future, and no one can rob him of that yet. The young man waits until everything is quiet. Then he packs up his clothes in his suitcase and walks out into the whispering, frosty wind to get away. Flight? It was flight, but not from these two who resembled human beings, since they wanted most of all for me to leave, so that they would be rid of me for the winter. The young man thinks he can flee from himself. Some believe for a very long time that it is possible. You see people who believe it even when they are over forty years of age, unhappy individuals, going off every three years or several times a year with a new woman or a new man, eternally fleeing from something inside.

I walked over uneven ground with withered straw. It was heavy going, and I stumbled and fell. Then I went down into a dried-out ditch that led to the main road. I had often walked there. The moon was coming up. It lay like a dark red fire behind a little woods. Far away a coyote was whining. At one point the ditch got narrow, and I put my suitcase up on my shoulder. It was there I got caught in a wolf trap.

This is being written on a midsummer day on Öland in the Baltic. The flies are buzzing in the room. I am living in the most beautiful place on one of the world's most beautiful islands. I bend over, look at the white scars on my left foot, then stare out over the Kalmar Sound which is calm and blue. Far away is a strip of smoke from a steamship. A friend of mine who is a geologist is standing a hundred yards away chipping at the chalk face. He's hunting fossils for a museum. I look down again at the white scars: Fossils! A sketch remains after something that was once blood and pain.

Here sits somebody trying to remember as precisely as possible: I stood in the wolf trap at least seven hours, perhaps ten to eleven hours. It had sprung around the heel on my left foot, right over the knuckles. It wasn't possible to get both hands down to open the trap, and my suitcase had squeezed itself against the injured leg when it had fallen down. The trap was fastened to a chain.

How does it feel to stand all night in a wolf trap? How do the brief click, the pain, the long minutes feel? The blood trickling gently and quietly, the pounding up in the knee when you have been standing long enough?

At times I passed out. I know I slept several minutes now and then since the moon was quite high. I was standing, leaning up against the one wall of the ditch, sleeping. My mouth was dry, I was thirsty, hot and cold and I was freezing. My jaws were tired after the many calls for help. You can get used to being caught in a wolf trap.

Stupidity has rusty, merciless teeth. It doesn't know it's cutting into flesh, nerves and bones. If you have become a sacrifice to stupidity, don't try to plead with it. It has no imagination. It only digs its teeth in harder. It cannot put itself in your place. It laughs at your miserable calls and comprehends them only as noise. What would stupidity have said if the same thing had been done to it? Stupid questions! It cannot learn the only human commandment: Do not do unto others what thou wouldst not have them do unto thee. Strike stupidity down!

But you cannot strike down a wolf trap. There you stand, and the night is long. The moon rises, becomes white and pale. You shout until you can manage no more. You let a dry tongue move over dry lips. You try to move ever so little so you can rest a while in another position and deaden the pain a bit, but give a start and scream. You weep in your miserable impotence, but the trap does not open. It sticks to its principles. You think about God, but the trap holds. You lose consciousness and reawaken with a pitiable child-like scream. The moon goes down. For the second time it becomes big and red, but that's not the end of your night watch. Oh, why did I go this way? Why didn't someone tell me to go another way? Was there anyone who said that? Indeed, everybody said that: Don't go that way! But you went that way, and here you stand with your fear and pain with one foot in stupidity's rusty jaw.

Daybreak came, but nothing happened, nothing except that now it was pounding up my thigh as well, and then it was a relief to think that it would be a while before it started pounding in my shoulder too. But then stupidity is sly. He took a jump from my thigh and started pounding in my head. For a long while he left the foot and the leg in peace, just held tight while he let it pound rhythmically in my skull. He ground stones in my head, then for a variation went outside and struck me with a hammer in my neck. Now and then with difficulty I opened my eyes and saw fine snow flakes dancing in the air. The first snow of the year. I carefully leaned my head back slightly and tried to get some in my mouth, but the fine flakes merely tapped me here and there on my face. I had a thought: It's too bad to catch a wolf in a trap. Would the blessed hunter never come and bash me in the head with a club?

Daybreak, but still no Ford car clattering along the road, and the farm? It was behind several hills with trees growing on them. No one would come from that direction. And—well, he who does not prosper in blood-brotherhood with stupidity, he ends up in a prison or in a psychiatric clinic. A wolf trap is more merciful. It lets you wake up in a hospital where a doctor stands pouring caustic things on your mangled foot. You give out one last protesting scream against fate and its wolf traps before you clench your teeth and let the doctor fiddle with your foot, as an elderly nurse also treats you like a new-born baby and pours water into the mouth of a poor fellow moaning he is thirsty, and the water runs over his throat and down onto the bed.

What does it all mean? The years pass, and it is gone. An Englishman was once asked what he thought would become of the English in a thousand years. He answered that they probably would be sitting, drinking tea. Just what I am doing now, even though I don't like tea, but there's no coffee to be had. The past? The wolf trap has certainly been sold for scrap iron long ago. The stupid farm couple are lying under a beautiful stone. The letter has been burned, and the woman? What has become of her?

Notes to "The Wolf Trap"

"Vargsaksen" (The Wolf Trap) came out originally in the Swedish newspaper *Dagens Nyheter, Söndagsbilagen* (August 8, 1943), but in Norwegian, not Swedish. Essentially the same text, with the omission of a few phrases and some punctuation differences, was published first in Norway in *Magasinet* (September 14, 1946). A final version, slightly shorter with several small sections left out and a few phrases added, appeared in *Årstidene* 9–10 (1954), *Magasinet* (March 30, 1960) and in *Dans, dans, Roselil* (1965).

Though based on the original, an occasional phrase or sentence is left out of the translation, and a number of other minor changes have been made, in accord with later versions. Also a few contemporary references have been omitted.

Both this story and the following one, "Horse Thieves," were written while Sandemose was a refugee in Sweden during World War II. This is why they both were published first in Swedish publications. Sandemose lived for a period on the island of Öland off the east coast of Sweden in the Baltic Sea, mentioned in the text, where he wrote "The Wolf Trap."

Horse Thieves

One day toward the end of April I was making my way from one prairie station to another in southern Saskatchewan. I had been walking for a long time on the dusty road without having been picked up. I was extremely annoyed. Usually there were a lot of cars on the roads, and they would always stop to pick up a pedestrian, but during that whole morning not a single one came by. I had been trudging along for four hours in a cold wind and burning sun without seeing any sign of life. The prairie in these regions was gently rolling with several sloughs here and there.

Around noon I caught sight of a rider coming from the south. He had with him two horses in addition to the one he was sitting on. The man waited for me when he reached the road. He turned out to be a Swedish-born Canadian about twenty years old. He had come over with his parents when he was eight and was now out looking for runaway horses, a herd of about fifty ponies. A pedestrian in Canada is such a remarkable sight that he asked me very curiously what the reason was for my walking here. I told him the truth, that I was out looking for work but didn't have any money for a train.

The Swede thought it would be nice to have company and asked me to come along with him. At the moment he was on his way to a Norwegian with second sight who lived further north. He didn't have any great confidence that the man could tell him anything about the horses, but now he had almost given up and wanted at any rate to try this last possibility.

I thought it was a good idea and probably also thought that this Swede who was familiar with the country might be able to find me something to do later on. First we sat down in the withered grass a little way from the road and ate some of his food. He had butter and bread and dried meat, and to go along with that we made a cup of tea. My spirits rose considerably when I had got something in my stomach, and we rode off to the north. The prairie is no riding ground, and I was a poor horseman. You had to be especially on the lookout the whole time for the holes badgers had dug in the ground. If a trotting horse got his foot into one of these holes, it was fairly certain the leg would break.

At last we came to a little farm with some young trees around it. There was nobody in sight. The Swede put his hand to his mouth like a funnel and shouted, "Is anyone there?"

Right afterward an old man with a long beard appeared in the door and said, "What are you bellowing about?"

The Swede asked if the old man was the Norwegian with the name Wise Ola. The old fellow answered irritably that yes, that was his name.

"Then you must be the one who can divine water?"

Ola answered, "Do you need a well?"

The Swede laughed and answered, "I don't need any well, but they told me on a farm south of here that you could divine water, and so I thought, if that Ola can divine water, then he can probably also divine horses, because fifty ponies of mine have run off, and I have the feeling they must be in these parts."

I now got to see a sight which I have amused myself over later, but which at the time merely seemed rather strange. Wise Ola looked at us for a while, then his face began to be distorted. He lifted his arms as if he were conjuring something up. He moaned, and in short looked as though he had lost his senses. Then he emitted some hoarse, unarticulated sounds before he began chanting, "Your name is Göran, and you're from South Dakota. Your name is Göran and you're from South Dakota. Your name is Göran and you're from South Dakota. You're looking for fifty-three horses. You're looking for fifty-three horses. You're looking for fifty-three horses. They are yours by right. You have bought and paid for them. They are yours by right. You have bought and paid for them. They are yours by right. You have bought and paid for them. They are in Canada. They are in Canada. They are in Canada. Get them in Sunny Valley. Get them in Sunny Valley. Get them in Sunny Valley."

Göran had been staring at him with open mouth, and now he said, "Damn, what a performance."

Wise Ola acted like he was waking up and said, "Did I say anything?"

Göran laughed and said, "Yes, you said that my name was Göran and that I was from South Dakota, but I knew that already. Who told you that anyway?"

"Oh, your name is Göran, but didn't I say anything about the horses?"

"Yes, you said that there were fifty-three, but there are only fifty, since I have three of them here. You said I should get them in Sunny Valley."

"So go get them."

Göran was still laughing. "Do you have dealings with the Devil?"

Ola answered seriously, "No, it's the *spirit* I have dealings with."

"Yes, yes," said Göran, "it doesn't matter to me, only if the horses are where you say they are. What do I owe you?"

Ola answered, "You can pay me the same as when I am using my divining rod. That's fifty cents."

※

It was out of the question riding to Sunny Valley, and we left the horses behind at the wise Norwegian's. I gathered that Göran was not penniless, but it wasn't in his book to pay for a train ticket. We went northeast, and late in the afternoon we stood by the railway line. We followed it a couple of miles until it made a curve where the train would have to slow down. We hid there in some bushes, and toward evening a freight train finally approached. It was no big deal getting up onto the narrow platform on the last car, but it was an awful job to hang on. The car jumped so that our backs were completely sore. I don't remember what happened right afterward, but Göran told me that same night what had gone on.

The next thing I recalled was something resembling the sound of a train, a sound which gradually became louder, and finally I woke up. I slowly stretched my hands over to something hard which I felt under my neck and realized it was a rail.

Then I suddenly was aware of what was about to happen. I didn't quite get to my feet, but threw myself away like a frightened animal. Above me I saw how the wheels under the train ground round, and I was on the point of losing consciousness one more time when I thought how my head could now be lying between the rails.

The train was gone. I sat there and wasn't very self-confident, but if the next morning I followed the tracks I would undoubtedly come to a station. A ways from the rail line I made a fire and soon fell asleep.

When I woke up in the broad daylight, a man was lying on the other side of the fire. He woke up as I stared at him. It was Göran. He hadn't wanted to wake me when he found me, probably because he himself was very tired. He told me that an official on the train had stuck his upper body out of a trapdoor above us and hit me on the head with a stick. Göran himself had not dared jump off a train which by that time was going full speed. He was fairly certain that I was dead, and he succeeded in moving forward in the train before the official could get him with the stick too. There were two chasing him, and when the train a good while later had slowed down, he had to attempt the leap. It went well, and most of the rest of the night he had walked around to see what had happened to me.

I can't say I had any great desire to repeat the experiment, but Göran wouldn't give in. That morning, one on each side, we jumped on a northbound freight and after great difficulties positioned ourselves back to back on an arrangement under the last car. That is the way we got to Sunny Valley.

ಸಿಣ

I have no special belief in people with second sight, and I have my own ideas about that wise Norwegian. If Göran's ponies actually were in Sunny Valley, and Wise Ola could tell us that, it's hardly any spirit who informed him.

It was a clear, moonless night. We went into the valley. We looked around for a farm where we could sleep, but there wasn't a house in sight, and we made a fire at the foot of an old maple tree.

I remember clearly that night as I lay looking up at the sailing moon. It's many years ago, and the world has become a different one since then. I was very young, but I had known for a long time that I wanted to write. Often young people who want to be authors believe more in what they read than in what they see. I remember I have written about these events before, there just north of the border to the United States. But what was it I wrote then? Yes, it must also have been about what I had seen, but it got horribly mixed up with everything I had *read*. That is the way is was for several years. When I published my first book, I had quite a chequered career behind me, but I saw it through the eyes of other authors, not through my own. I repeat: I believed more in what I had read than in what I had seen. When I wrote about my meeting with Göran earlier it got mixed up with a considerable amount of romanticism. The remarkable thing is that I had a great deal of success the moment I began writing, when I related everything that others had already related. For a long time it was different, when I allowed myself to tell what I actually had seen.

Well, this report about my trip as a blind passenger and the hunt for Göran's runaway horses is perhaps not especially remarkable, the way I now tell it and the way it really happened, but I can't see now at any rate that it would be better by being furnished with screeching Indians or flapping vampires.

That which I constantly return to in my mind is the night there under the old maple tree, by the fire, under the sailing moon. Always what we remember most clearly and with the greatest pleasure is not events but images.

I didn't fall asleep until toward morning and woke up hearing footsteps. It was at daybreak. Göran had been away. It was his footsteps that woke me. He stood quietly and looked down at me, grinning. "That there Norwegian sure was right. My horses are a little farther up the valley here. I walked around among them. They had my brand, and they all seem to be there. What the hell shall we do? Somebody has taken them. They're in an enclosure."

It was my opinion that someone had been taking care of the strange horses and would hand them over to the owner when he came by. Göran was of another opinion. The horses had been stolen, and since we were only two men as opposed to undoubtedly many, Göran had no other choice but to steal back his own horses.

This of course sounded very exciting, but I had reason to be hesitant, since then I would have to ride a horse without a saddle, and I wasn't exactly a circus acrobat. But objections were useless as far as Göran was concerned.

A half hour later we had driven the horses out of the enclosure and were on the way to the southwest.

※

We rode the whole day without a rest. Göran had the entire job of keeping the ponies together. For my part, I had enough to do keeping myself on horseback. It was I who said stop toward evening. Göran would have preferred to keep going through the night. But it was absolutely impossible for me to continue. I was as though crushed in my crotch and was bleeding several places on my body from the bumps I had received the many times I had fallen off. I suggested that Göran continue on alone, if he would give me a couple of dollars and a bit of food. I expect now that he didn't think it was a good idea leaving me behind alone on the prairie. At any rate he didn't say anything, and we struck camp for the night.

※

That was the last night I was together with Göran. He was right that we were not yet sufficiently far away. Before we got any farther the next morning, a half dozen riders appeared from all directions. There was no question of escaping. Besides, they were all armed with rifles or shotguns. We got to our feet and looked pretty dejectedly at the men who encircled us. Göran had got up.

"What's your name?" asked one of the men, and pointed at Göran.

Now and then funny things happen, but a long time can pass before you see the comical. You have to remember that I was in a condition as if I had spent a day with the Gestapo. I had absolutely no sense for jokes. Two weeks passed before one morning I started laughing at what Göran answered.

"What the hell business is it of yours what my name is? Do you collect autographs, maybe?"

"Shut your trap, you horse thief!" yelled the man.

"Are you calling *me* a horse thief?" screamed Göran. "Say that one more time and I'll..."

He stopped in mid-sentence, perhaps to figure out what he should do. The leader lifted his rifle a little and said, "Now you answer what I ask you, or I'll give you an autograph that says bang."

I was still sitting on the ground and had a definite feeling that it was best not to keep my head up there among the rifle barrels. Sitting on my back I was witness to a development of the case which was equally surprising for all parties. It was the sheriff and his men who had captured us. The horses had been in a municipal enclosure, and the owner had been searched for already in the local newspapers. During considerable laughter from the whole group, the raging Göran had to pay for the advertisements and the inconvenience the sheriff had had with the horses. In addition, Göran had taken the law into his own hands when he had appropriated the horses without permission. The sheriff demanded two dollars for each of his companions and five dollars for himself.

Right from the beginning of my friendship with Göran I had been clearly aware that he had money, but now he screamed in a blind fury, "Where in deepest hell am I supposed to have got so much money? Do you think I go around with a printing press under my arm? This here is twenty-seven dollars. Do you think I'm a millionaire?"

The sheriff laughed. "No, no, then we'll take one and a half horses."

"One and a half horses?"

"Yes," said the sheriff. "Twenty dollars for one of your nags there, and that leaves seven dollars. That comes to about one and half horses. But you have a nice young stallion, so we'll be satisfied with him."

That is the way it was settled. Then the men got off their horses and we ate breakfast together as though nothing had happened. One of the men agreed to accompany Göran. One of the others offered me work on his farm, and I followed them back to Sunny Valley.

Notes to "Horse Thieves"

"Hästtjuvar" (Horse Thieves), *Folket i bild* 1 (January 1, 1945), is Sandemose's only Canada article to have appeared in Swedish before it appeared either in Norwegian or Danish, though it is likely a translation of a Norwegian original. The Norwegian version came out in *Magasinet* 1–2 (Oslo) (January 4, 1947) as "Hestetjuver," and this is probably the original that the Swedish translation was made from. The translation is based on the Norwegian "Hestetjuver" with a few changes in the paragraphing.

This story about a man riding the rails up to Canada to look for his runaway horses, having to steal them from a municipal corral and getting caught and fined by the sheriff is found in the first part of the novel *Ross Dane*. Here Ross is the one searching for the horses. On his way to retrieve them he meets a Métis, Charles Villeneuve, who accompanies him.

BIBLIOGRAPHY

Books and Articles by Aksel Sandemose

"Barndom" (Childhood), *Arbeidets* Jul (1934).

"Billeder fra en lang reise" (Pictures from a Long Journey), *Aschehougs Magasin* 7 (July 1935).

"Borgerkrig" (Civil War), *Arbeidets* Jul (1936).

"Canada som Fremtidsland," *Hareskov Grundejerblad* (July 15, 1927).

"Den blinde Gade" (The Blind Street), *Forum* (March 1923).

"Den flyvende Hollænder" (The Flying Dutchman), *Berlingske Tidende*, Aftenudgave (August 23, 1928).

Det svundne er en drøm (The Past is a Dream) (Oslo: Aschehoug, 1946).

En flyktning krysser sitt spor (A Fugitive Crosses His Tracks) (Oslo: Tiden Norsk Forlag, 1933).

En flyktning krysser sitt spor. Espen Arnakkes Kommentarer til Janteloven (A Fugitive Crosses His Tracks. Espen Arnakke's Commentary on the Law of Jante) (Kjørkelvik, Risør: Aksel Sandemose, 1955).

"En kanadisk Præst" (A Canadian Pastor), *Fyns Venstreblad* (April 15, 1928).

"En Pige gaar til Canossa" (A Girl Eats Humble Pie), *Søndags B.T.* 33 (August 18, 1929).

"En rytter på prerien" (A Rider on the Prairie), *Stavanger Aftenblad* (January 20, 1934).

En sjømann går i land (A Sailor Goes Ashore) (Oslo: Gyldendal, 1931).

"En vandrer får influensa" (A Wanderer Catches Influenza), *Helgelands Arbeiderblad* (Christmas 1933).

"En vandrer.får influensa" (A Wanderer Catches Influenza), *Social-Demokraten, Hjemmets Søndag* (June 7, 1936).

"En vandrer.får influensa" (A Wanderer Catches Influenza), *Tidens Tegn, Lørdagsavisen* (February 1, 1936).

"Fattige Folk paa Rejse" (Poor People Travelling), *Sorø Amtstidende* (July 4, 1928).

"Flytning paa Prærien" (Moving on the Prairie), *Dagens Nyheder* (August 22, 1928).

"Flyttedag" (Moving Day), *Social-Demokraten, Hjemmets Søndag* (August 8, 1937).

Fortællinger fra Labrador (Stories from Labrador) (Copenhagen: Gyldendal, 1923).

"Fra Belle-Isle til Montreal" (From Belle-Isle to Montreal), *Berlingske Tidende*, Aftenudgave (October 8, 1927).

"fra Kjørkelvik," *Aktuell* 24 (November 26, 1949).

"Grækernes Flytning" (The Greeks' Move), *Social-Democraten* (December 24, 1928).

"Han gad ikke flytte sig" (He Couldn't Manage to Move), *Dagbladet* (May 16, 1935).

"Hesten" (The Horse), *Fram, Norsk Magasin* 3 (February 6, 1943).

"Hesten" (The Horse), *Social-Demokraten* (July 4, 1937).

"Hestetjuver" (Horse Thieves), *Magasinet* 1–2 (Oslo) (January 4, 1947).

"Hjem til Danmark!" (Home to Denmark!), *Dagens Nyheder* (June 10, 1928).

"Hjemløse Fugle" (Homeless Birds), *Morsø Folkeblad* (July 2, 1921).

Horns for Our Adornment, translated by Eugene Gay-Tifft (New York: Alfred A. Knopf, 1938).

"Hästtjuvar" (Horse Thieves), *Folket i bild* 1 (January 1, 1945).

"Høst i Canada," *Berlingske Tidende*, Aftenudgave (December 23, 1927).

"I Canada skal du æde dit Brød i dit Ansigts Sved" (In Canada You Shall Eat Your Bread in the Sweat of Your Brow), *Hjemmet* 29 (Copenhagen) (July 18, 1928).

"I Pennsylvanien" (In Pennsylvania), *Morsø Folkeblad* (October 14, 1927).

"Jeg har vondt både her og der, og selv er jeg ikke frisk heller" (I've Got a Pain Here and There, and I'm not Really Well Myself), *Arbeiderkvinnen* 2 (February 1937).

"Julemorgen" (Christmas Morning), *Social-Demokraten, Hjemmet Søndag* (December 19, 1937).

Klabavtermanden, Fortælling fra Havet (The Klabavtermand, Story from the Sea) (Copenhagen: Gyldendal, 1927).

"Kulturen paa Prærien" (Culture on the Prairie), *Aarhuus Stiftstidende* (June 11, 1928).

"Livet paa Canads Prærie I–III" (Life on Canada's Prairies I–III), *Aarhuus Stiftstidende* (May 2, 3, 4, 1928).

"Lykken" (Happiness), *Kring jul. Radiogavefondets julehefte* (1951).

"Lyckan" (Happiness), *Lørdagsexpressen* (December 23, 1944).

"Lykken" (Happiness), *Social-Demokraten, Hjemmets Søndag* (February 6, 1938).

"Medicinmænd" (Medicine Men), *Berlingske Tidende, Søndagsnummer* (April 15, 1928).

Mænd fra Atlanten (Men from the Atlantic) (Copenhagen: Forlaget af 1924, 1924).

"Norske amasoner. Fortelling fra Kanada" (Norwegian Amazons. Story from Canada), *Hjemmet* 12 (Oslo) (March 19, 1932).

"Norske Amazoner" (Norwegian Amazons), *Hjemmet* 19 (Copenhagen) (May 12, 1934).

"Nybyggere i Canada" (Pioneers in Canada), *Morgenbladet* (July 18 and July 20, 1929).

"Paa Billig-Billet" (On a Cheap Ticket), *Aarhuus Stiftstidende* (April 7, 1930).

"Paa Skovarbejde i Vest-Canada" (Working as a Logger in Western Canada), *Hjemmet* (August 15, 1928).

"Porten til Canada" (The Gateway to Canada), *Sorø Amtstidende* (June 5, 1928).

"Prærien—for lenge siden" (The Prairie—Long Ago), *Aktuell* 4 (January 25, 1965).

"Præriens Kvinder" (Prairie Women), *Aarhuus Stiftstidende* (March 22, 1928).

"Præriens Nat" (The Prairie Night), *Berlingske Tidende, Søndagsnummer* (March 25, 1928).

"Racekamp" (Racial Struggle), *Politiken* (June 12, 1935).

"Redvers," *Berlingske Tidende*, Aftenudgaven (August 20, 1928).

Ross Dane (Copenhagen: Gyldendal, 1928).

Ross Dane, translated with an introduction by Christopher Hale (Winnipeg: Gunnars and Campbell, 1989).

"Rum nr 14" (Room no. 14), *Folket i bild* 1 (January 3, 1943).

"Sandemose: Det er Arbejdsglæde" (Sandemose: It's Joy of Work), *Hjemmet* (December 18, 1928).

Sandemose Forteller (Sandemose Relates) (Oslo: Tiden, 1937).

"Sandheden om Canada" (The Truth About Canada), *Aalborg Venstreblad* (January 24, 1929).

"Saskatchewan I–II," *Berlingske Tidende* (July 9–10, 1928).

"Se selv! Canada-Oplevelser" (See for Yourself! Canada Experiences), *Sorø Amtstidende* (June 15, 1928).

September (Oslo: Tiden, 1939).

"Simon Hjortnæs, Danskernes Konge i Canada" (Simon Hjortnæs, King of the Danes in Canada) *Hjemmet* 1 (Copenhagen) (December 24, 1929).

Storme ved Jævndøgn (Storms at Equinox) (Copenhagen: Gyldendal, 1924).

"Tidlig vår" (Early Spring), *Magasinet* 17 (Oslo) (April 27, 1957).

"30 Juni" (June 30), *Göteborgs Handels-och Sjöfarts-Tidning* (May 24, 1935).

Ungdomssynd (Sin of Youth) (Copenhagen: E. Jespersen, 1924).

Varulven (The Werewolf) (Oslo: Aschehoug, 1958).

"Vinter og Vaar" (Winter and Spring), *Politiken, Magasinet* (June 17, 1928).

"Winnipeg," *Berlingske Tidende*, Aftenudgaven (December 30, 1927).

Årstidene. Brev fra Kjørkelvik (The Seasons. Letters from Kjørkelvik) (Oslo: J. Chr. Gundersen, 1951–55).

Books and Articles by Other Authors

Across Border and Valley. The Story of Maryfield and Fairlight and Surrounding Districts, Vol. 2. (Maryfield: Maryfield and District Historical Society, 1984).

Atlanten har så mange mil. Strejflys over Sandemose og hans forfatterskab (The Atlantic has so Many Miles. Glimpses of Sandemose and his Authorship) (Copenhagen: Aschehoug, 1986).

Bender, Henning and Birgit Flemming Larsen (eds.). *Danish Immigration to Canada*, Udvandrerarkivets Skriftserie: Udvandrerhistoriske Studier Nr. 3. (Ålborg: 1991).

Bergstedt, Harald. "Aksel Sandemose: Ross Dane," *Social-Demokraten* (December 23, 1928).

Birn, Randi. *Aksel Sandemose—Exile in Search of a Home*, Contributions to the Study of World Literature, Number 2. (Westport, CT and London, England: Greenwood Press, 1984).

Bojesen, Palle Bo. *New Denmark, New Brunswick, Canada: Udviklingen i en dansk udvandrerkoloni 1872–1914* (New Denmark, New Brunswick, Canada: The Development in a Danish Emigrant Colony 1872–1914). (Århus: Aarhus Universitetsforlag, 1993).

——. "New Denmark—The Oldest Danish Colony in Canada," *Danish Immigration to Canada*, 49–70.

Brix, Hans. "En Fortælling" (A Story), *Dagens Nyheder* (April 16, 1927).

Broe, Axel. "Aksel Sandemose," *København* (October 2, 1928).

——. "Klabavtermanden," *København* (March 15, 1927).

"Canada som Indvandringsland: Beretning afgivet af den til Undersøgelse af Betingelserne for dansk Udvandring til Canada udsendte Delegation" (Canada as a Land for Immigration. Report Submitted by the Delegation Sent out to Examine the Conditions for Danish Immigration to Canada), *Udenrigsministeriets Tidskrift* (January 3, 1924).

"Carl Møllers Legat," *Nationaltidende* (April 26, 1927).

Chr. R. "Ross Dane," *Politiken* (November 3, 1928).

Christensen, Rolf Buschardt. "Danish Folk Schools in Canada," *Danish Immigration*, 106–24.

"Danish Settlers and Sea Thirst," *Weekly Manitoba Liberal* (Portage la Prairie, March 15, 1928).

"Danish Settlers in Prairie Provinces Terribly Sea-Sick," *Montreal Herald* (February 10, 1928).

"Danish Settlers on Western Farms Suffer Sea Thirst," *Free Press Weekly Prarie Farmer* (Winnipeg, March 7, 1928).

Dickson Koloniens Historie. Et Mindeskrift om vore Pioneerer (History of the Dickson Colony. A Memorial Volume about Our Pioneers) (Blair, NE: 1948).

E.j. "Axel [sic] Sandemose fik i Gaar Aarets Humorist Legat. Arbejdsmanden, som blev Digter" (Axel Sandemose Received Yesterday the Year's Humorist Grant. The Working Man Who Became a Poet), *Social-Demokraten* (April 26, 1927).

E.j. "En Roman fra Kanada" (A Novel from Canada), *Aalborg Amtstidende* (December 11, 1928).

Engelstoft, Povl. *Den nye Litteratur* 6 (Aargang, 1928–29): 39.

Estvad, Leo. *Aksel Sandemose først i 20'rne* (Aksel Sandemose Initially in the 20s) (Copenhagen: Carit Andersen, 1967).

Flor, Kai. "En Bog om Søen" (A Book About the Sea), *Berlingske Tidende* (April 22, 1927).

Frimand, John. "Til Canada" (To Canada), *Aalborg Venstreblad* (January 1, 1928).

From Danaview to Standard (Standard, AB: Standard Historical Book Society, 1979).

"Fun and Frolic Being Towed across Canada in Motorless Car," *Winnipeg Free Press* (September 17, 1927).

Geismar, Oscar. "Aksel Sandemose: Ross Dane," *Fyns Venstreblad* (October 13, 1928).

Gelsted, Otto. "En Dansk-Amerikaner" (A Danish-American), *Ekstra Bladet* (December 12, 1928).

———. "En Søroman" (A Sea Novel), *Extra Bladet* (April 1, 1927).

Greene, B.M. (ed.). *Who's Who in Canada 1927* (Toronto: International Press Ltd., 1927).

Grub-Axe to Grain (Spruce View, AB: Spruce View School Area Historical Society, 1973).

Haavardsholm, Espen. *Mannen fra Jante. Et portrett av Aksel Sandemose* (The Man from Jante. A Portrait of Aksel Sandemose) (Oslo: Gyldendal, 1988).

Hale, Christopher. "Danes" in *Encyclopedia of Canada's Peoples*, 406-13.

———. "Happy, Holy or Anglican: Danish Churches in Canada," *Religious Studies and Theology* (1998): 47-58.

———. "The Image of the Prairie Woman in Aksel Sandemose's Diary and Published Work," *Atlanten har så mange mil*: 139-49.

Hemstitches and Hackamores: A History of Holden and District (Holden, AB: Holden Historical Society, 1984).

Henriksen, Hans. "Aksel Sandemoses Ny Bog. *Ross Dane*" (Aksel Sandemose's New Book. *Ross Dane*), *Morsø Folkeblad* (October 10, 1928).

The History of Dalum (Drumheller, AB: The Big Country News, 1968).

Houmark, C. "Det middelmaadige Geni" (The Mediocre Genius), *Berlingske Tidende* (November 24, 1928).

Jensen, Martin. "Østergaard, Johannes and Sorine," *Across Border and Valley*, 972.

Kristensen, Tom. "Efteraarets Bøger" (Autumn Books), *Tilskueren* (November 1928): 323.

———. "Aarets Humorist" (Humourist of the Year), *Politiken* (April 26, 1927).

———. "Aksel Sandemose," *Politiken* (May 16, 1927).

Levin, Poul. "Nord og Syd" (North and South), *Tilskueren* (May 1927): 355.

Linck, Olaf. *Kanada det store Fremtidsland* (Canada the Great Land of the Future) (Copenhagen: E. Jespersen, 1926).

Magocsi, Paul Robert (ed.). *Encyclopedia of Canada's Peoples* (Toronto: University of Toronto Press, 1999).

Mikkelsen, C. *Canada som Fremtidsland* (Canada as Land of the Future) (Copenhagen: Aschehoug, 1927).

M.u. "Literatur," *Aalborg Stftstidende* (November 13, 1928).

Møller, H.O. Frimodt. *Dansk Bosættelse i Canada* (Danish Settlement in Canada) (Copenhagen: Dansk Traktatselskabs Forlag, 1927).

Nissen, Margrethe, Esther Thesberg and Andy Kjaersgaard, "A History of Dickson, Alberta, Canada," *Danish Emigration*, 71-90.

Nordberg, Carl-Eric. *Sandemose. En biografi* (Sandemose. A Biography). (Oslo, Copenhagen and Stockholm: Schønbergske, 1967-1968).

Olsen, Poul Erik. "Emigration from Denmark to Canada in the 1920's," *Danish Emigration*, 125-45.

Paulsen, Frank. *Danish Settlements on the Canadian Prairies: Folk Traditions, Immigrant Experiences, and Local History*, National Museum of Man Mercury Series. Canadian Centre for Folk Culture Studies, Paper no. 11 (Ottawa, 1974).

Reflections—Dalum and Area. (Dalum, AB: Dalum History Book Committee, 1990).

Simonsen, Henrik Bredmose. "The Early Life of the Danish Churches in Canada," *Danish Immigration*, 91–105.

———. *Kampen om danskheden. Tro og nationalitet i de danske kirkesamfund i Amerika* (The Struggle for Danishness. Faith and Nationality in the Danish Church Congregations in America) (Århus: Aarhus Universitetsforlag, 1990).

Storm, Ole. *Janteloven. Sandemose. En biografi* (The Law of Jante. Sandemose. A Biography) (Copenhagen: Gyldendal, 1989).

Söderhjelm, Henning. "En ung dansk författare" (A Young Danish Author), *Göteborgs Handels-och Sjöfarts-Tidning* (March 28, 1927).

Udmark, John Andersen. *The Road We Have Covered* (New York: Modern Age Books, 1940).

Væth, Johannes. *Aksel Sandemose og Jante* (Aksel Sandemose and Jante) (Copenhagen: Vinten, 1965).

———. "Blade af Axel Nielsens dagbog" (Pages from Axel Nielsen's Diary), *På sporet af Sandemose*: 37–41.

———. "Lykkemand eller nidding" (Lykkemand or Nidding), *På sporet af Sandemose*: 66–70.

———. "Om Sandemoses læreår" (Concerning Sandemose's Apprenticeship), *Atlanten har så mange mil*: 10–11.

———. *På sporet af Sandemose* (Nykøbing: Forfatterforlaget ATTIKA, 1975).

Wamberg, Niels Birger, "Johannes V. Jensen og Aksel Sandemose" (Johannes V. Jensen and Aksel Sandemose), *Sandemoses ansikter*: 61–77.

———. (ed.). *Sandemoses ansikter* (Faces of Sandemose) (Oslo: Aschehoug, 1969).

Letters and Documents in Gyldendal Archives, Copenhagen

Letter, Gyldendal Publishers to Housing Co-operative "Paa Bjerget," Copenhagen, August 11, 1927.

Letter, Aksel Sandemose to H. Jerichow, Copenhagen, May 22, 1926(?).

Letter, Aksel Sandemose to H. Jerichow, Copenhagen, February 11, 1927.

Letter, Aksel Sandemose to H. Jerichow, Copenhagen, May 22, 1927.

Letter, Aksel Sandemose to H. Jerichow, Copenhagen, May 23, 1927.

Letter, Aksel Sandemose to H. Jerichow, Blidstrup, July 29, 1927.

Letter, Aksel Sandemose to H. Jerichow, Copenhagen, March 15, 1928.

Letter, Aksel Sandemose to H. Jerichow, Paa Bjerget, October 28, 1928.

Letter, Aksel Sandemose to S. Schmidt, Calgary, Alberta, December 17, 1927.

Letter, Aksel Sandemose to S. Schmidt, Father's Point, August 19, 1927.

Letter, Aksel Sandemose to S. Schmidt, Calgary, December 17, 1927.

Letter, Aksel Sandemose to S. Schmidt, Erie, January 16, 1928.

Letter, Aksel Sandemose to S. Schmidt, Paa Bjerget, April 25, 1928.

Letter, Aksel Sandemose to S. Schmidt, Paa Bjerget, October 29, 1928.

Letter, S. Schmidt to Aksel Sandemose, Copenhagen, January 17, 1928.

Letter, S. Schmidt to Aksel Sandemose, Copenhagen, March 22, 1928.

Letter, S. Schmidt to Aksel Sandemose, Copenhagen, July 7, 1928.

Letter, S. Schmidt to Aksel Sandemose, Copenhagen, November 11, 1928.

Letter, M. B. Sorensen to Aksel Sandemose, Copenhagen, July 24, 1927.

Reader Assessment, Reader Ludvig Holstein's of *Folket paa Prærien* by Aksel Sandemose.

Letters and Documents in the Royal Library, Copenhagen

Sandemose, Aksel, *Rejsedagbog* (Travel Diary) also referred to as Canada diary.

Johannes Væth Collection of Photocopies

Diary fragments, Aksel Sandemose, 1916–17.

Diary fragment, Aksel Sandemose, 1929, handwritten copy.

Letter, *Berlingske Tidende* to Aksel Sandemose, Copenhagen, November 6, 1926.

Letter, Jørgen Bukdahl to Aksel Sandemose, Oslo, no date.

Letter, Jørgen Bukdahl to Aksel Sandemose, Oslo, no date.

Letter, H.H. Congdon to Aksel Sandemose, Halifax, February 15, 1930.

Letter, Gunnar Gunnarsson to Aksel Sandemose, Gentofte, January 8, 1927.

Letter from Valdemar Henriksen, Johannes Væth, Vils, Denmark, October 11, 1966.

Letter, P. Hess to Aksel Sandemose, Copenhagen, February 10, 1927.

Letter, Axel Laursen to Aksel Sandemose, Copenhagen (?), January 14, 1926.

Letter, William Walter Ludlow to Aksel Sandemose, Joe Batt's Arm, March 7, 1928.

Letter, Aksel Sandemose to Jørgen Bukdahl, Copenhagen, January 10, 1926.

Letter, Aksel Sandemose to Jørgen Bukdahl, Copenhagen, January 12, 1926.

Letter, Aksel Sandemose to Jørgen Bukdahl, Copenhagen, March 10, 1926.

Letter, Aksel Sandemose to Jørgen Bukdahl, Copenhagen, June 5–6, 1926.

Letter, Aksel Sandemose to Jørgen Bukdahl, Copenhagen, August 5, 1926.

Letter, Aksel Sandemose to Jørgen Bukdahl, Copenhagen, April 20, 1927.

Letter, Aksel Sandemose to Department of Industries and Immigration, Halifax, Nova Scotia, Copenhagen, January 27, 1930.

Letter, Aksel Sandemose to Hans Helge Jensen, Maryfield, Saskatchewan, September 18, 1927.

Letter, Aksel Sandemose to Hans Helge Jensen, Calgary, December 17, 1927.

Letter, Aksel Sandemose to Poul Munk-Madsen, Father's Point, August 20, 1927.

Letter, M.B. Sorensen to J.S. Dennis, Copenhagen, April 14, 1928.

Letter, M.B. Sorensen to P.L. Sanford, Copenhagen, January 29, 1930.

Letter, Henning Söderhjelm to Aksel Sandemose, Göteborg, May 17, 1927.

Letter of conveyance, Aksel Sandemose to Co-operative Housing Society "Paa Bjerget," Copenhagen, June 7, 1927.

NKS

Letter, Aksel Sandemose to M.K. Nørgaard, Copenhagen, April 28, 1927, NKS 2632 2°.

Udvandrerarkivet, Ålborg

Letter, Aksel Sandemose to Godtfred Madsen, Paa Bjerget, February 26, 1929.

INDEX

A
Alberta, 63, 114–115; Calgary, 4, 34–35, 70; Camrose, 30–31; Dalum, 4, 32, 70, 101–104; Dickson, 2; East Coulee, 33, 131–134, 147–148; Edmonton, 31; Holden, 3–4, 29, 30, 36, 100–101; Home Coulee, 4, 31; Standard, 2, 6, 7; Wayne, 6, 31–33, 102, 133
Alida, SK, 3, 6, 25–27, 57
Andersen, John, 32–33, 131, 132, 133, 134

B
Beaver Coulee, 1, 4
Belle-Isle, QC, 82
Bergstedt, Harald, 40
Berlingske Tidende, 15–16, 19, 21, 42
Blandt Soens Vagabonder, 13
Brandon, MB, 36
Brix, Hans, 17
Broby, Svend, 41
Broe, Axel, 40–41
Bukdahl, Jorgen, 15, 16, 17

C
Calgary, AB, 4, 34–35, 70
Camrose, AB, 30–31
Canada, Government of, 4–5
Canada som Fremtidsland (Mikkelsen), 6–7, 7–8, 24
Canadian National Railways, 27–28, 42, 43
Canadian Pacific Railway: considers hiring Sandemose, 41, 42–43; funds Sandemose travel, 19, 27; and prairie settlement, 2, 3, 4, 5, 45n7, 65
Carl Mollers Legat, 17–18
Carstensen, Johannes, 15
Chaffey, Charles, 12
Christensen, Hans, 30
Christensen, Mads, 21
Christensen, Mathias Gammelgaard, 4
church, 2–3, 4, 32, 71, 72–73, 103–104
Congdon, H.H., 44

D
Dalum, AB, 4, 32, 70, 101–104
Damskov, Niels, 3, 6, 7, 26, 45n7
Dana (school), 4, 34, 35
Dannevirke, SK, 3, 25, 26, 68, 69, 138
Dansk Folkesamfund, 4, 32, 104
Denmark: emigration to Canada, 5–6, 55–57, 61–62, 66–68, 85, 92–94, 138; settlement in Canada, 2–8, 68, 69–70, 71, 72, 100, 101–103
Dennis, J.S., 36, 41
Dickson, AB, 2
doctors, 105–109
Dresen, Carl, 33

E
East Coulee, AB, 33, 131–134, 147–148
Edmonton, AB, 31
Elliott, Frank J., 95
Elm Creek, MB, 23–24
Estvad, Leo, 13

F
farming, 60, 61, 65, 66, 74, 111–112, 138. *see also* harvesting
En flyktning krysser sitt spoor, 1, 9, 10, 13, 142
Den flyvende Hollænder, 16–17
Fortællinger fra Labrador, 14, 16
Fremming, Danish Vice-Consul, 28, 34
Frimand, John, 42
"From Belle-Isle to Montreal", 21, 82–84

G
Geismar, Oscar, 41
Gormsen, Marius, 5
"Grækernes Flytning", 37–38
Grundtvig, F.L., 104
Grundtvig, N.F.S., 2, 104
Gunnarsson, Gunnar, 16
Gyldendal, 13, 14, 15, 16, 19, 31, 39–40, 41. *see also* Jerichow, Herbert; Schmidt, S.

H

Hamilton, ON, 36
harvesting, 85–87, 88–89. *see also* farming
Headingly, MB, 39
Henriksen, Hans, 40
Henriksen, Valdemar, 28–29
Hjortnæs, Karen, 137
Hjortnæs, Simon: background, 3; early Danish success story, 6, 7; Sandemose's view of, 57, 100, 135; Sandemose's visit with, 25–26, 29, 135–139
Hjortnæs, Mrs. (Simon's mother), 25, 137
Hoel, Sigurd, 12
Holden, AB, 3–4, 29, 30, 36, 100–101
Holstein, Ludvig, 39–40, 40
Home Coulee, AB, 4, 31
horses, 74–77, 103–104, 121–122, 150
Hotel Palliser, Calgary, 34, 35
hotels, 123–125, 126
hunting: coyotes, 97–98, 117–118, 132–133; ducks, 39, 119–121, 140–141; rabbits, 30–31, 113–114

J

Jakobsdatter, Amalie, 8, 9, 10, 11, 13
Jensen, Hans Helge, 89
Jensen, Johannes V., 14
Jensen, John M., 20
Jensen, Martin, 22
Jerichow, Herbert, 16, 18, 19, 39, 41
Jespersen, Mr., 39
Jorgensen, Petra, 109
Jorgensen, Thora, 31, 32, 49n138
Juhl, Mrs., 32
Juhl, Pastor, 31–32

K

Klabavtermanden, 16, 17, 40
Knudsen, Jens, 4, 34, 67
Kristensen, Tom, 17, 40

L

La Cour (CNR official), 42, 43
Lake Manitoba, MB, 28, 39, 140–141
Larsen, Ejner, 48n101
Larsen, Pastor, 25
Linck, Olaf, 6, 18
Ludlow, William W., 12, 37

M

Madsen, Godtfred, 7, 24–25, 26, 42, 109
Madsen, Rasmus, 6, 7, 25
Mænd fra Atlanten, 14, 15, 39
Manitoba, 63; Brandon, 36; Elm Creek, 23–24; Headingly, 39; Lake Manitoba, 28, 39, 140–141; Ostenfeld, 3, 27; Poplar Point, 141–142; Reston, 27; Souris, 24. *see also* Winnipeg, MB
Maryfield, SK, 21–22, 89, 116–117
Mikkelsen, C. (author), 6–8, 24, 36
Mikkelsen, Carl (immigrant), 27, 28
Mikkelsen, Christine, 27
Mikkelsen, John, 27, 28
Moller, Carl, 17
Montreal, QC, 38, 47n82, 48n115, 83
Munk-Madsen, Poul, 20, 47n68
Murray, Bill, 48n99

N

New Denmark, NB, 2, 7
Newfoundland, 12, 37, 44, 82
Nielsen, Anton, 20, 35, 37
Nielsen, Jorgen, 8, 9, 10, 11
Northcliffe, Lord, 12
Norway, 44, 71, 72, 100
Nova Scotia, 41, 44

O

Obstfelder, Sigbjorn, 13
Olsen, Arnold, 45n20
Ontario, 36, 107
Ostenfeld, Henrik, 3
Ostenfeld, MB, 3, 27
Ostergaard, Axel, 49n143
Ostergaard, John, 21–22, 89
Ostergaard, Peter, 32
Ostergaard, Sorine, 22

P

Pallesen, Peter, 6, 7, 34, 56
Paris, Anna, 9, 10–11, 20, 35, 36–38
Paris, Paul, 36–38
Paulsen, Frank, 3
Petersen, Charles Waldemar, 34
Poplar Point, MB, 141–142
prairies: climate and landscape, 63–64, 96–97, 114, 117, 128, 133; people, 71, 72, 110, 116–117, 118; settlement of, 65–66, 68–69, 119; work on, 60–61, 85, 116–117, 121, 128, 129–130
Press, H.S., 28

Q

Quebec City, QC, 83

R

racism, 30, 116, 143–145
Rasmussen, Mrs. (Pastor's wife), 104
Rasmussen, Peter (chairman of church congregation), 32
Rasmussen, Peter (Pastor), 4, 30, 31–32, 33, 100, 101, 102, 103
Rasmussen, Reinhold, 103
Redvers, SK, 3, 24–25, 123–127
Reston, MB, 27
Reventlow, Christian, 5
Ross Dane: events from travels included in, 1, 77, 99, 108, 122, 148; notes on, 17, 48n, 101; real life people in, 3, 30; writing of, 33, 39–41

S

Sacco, Nicolo, 94, 95
Sandemose, Aksel: background, 1, 8; changes his name, 8–9; concepts of lykkemand and nidding, 16–17; considers emigrating to Canada, 29, 41–44, 150; as a drinker, 11, 43; early writing struggles, 13, 14–16, 17–18; growing up in Denmark, 9–11; haunted by spirits, 38–39, 119, 133, 147–148; illness, 24, 35, 37; jobs other than writing, 11–12, 13, 14–15, 88–89; journey to Canada, 18–20; looks to leave Denmark, 15–16, 41–42, 43–44; money problems, 14–16, 17, 18, 19, 28–29, 31, 35–36, 37, 43; publishes *Ross Dane*, 39–41; relations with his sister, 10–11, 36–38; reviews Mikkelsen's book, 7–8; travel in Alberta, 29–35; travel in Manitoba, 23–24, 27, 28, 36; travel in Saskatchewan, 22–27, 29; travel in the US, 20–21, 36–38; views of, 32, 36, 37; and women, 11, 12–13, 13–14, 20
Sandemose, Bjarne, 115
Sandemose, Dagmar (Ditveldsen), 13–14, 19, 42
Sandemose, Iben, 115
Saskatchewan, 63, 116–122, 149; Alida, 3, 6, 25–27, 57; Dannevirke, 3, 25, 26, 68, 69, 138; Maryfield, 21–22, 89, 116–117; Redvers, 3, 24–25, 123–127; Saskatoon, 29; Wawota, 122
Saskatoon, SK, 29
Schmidt, S., 20, 35, 39, 41, 88, 89
Scott, George A., 95
September, 1
En sjomann gar i land, 1
skunks, 128–129
Sorensen, M.B., 5, 7, 18, 19, 25, 41, 43–44
Sorensen, Oscar, 31, 49n140, 101, 102
Sorensen, Peter, 3, 29–30, 36, 100, 113, 146
Souris, MB, 24

St. John, NB, 38
St. Lawrence River, 82–83
Standard, AB, 2, 6, 7
Storme ved Jaevndogn, 14, 16, 17
Strate (immigrant), 26
Det svundne er en drom, 1, 13

T

Thorkil (farmer), 33
Toronto, ON, 107
train travel, 78–80, 88, 90, 110–111, 112

U

Ukrainians, 30, 143, 145
Ungdomssynd, 14, 39
United Church, 2–3, 4
United States and Danish settlement, 2, 3, 4, 66, 104

V

Vanzetti, Bartolomeo, 94, 95
Varulven, 1, 13
Væth, Johannes, 9, 16, 46n25
Vi pynter oss med horn, 13

W

Wawota, SK, 122
Wayne, AB, 6, 31–33, 102, 133
Weltzer, Johannes, 17, 18
wildlife (*see also* hunting): abundance of, 64, 114–115; bear, 149–150; fowl, 117–118, 131; skunks, 128–129
Winnipeg, MB: in Sandemose's articles, 88, 90–92, 93–95, 140, 142; in Sandemose's diaries, 21, 27, 28, 89
winter, 30, 63–64, 96–97, 114, 133–134
women, 54–55, 56, 57, 98